DINÉ TAH

MY RESERVATION DAYS

1923–1939

ALWIN J. GIRDNER

RIO NUEVO
PUBLISHERS

Rio Nuevo Publishers®
P.O. Box 5250
Tucson, AZ 85703-0250
(520) 623-9558, www.rionuevo.com

Photographs: front cover and pages 2, 13, 67, 76, 81, 84, 115, 119, 122, 130, 150, 153, 168, 171, 199, 234, 240, 258, 270, 329, 338, 343, 346, and 356 courtesy Girdner family; all others courtesy Northern Arizona University, Cline Library, Girdner, Alwin, and Barker, Florence collections.

Map by Matthew Girdner.

Half title page: Cousins David, Bob, and Ruthie Campbell and Alwin, circa 1928.
Frontispiece: Edge of Monument Valley.

Book design: Rudy Ramos Design.

Printed in the United States of America.

10 9 8 7 6 5 4 3 2 1

Library of Congress Cataloging-in-Publication Data

Girdner, Alwin J., 1923-
  Diné Tah : my reservation days 1923-1938 / Alwin J. Girdner.
     p. cm.
  ISBN-13: 978-1-933855-56-1 (pbk. : alk. paper)
  ISBN-10: 1-933855-56-8 (pbk. : alk. paper)
 1. Navajo Indians--Missions. 2. Navajo Indians--Religion. 3. Navajo Indians--Social life and customs.
 4. Plymouth Brethren--Missions--Navajo Indian Reservation. 5. Missionaries--Navajo Indian Reservation--Biography. 6. Navajo Indian Reservation--Religious life and customs. 7. Navajo Indian Reservation--Social life and customs. I. Title.
  E99.N3G53 2011
  979.1004'9726--dc22
                        2011013129

To Marjorie Jo Wilson Girdner,

my dear wife and partner of 58 years whose words of encouragement gave me the confidence to put down on paper for my family the retelling of my many bedtime stories. Early in my young family's life our nighttime routine would be for me to sit on the end of the children's beds and recount stories of growing up on the Navajo Reservation while Marjorie enjoyed some rare, peaceful evening moments. Often, however, her peace was interrupted by young Allen who would bail out of bed at the end of the evening's tale and run in to tell his mother, in exaggerated detail, his version of my story. Thank you for believing in me, Marjorie.

This is for you.

Contents

Con and Grace, Alwin's hosts the night of the big wind.

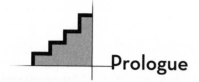

Prologue

The story of my life on the Navajo Reservation began on a cold night in December of 1924. A howling sandstorm blew up around Immanuel Mission, a tiny, two-room abandoned trading post that sheltered my family of six adults and one baby, new missionaries to a remote corner of the vast Four Corners region of northern Arizona.

About three o'clock in the morning Mother woke to a crashing sound and, to her horror, saw a corner of the roof lifting up and down, pounding loose some of the stone blocks of the wall.

She jumped up, screaming, "Glen, Glen, wake up!" and just as Dad sat up, a stone fell onto their bed, grazing his head and slicing an ugly gash in his scalp. Mother lit a lamp, snatched me from my crib, and wrapped me in a blanket, and Dad, ignoring the blood dripping down his face, rushed out into the storm.

A young Navajo couple, Grace and Con, were camped in a temporary shelter built in front of a small cave in the side of an arroyo about 100 yards north of the Mission, and Dad ran down the wash, stopped at their hut, and shouted. Con raised the blanket, peered out into the dark, and was astonished to see, shivering in the wind just outside his hogan, the bleeding white man known as *damoo lichíí',* or Red Sunday, clutching his bundled-up baby.

I was only fourteen months old at the time but still have a distinct memory of being carried in the dark and being handed through a hanging blanket door to a young woman who was nice and warm and began soothing me as Dad left. This may be from hearing the story retold countless times in my youth, but I can still feel that cold wind, the warm hut, and those soft, comforting Navajo words.

Next morning the missionaries started clearing away the wreckage and found that a forty-pound rock had crashed into my crib, doing substantial damage to the crib but fortunately not to me. Had I remained in that little crib this would be a short story—ending here.

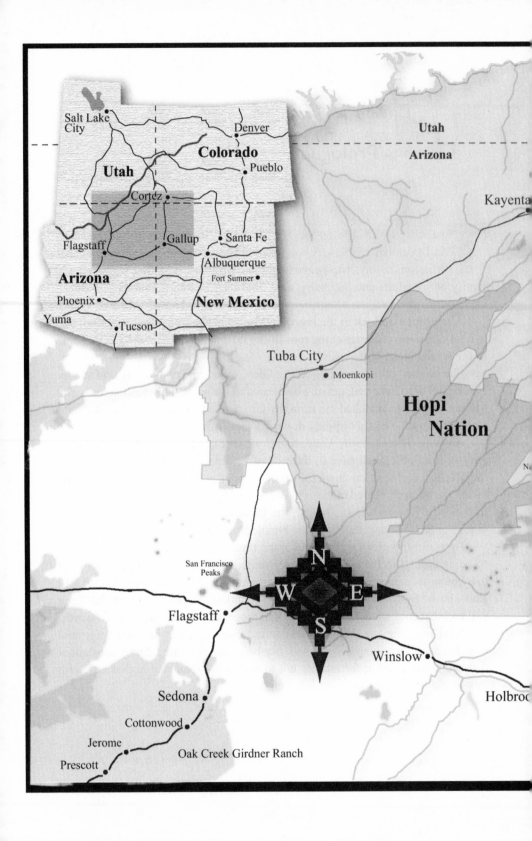

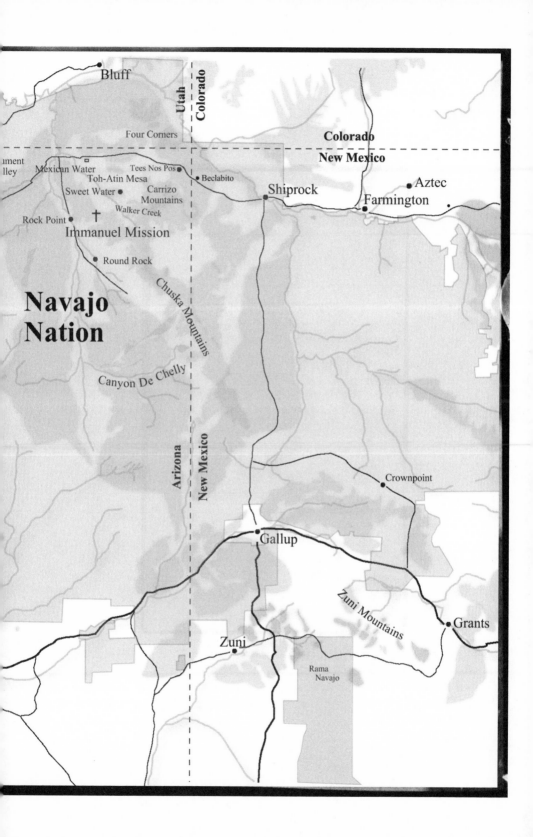

Clara Holcomb and Hazel Fairfield, 1923.

Introduction

As I begin this saga, I would like first to define my purpose in setting down these recollections of a time long since gone. This is not a definitive account of Immanuel Mission or of the Navajo people, but rather an account of early missionary activity, told through stories of people and events as seen by a small boy living in one corner of the Navajo Reservation before World War II changed forever the customs, the way of life, and even the language of the native people living in that lonely land.

In writing this account, I have drawn from my own memory, family records, and long discussions with my father, Glen C. Girdner, who also wrote extensive notes to prepare his record of those early days. He described his record as "an account of some of the more outstanding events and maybe a few short stories of the mission activities up to the time of our leaving there in 1939."

His "manuscript," as he called it, was not completed before his death in 1988, at the Arizona Pioneers' Home in Prescott, Arizona. It consisted largely of notes, written in his painstaking handwriting on sheets of paper, backs of envelopes, and small scraps of blank paper he frugally cut from the backs of periodicals and newsletters. I know these notes are true and accurate to the best of his knowledge, as in the preamble to the typed material, he states: "I'm writing this from memory as I don't like fiction mixed with my facts: I'll take them straight, please."

The missionary nurse Florence Barker also kept a record of her five years at the founding of Immanuel Mission and took several hundred pictures, as did my aunt Clara E. Holcomb. These journals and pictures are now at the Cline Library at Northern Arizona University. I have also drawn extensively from reports by H. A. Holcomb and Clara Holcomb, published by the Gospel Missionary Union, now Avant Ministries, in issues of the *Gospel Messenger* from the early 1900s.

In the 1920s it was almost impossible to write anything in Navajo that would be easily recognized, mainly because at that time there was no standardized written Navajo, and words were transcribed in wildly different ways. However, writing and spelling of the Navajo language has developed over the years, and the early attempts to reduce the language to a written form have gradually become more standardized. As an example: the name of the tribe was spelled

Marie and Glen teaching Alwin to walk on the Reservation.

"Navaho" for a time, but subsequently the Tribal Council officially endorsed "Navajo." In this work I have generally used the spelling system established in *The Navajo Language* by Robert Young and William Morgan, but passages from the Florence Barker journals and Glen Girdner's manuscript are in their original spelling.

There are no capital letters in written Navajo, but when a Navajo term has been adopted into English as a proper noun, such as a personal or place name, I have added capitalization in my text. In writing about these bygone Reservation days, I also occasionally use the word "Indian" instead of "Native American," which seems anachronistic in describing the early twentieth century. Most often, however, I speak more specifically of Hopi, Navajo, or Diné.

Literally translated, the word "Diné" means "the people." "Diné Tah" (sometimes spelled as a single word, and pronounced, approximately, "dih-NEH tah") means "among the people" or "among the Navajo," but it has also come to mean the land or homeland of the Navajo people. That homeland comprises parts of Arizona, Utah, Colorado, and New Mexico—a total area the size of New England—and is a land of great beauty and equally great geographic and climatic variety.

1   The Color of Yesterday

Pictures of the past are all in black and white or, worse, sepia. TV and movies also often show flashback episodes this way, so most people visualize the "olden days" as being lived without color and imagine everyone walking about in black and white.

I remember my early days in the Navajo country as full of color, bright and vivid. The skies were almost always a clear, deep blue, and mornings and evenings were spectacular, with deepening shadows throwing details of the mountain peaks and canyons and the red mesas into sharp relief. In the foreground the high desert hills and sandy soil were covered with sage-green and gray bushes, punctuated here and there with dunes of red sand.

I was an early riser and in my preteen years went out in the arroyos or washes, as we called them, climbing around the mesas early in the morning before anyone else was stirring. This was the time of day to find arrowheads, broken pieces of pottery, and, occasionally, larger artifacts such as grinding stones—which we called metates—or maybe even a fragment of pipe, in ancient Anasazi (now commonly referred to as Ancestral Puebloan) camping sites.

As the darkness receded, rabbits and small birds would rustle in the bushes and an occasional coyote would scream a last great howl before trotting off to his siesta. And sunrise was an awesome time, absolute silence as the clear gray of the dawn gradually lightened to pink that quickly became yellow, then brightened into splendid color as the rays of light came over the mountain.

As the sun moved up toward the zenith, the color of the desert would slowly fade, and brilliant sunshine would build up heat until by late morning almost all birds and animals had disappeared into their own shelter, not to reappear until shadows were long and the breeze of the evening cooled the air. Sunsets came quickly, with great masses of clouds blazing in the western sky as the sun sank very slowly, then suddenly dipped below the mesa in a glorious burst of red and gold that filled the entire sky with glory, and then was gone.

In describing these old days I might paraphrase Southwestern artist and author Tom Lea in his book *Wonderful Country*: "Oh, how I wish I had the power to describe the wonderful country as I saw it then."

2 ⌐ The Long Walk

My own story is one thread in a history that reaches back many centuries. The Navajos are an Athabascan people and relatively new to the Southwest, compared to the Pueblo people of the Hopi mesas and Rio Grande Valley. Like their Apache cousins, Navajos were a nomadic people, hunters and gatherers who lived off the land and took whatever they could find as they moved about their vast domain. Navajos and Apaches speak similar versions of Athabascan, which is also spoken by more than thirty other tribes in Canada, Alaska, and the west coast, and thus the highest mountain in North America has an Athabascan name—Denali, the "High One."

Michael LaCapa, an accomplished artist, storyteller, and educator of Apache–Hopi descent, once described the Navajo and Apache attitude: "When they rode over a hill and saw someone's stray cows they shouted in delight, 'Oh look what the gods have provided for us!' and rounded them up for dinner." The Navajo lifestyle allowed appropriating whatever came to hand, but they also had a high sense of responsibility to their family and clan members, and whatever they had the good fortune to find was consumed immediately—shared equally with everyone in the extended family.

Independent and self-supporting, the Navajos distrusted outsiders but were always open to anything that would enhance their own way of life, and they adapted many things from other peoples, particularly the Pueblo Indians, from whom they learned weaving, pottery making, and farming. After the Spanish introduction of the horse to the Rio Grande Valley, the Navajos were able to greatly improve their condition by raiding far and wide throughout the Spanish settlements and neighboring tribes for horses, cattle, sheep, and occasionally women.

The concept of all Indians living in peace before the intrusion of the white man is not entirely accurate, considering the almost constant warfare between the various Indian tribes long before the arrival of the first white men. The Navajos had been in intermittent conflict with the Comanches, Utes, and other tribes for years before the arrival in 1598 of Juan de Oñate and his settlers from what is now Mexico. In 1846, at the end of the U.S. war with Mexico, General Stephen Watts Kearny, with 1,700 troops of the Army of the West, invaded Santa Fe, and a third culture was introduced into the area, with new ideas of private ownership of land and property that added another dimension to the uneasy cultural balance.

Navajo raiding of villages, and counter-raids on the Navajos by the Utes, Comanches, and Mexicans, continued after the arrival of the new American forces. The Americans became involved soon after they marched into Santa Fe with Kearny, and warfare and desultory raids and counter-raids continued. It should be noted, however, that the Navajos did not indulge in "recreational killing" as did some of their Apache cousins. I discussed this subject extensively in my University of Arizona master's thesis from 1950, "Navaho–United States Relations."

Captive women and children were usually treated well by the Navajos and incorporated into the tribe, so many Navajos are descendants of women taken in raids. In time new clans appeared as the *naakaii,* from Mexican captives, and the *mą'ii deeshgiizhnii,* from Jemez Pueblo people who sought refuge with the Navajos when the Spanish returned to New Mexico after the Pueblo Revolt of 1680.

U.S. troops made a number of expeditions into Navajo country, and a number of "treaties" were concluded between them, but the Americans did not seem to comprehend the fact that the tribe had no overall chief but consisted of individual groups with their own headmen who had influence only in their own areas, and so any agreement by one group of Navajos was not necessarily binding for all other bands of Navajos. The thumbprint of one or more "chiefs" of one group of Navajos on a paper did not particularly affect other groups of Navajos, particularly bands of young "have nots" who continued taking the easiest way of getting sheep, cattle, horses, and wives by raiding their neighboring Pueblos.

These raids resulted in thousands of sheep being stolen and a number of women and children taken captive. In this desultory warfare, killings were only incidental, as most raids were motivated by the temptation of free livestock. Fort Defiance was established by the army at *tséhootsooí* in Navajo country to control these ambitious young men, and a number of military excursions into the area continued.

Relations between the Navajo and the U.S. worsened over time. "Uncle Dick" Wootton, who was a scout and guide for Colonel Newby's expedition to "whip the Navajos into better behavior" in March 1848, described the Navajos as the most industrious of all the Indian tribes, who did less fighting but were also the "greatest lot of thieves among the Indians" (quoted in *Uncle Dick Wootton* by Howard L. Conrad). Then, in April of 1860, a large organized Navajo attack was made on Fort Defiance before dawn. "Two thousand yelling Navajos poured a heavy fire of arrows and bullets into the fort and forced their way into the sutler store," according to Senate Executive Document 1, 36th Congress, Second Session, and it was decided that military action was called for.

In October, Colonel Edward R. S. Canby, under orders to "seize and destroy the crops," led two detachments of six mounted and nine infantry companies, accompanied by Ute and Pueblo Indians to act as spies and guides, into Navajo country. The Navajos fled west of the Hopi villages to the Little Colorado River with their flocks and herds, but a number of Navajo mounted parties followed the pursuing troops, watching them from the high mesas along the route. The Utes, moving ahead of the troops, killed six Navajos; captured women, children, hundreds of horses, and several thousand sheep; and promptly deserted. "They are satisfied and have gone home," said Canby, according to Max L. Heyman Jr. in *Prudent Soldier: A Biography of Major General E. R. S. Canby.*

The troops remained in the field until an armistice was agreed upon and Canby returned to Fort Defiance. However, following Canby's inconclusive campaign, several volunteer New Mexico groups, one with over 300 men, burned crops, raided the Navajo country, and returned with many flocks and captives, mostly women and children. Acts of violence continued with raids by the younger, irresponsible Navajo men who had no property to lose, followed by retaliatory excursions made by Mexicans, often on peaceful Navajos attending their flocks.

CALIFORNIA COLUMN

At the start of the Civil War, Colonel James Henry Carleton, who had served in New Mexico with the First Dragoons, was stationed in California, where he recruited what became the First Volunteer Infantry, and in July of 1861 he led the "California Column" from the Los Angeles area across the deserts of Arizona and New Mexico to check the Confederate threat to the Rio Grande Valley. A skirmish, now known as the Battle of Picacho Peak, was fought in what is now southern Arizona before Carleton moved his California Column on to Tucson and bartered with the Pima and Maricopa Indians for food and forage before moving on again to Las Cruces, New Mexico.

Confederate General Henry Hopkins Sibley, on learning of the California Column advance, abandoned all plans for the occupation of New Mexico and retreated back into Texas, and Carleton reached Santa Fe in September of 1862. General Canby was reassigned to another command in the Union Army, and Brigadier General Carleton assumed command of the Department of New Mexico. The Navajos had meanwhile taken advantage of the Civil War to increase raiding, and in November 1863, General Carleton ordered that both the Navajo and the Mescalero Apache tribes be removed from their traditional homelands to a new, permanent reservation on the Pecos River in eastern New Mexico, where they were to learn how to become peaceful farmers.

KIT CARSON

A longtime mountain man with an intimate knowledge of the ways of Indians, Christopher "Kit" Carson, was assigned a contingent of troops and ordered to organize a campaign to round up the thousands of Navajos hidden away in their far-flung canyons and mountains. Carson reluctantly followed Carleton's orders and moved his troops into Navajo country, tearing down hogans, cutting down peach orchards, destroying crops, and killing anyone who resisted.

After Carson succeeded in invading the stronghold of Canyon de Chelly, he then marched captives in several groups on the "Long Walk," over hundreds of miles, to their new home in New Mexico. This was at Bosque Redondo near Fort Sumner, or *hwééldi,* as the Spanish word *fuerte* (fort) sounded to the bewildered Navajos.

The first group of the Navajos, with their headman Delgadito, were taken from Fort Defiance to Los Pinos, then up the Rio Grande past Albuquerque to Santa Fe and marched through the streets of the capital. It has been said that this was ordered by Carleton to show the Navajos as defeated prisoners of the army; however, the circuitous route up the Rio Grande and then down the Pecos to Fort Sumner actually provided better access to water on the way across the desert.

Some bands escaped capture by fleeing to Navajo Mountain, the Four Corners area, and other remote places and were never found, but over the years many of these people were forced to join the rest of the tribe in a new life at Fort Sumner, trying to farm the flatlands so far from their traditional mesas and mountains. Eventually some 9,000 Navajo men, women, and children were interned. As the campaign ended, General Carleton had Fort Defiance evacuated and abandoned as a military post and moved all troops and all supplies to Fort Wingate.

Conditions were miserable at Bosque Redondo. The farming projects failed, leaving the people near starvation, and the confinement with their traditional enemies, the Mescaleros and the Jicarilla Apaches, led to acts of violence between the tribes. It was later reported that over 1,500 internees died during those desperate four years at Fort Sumner. Carleton made provisions for both a school and hospital, and a small Catholic church was established, but very few of the detainees found these amenities useful and seldom attended any of them. Navajos particularly feared the hospital, as it was a place where people died and was therefore full of evil spirits.

The Navajo confinement was not well-accepted by many of the other people of New Mexico, and the policy of internment began to draw criticism from the *Santa Fe New Mexican* and other newspapers, which didn't oppose the reservation as much as they did the relocation of Navajos to New Mexican lands. The confinement also removed the only remaining source of slaves. José Chaves, who had already served eight sessions as president of the New Mexico territorial council, successfully campaigned to remove the Navajos already at

Roy Scott.

Bosque Redondo to their own tribal area, and in the election of 1865 and as the New Mexico territorial delegate to the 39th U.S. Congress, he took the problem to the U.S. Senate.

TREATY OF 1868
A senate judiciary committee then investigated Indian slavery in New Mexico Territory. An act of congress subsequently prohibited peonage in the territory, and this was followed in 1868 by the appointment of a federal peace commission headed by Lieutenant General William T. Sherman. The new peace commission made the long trip across the plains to Bosque Redondo and began negotiating an agreement to move the Navajos home to their beloved Diné Tah (or homeland) if they would maintain the peace in the future.

After an intense period of discussion, an agreement was reached with Barboncito and the other eleven headmen. Some 3,500 Navajos were released, and on June 1, 1868, the treaty was signed, and after four long, miserable years of captivity, over 8,000 Navajos walked the long trail back to Fort Wingate and their new reservation on their traditional lands on the Colorado Plateau, completing the period now remembered as the "Long Walk from *hwééldi*." Three groups of Navajos from the main group did not complete the return journey but split off to form small settlements along the way: Canoncito, Ramah, and Alamo on the western edge of New Mexico.

The raiding days of the Diné were over, and, except for a few small local incidents, there was lasting peace on the new reservation. The Navajos had no desire to repeat the four years of captivity and terrible conditions at Bosque Redondo, and the cessation of raids and taking of slaves by the New Mexicans gave little cause for retaliatory raids on their neighbors along the Rio Grande.

An epitaph for the Fort Sumner attempt to solve the Navajo problem was suggested at that time:

> *If so soon I am done for*
> *I wonder why I was begun for.*
> —quoted by JOHN WATTS,
> *Welcome to Navajo-Land Magazine,* Navajo
> Nation, Window Rock, Arizona, n.d.

STORIES OF *HWÉÉLDI*

During our early years at Immanuel Mission, stories of the Long Walk were still being told by the few survivors and occasionally by second-generation Navajos who had heard them from their elders. I remember listening to Navajo tales about the experiences of family members when they were first exposed to the strange ways of the *bilagáana* (the Navajo name for "American"). When cups and plates were issued, they punched holes in the flat disks and wore them as pendants around their necks, and how terrible they found the bars of soap they mistook for *bilagáana* food! They had also tried to eat coffee beans, and they boiled raw white flour into a soup that only made them sick.

Most of these stories were told in a joking manner, and few hostile feelings were displayed about that terrible time in the past. They saw some advantage in the fact that the Diné had learned to eat the strange new foods and became addicted to the coffee and also learned to make a frybread that soon became a Navajo staple as well as a tourist attraction.

Today there are many stories in print about the treatment of the captives on the Long Walk and at the "concentration camp" of Fort Sumner. Accounts of Navajo stragglers and women with babies being shot by the soldiers on the march and of women and children being mistreated still appear in a few publications.

But at Immanuel Mission, seventy-five years ago, we heard very little resentment or hostility expressed by Navajos about their parents' treatment by Carson, *biee'lichii'ii,* or by his soldiers, either at *hwééldi* or on the long marches between their country and Fort Sumner. A few accounts did mention the Utes and the Apaches taking advantage of the people during that terrible time, raiding and plundering the defenseless Navajo camps and carrying off women and children as slaves, but I heard no stories of brutal treatment by the

The Navajos in our remote Four Corners area, however, did not experience as much tribulation as the rest of the tribe, as they were isolated from most of the action—and many families succeeded in avoiding capture altogether.

Louisa Wade Wetherill, who was at the Kayenta trading post while I was on the Reservation, knew an old Navajo man, Wolfkiller, who told many stories of the Navajo people and their years at *hwééldi*. She recorded them at the time, but they were not published until 2007 in *Wolfkiller*.

Wolfkiller's comments about the Long Walk were similar to those we heard at Immanuel Mission, such as this observation: "Grandfather told the ones who had complained that it was their own fault. He said they had not tried to control their young men, so the whole tribe must suffer." And:

> We only wanted to live our lives as we had been doing for many years. I said that we knew our past record was against us and that some of our people had brought the trouble on themselves and deserved the punishment they were getting, but we who did not want trouble felt that we did not deserve to be punished for the sins of someone else. Now we had decided there was nothing for us but to go with them.

I personally knew only two survivors of *hwééldi: tsinaabǫǫs sani,* the grandfather of the extended *tłízí lizhin* family, and an old lady we called "Sister Sorry" for her mournful demeanor. But, as a youngster, I had little conversation with either of these two old-timers. I came to regret this later when, as a graduate student at the University of Arizona, I was writing a thesis on early Navajo history.

Navajos distrusted outsiders, but they also were adaptive and quick to learn and soon applied any practices or new methods they thought would enhance their way of life. Over time, sheep, rugs, silver, and even religious practices of the Pueblos and other cultures were incorporated into their daily lives, and the tribe thrived. When the first buildings were put up at Immanuel Mission, a number of Navajos were found to be quite skilled and worked very well with Dad at everything from mixing adobe to nailing tarpaper on the roof.

"Sister Sorry."

3 At Home in a Hogan

avajos never lived together in large groups or villages, as did their Pueblo neighbors, but always in separate, small groups of hogans scattered through the far-flung hills and canyons of the lonely, enormous Reservation. Many of these homes were almost invisible, tucked away among the trees, bushes, and scrub vegetation.

The most important factor in any hogan location was the availability of water, and hogans always had a source, usually a spring or a very small stream somewhere in the vicinity, but often it had to be hauled by the bucketful for considerable distances, usually over 100 yards and sometimes several miles. After the arrival of the *bilagáana,* a few families acquired wagons and larger barrels, tubs, and other containers so water could be transported from more distant sources, but it always remained scarce and was doled out in very small portions for drinking, cooking, and washing.

Navajos used water by the cupful, in contrast to the average white person's consumption, which is estimated now at nearly seventy gallons a day. As a result there was seldom the luxury of washing either their persons or their clothing, and new items were often put on over the old garment and neither removed for months, as everyone slept clothed. In spite of this, Navajos were almost always neat in their appearance.

All hogans were built facing east, usually with a blanket-covered doorway and a packed earth floor, with a fire for cooking and heat in the center of the hogan and a round smoke hole in the center of the roof to let the smoke out. Cooking was almost always done over the open fire. Sheepskins, blankets, any food, and all of the family's worldly goods were stored around the sides of the hogan between the supporting logs, and a few large goods and equipment would be suspended a little above the people's heads, as everyone sat on sheepskins on the hard-packed dirt floor.

When I was on the Reservation, most hogans were of the cribbed-log, round style, but the older fork-stick hogans were not uncommon. Building a hogan was usually a cooperative effort by a number of Navajo men and often was something of a festive occasion as the men worked together to put together the rather complicated structure. In summertime a Navajo family would often erect

Navajos at an old-style hogan in the foothills.

a *chaha'oh,* once described by Aunt Clara as "a brush hut built only for shade, sometimes only three sticks in the ground between a wagon wheel and some sacks of wool, on which were hung three or four yards of muslin."

VISITING ETIQUETTE

Approaching a hogan on camp visits, we observed the Navajo custom of taking time as we came near, so the people would know someone was coming and could prepare for visitors, even though they were well aware of our approach long before anyone arrived, as most camps had a pack of mangy, half-wild dogs that barked ferociously at all strangers.

After a time, someone, usually a man, would lift the blanket and come out to shout at the dogs, sometimes throwing a stick or stone and ordering quiet. Sometimes this would be effective and the animals would slink a few yards away, still snarling and sniffing suspiciously at the intruders. The man would then welcome the guests without any loud greetings, and, after shaking hands and making a bit of conversation, would invite us into his hogan and offer us sheepskins. Men sat on the left side, on the floor, and women sat to the right.

NAVAJO DOMESTIC LIFE

Navajo society was matrilineal, and a new husband moved to the wife's camp after they were married, usually into their own hogan not far from the family hogan and the new mother-in-law. Children that came along would belong to the mother's clan.

Navajos communually erect a hogan as Florence Barker observes on Lael.

The husband was often occupied in religious ceremonies and rode out to take part in important sings and other gatherings, but the hogan was entirely the domain of his wife, the woman of the family. Although he usually built the hogan and he lived in it, his wife was in charge of daily life and owned almost everything except his personal belongings and his prized horses. Horses, sometimes large herds of them, were owned by the man, and the more horses a man owned, the more successful he was in the eyes of his kinfolk.

Livestock was usually individually owned, but most of the sheep seemed to belong to the wife. Children often had a few animals of their own that they had been given to raise for themselves, but their mother was in charge and responsible for all maintenance of sheep and usually assigned the task of herding to the older children. The woman was often the major source of outside income, too, through the rugs she wove on a frame fashioned by the man. Weaving was done in the hogan in wintertime and outside during the hot weather, usually under a *chaha'oh*, or shade, that had also been built by the man.

There were no cupboards or sink in a hogan and usually very little water. All preparing and cooking of food was done on the ground over the fire in the center of the hut, although occasionally some sort of stove, such as a metal drum with holes cut in the top, stood in the center of the hogan. Most hogans featured one indispensable little item, a little rack made of wire that stood maybe ten inches above the open flame, which cooks used in preparing all food that was not boiled.

A few pots and pans were the basic utensils in the hogan, and the Navajo wife shaped *náneeskaadí,* Navajo frybread, by slapping the dough, sometimes on her knee, to form round patties before cooking them on the wire rack. She prepared the mutton and whatever other foods there were, and the family ate it without benefit of any table. All meals were served on the wife's schedule, and the man ate whatever the woman prepared whenever she decided to prepare it. At that time a few Navajo men had more than one wife, and occasionally when a man married a widow he would eventually take her daughter as a second wife when she grew older.

Social behavior was gently taught to children by instruction in the Navajo way of doing things, and a child was almost never struck, but I have seen a frustrated mother get attention from an unruly child by shouting a warning "*jishcaa!*" (or "grave," meaning that the child was treading on dangerous or forbidden ground). In the hogan, everyone sat on the ground, usually on a sheepskin, and everyone also slept on the ground, on sheepskins, usually with blankets for covers. There was very little privacy and everyone was aware of the sleeping habits of all the others in the hogan.

THROW HIS SADDLE OUT

Divorce was easy, as the accepted Navajo custom at that time was that a woman could get rid of an undesirable mate by "throwing his saddle out." She would just put his saddle and other personal equipment and belongings outside the hogan door and when he returned he immediately would know he was dismissed and usually did not enter the hogan but just rounded up his horses and left, riding his horse and wearing his clothes, jewelry, and hat. All "real estate," sheep, and household goods remained with his recent wife.

Dad wrote a succinct comment on this custom: "To a degree the wife has the last word and cases are seen when the woman sets her husband's saddle outside the hogan and that is 'it.' Some men have given up and never returned. Others have made satisfactory apologies and promises and were received back again."

One day I witnessed a case when the local elders of the tribe were involved in a divorce. Fifteen or twenty men gathered for a meeting in the yard just outside the adobe main building at the Mission, and the discussion began. The talking went on and on and on for most of the day, as Navajos did not stop with a majority vote but continued talking until everyone present agreed.

I never knew just what the problem was nor how it was resolved, but finally the woman stood up, wrapped her Pendleton blanket around her, and solemnly walked around the circle, shaking hands with everyone present. The meeting then broke up and everyone departed. Curiously, I don't remember the ex-husband even being present at this meeting.

4 Navajo Ceremonies

Religion and ceremonies were part of all Navajo activities, social as well as religious, and at all times they were aware of *hôzhô*. *Hôzhô,* the need for balance and harmony between man and nature, was expressed in their oral history, stories, chants, and songs. The "sing" was a religious ceremony performed by a trained shaman or medicine man, which included chants and sometimes sandpaintings that had to be executed exactly right, as a mistake could cause great harm.

Navajos did not accept coincidences in life and believed that all things were interrelated, and that illness or misfortune could well have been caused by something done, even years ago, that had upset their harmony. It could only be restored by a ceremony to bring *hôzhô* back into their life.

Hundreds of books have been written about Navajo legends, customs, and ceremonies, beginning with the early reports of army personnel stationed near the Navajo country. One of the first was written by Dr. Jonathan Letherman, who spent three years at Fort Defiance. His impressions, published in 1855, were neither particularly well informed nor very complimentary, either of Navajo ceremonies or of their religious practices. "Of their religion," he wrote, "little or nothing is known, indeed all inquiries tend to show that they have none." He went on to report that Navajos had frequent gatherings for dancing but described their singing as "a succession of grunts and anything but agreeable." Although Major Letherman was ignorant of Navajo culture, he had a very successful career after leaving New Mexico. He changed his name to Letterman, served as medical director of the Army of the Potomac during the Civil War, and later as a professor of chemistry at West Point Military Academy. The largest army hospital at San Francisco during World War II was also named after him.

Dr. Washington Matthews, a military surgeon stationed at Fort Wingate from 1880 to 1884, also became interested in Navajo legends, language, and customs and made an early study of their religion with the goal of preserving something of their culture before it disappeared. He is credited with publishing fifty-eight pioneering monographs. Christian Barthelmess, a soldier-musician and photographer, was also stationed at Fort Wingate at that time and worked with Dr. Matthews to "put into writing both the words and music which the

Indians, having no written language, had previously preserved solely by word of mouth."

Father Berard Haile, a Franciscan priest, arrived at St. Michaels in 1900, and developed an intense interest in Navajo tradition and beliefs. Over the years he contributed extensively, not only to linguistics and development of a written language, but also to understanding many Navajo religious ceremonies and myths.

Father Haile was considered by many during my time on the Reservation as perhaps the foremost of scholars in the field. He published extensively until his death sixty-one years later, and a bibliography of his work would include over forty books and as many, or more, articles in periodicals. Father Berard was criticized by some for his approach in ministering to the Navajos but explained his method in a letter to John B. Wuest, OFM, which was published in the *Provincial Chronicle* in 1948. Writing during his golden sacerdotal jubilee year, Father Berard said:

> It seemed to me that one had to study [Diné] customs, their outlook on life, on the universe, [on] natural phenomena, [and] their concepts on the origin of man, vegetation and animals, before one could approach them on religious matters. Here were human beings, intelligent, ingenious, industrious, religious, enormously so; why then, approach them on a "You're all wrong, listen to me" basis? Traditions of such long standing cannot be uprooted by such matter-of-fact statements as we are accustomed to, owing to our training. I did not convert from theology to anthropology but did feel that all theology needed some anthropology to help mission work along.

Protestant missionaries believed the Navajo ceremonies to be heathen and were dedicated to freeing the Navajos from the concepts of evil spirits, witches, taboos, and curses that so permeated their daily life. They also opposed all pagan practices and ceremonies, including primarily social gatherings that had ceremonial or religious elements.

Occasionally a ceremony was held near Immanuel Mission and, although curious about Navajo beliefs, I did not ask questions and was therefore completely unaware of the myths and rituals involved in any Navajo social activities and ceremonials, as I had never attended anything but weddings. Almost all my knowledge of Navajo traditions and religion came from general Navajo conversations that I occasionally overheard, and from the often futile efforts of Yellowhair, the Navajo who lived with us, to instruct me in his culture.

Of all the Navajo ceremonies, the only ceremony with which I ever had personal contact was the popular Navajo social event, known to the outside world as a "squaw dance," which occurred during the nights of the *ndaa'*, or

Three young men resting on their way home from a local sing.

Enemy Way ceremony, that was held during the summer months. This was a girls' tag dance, and any man who declined an invitation from a girl to dance with her had to pay a cash penalty. It was one of the very few social occasions where there was any contact at all between unmarried young people, and even that was generally limited to her holding the edge of his jacket to keep him from "escaping," and all activity was well chaperoned by the entire group.

When I was about eight a sing was being held at a camp just south of the Mission, and early one morning while I was out at the woodpile, loading my wagon with the day's supply of fuel, a line of Navajos came quietly riding along the trail just beyond our western fence.

I didn't recognize any of the men, but noticed one well-dressed young woman was riding with them, holding a juniper pole decorated with a bright tangle of burnt weeds, eagle feathers, and deer hoofs bound by buckskin at the top, with colored red bayeta yarn fluttering down from it. One of the men also carried a pot drum. I was curious about the strange parade but didn't learn until years later that a juniper "rattle stick," a carefully selected and a decorated pole, was sometimes carried to the hogan of the friend or clansman who sponsored the ceremony.

On another bright summer morning, we noticed from the front porch that groups of mounted men were arriving at a Navajo camp not far from the Mission, and a lot of activity took place over the next several days, indicating a sing was under way. It was a long ceremony and took several days to perform.

During the warmer months I usually slept outside under a tamarisk hedge just outside our downstairs room, and several nights after the sing began, I was awakened just before dawn by gunfire somewhere near the Navajo camp where the sing was being held. Not long after, I heard loud conversation and laughter as several groups of young men rode up the trail past the Mission on their way home, and I knew the ceremony was over. I lay there until sunrise, wondering what had happened, and only years later did I learn that the squaw dance concludes with a scalp shooting ritual to "kill the ghost of the scalp."

The Enemy Way later became very well known in the Anglo world as it was often used for young men returning to the Reservation after service in the armed forces during World War II, to free them from the evil spirits of the dead they had been exposed to overseas. Tony Hillerman originally titled one of his early books about Navajo tribal police "The Enemy Way," but the publishers, in their wisdom, published it as *The Blessing Way*, an entirely different ceremony.

As most Navajo singing was done in connection with religious activities, and as I never attended a "sing," I officially knew very little about their music. But in actuality my younger brother Danny and I were familiar with many of the chants, as Yellowhair often chanted softly as he worked and every night from his bed after he retired at night. His room adjoined ours, so Danny and I learned many Navajo chants, whether we wanted to or not.

In *To the Foot of the Rainbow*, the anthropologist Clyde Kluckhohn vividly described first hearing Navajo singing as a young man in 1925: "The singing began again—weird melodies which reflected and portrayed the strange spirit of the desert; shrill fitful voices intoning the call of the hunted; then a deep, snarling, vibrating prelude to a swinging melodious chant."

At Immanuel Mission we would occasionally hear the wild, lonesome sound of the "riding song" of Navajo men riding past at night, which they sang to protect themselves from the unknown spirits that might be around in the darkness. And I often experimented with the Navajo way of singing. The Navajos were intrigued and highly amused by my vocal efforts, and one day I was walking across the yard singing a riding song at the top of my voice when I heard a burst of laughter from a group of young Navajo men sitting on the back porch of the adobe building.

Embarrassed, I stopped in mid-chant, but they all shouted for me to continue as they couldn't believe a six-year-old white kid could be singing one of their songs. One young fellow even offered to sing with me and started a chant, but I was too shy to perform for a Navajo audience.

5 Different Words of God

When my family came to Diné Tah in the early twentieth century, they were not the first missionaries to arrive there.

My father once described religion to me in a way that bears repeating. He explained faith as two men standing beside two separate columns that both rose up into the sky farther than either man could see, but each believed he stood at the foot of the one true way to heaven. Beyond their sight, however, the pillars actually joined together in an arch. Eighty years later, my own vision has expanded to one of many, many pillars that support a great invisible dome above us all.

As soon as the Spanish colonists reached New Mexico, they immediately set about converting the native people to a new way of life based on Christian principles. First came chaplains with the invading conquistadors, soon followed by zealous priests from Spain, France, and Italy, who over the years dedicated their lives to improving the Indians materially as well as spiritually. They established a mission at Santa Clara as early as 1627.

These zealous Catholic missionaries had a degree of success with the more peaceful pueblos along the Rio Grande, who simply adapted the new faith to their ancient practices and ceremonies and continued living much as they had before the invasion. The nomadic, more warlike Navajos, however, refused to settle down and persisted in moving about in the old hunting, gathering, and raiding way of life, rejecting altogether the idea of living in villages and farming.

A few Franciscans worked among the Apaches de Navajo, as they called the Diné in those days. Fray Miguel de Menchero had a mission at Cebolleta, New Mexico, below *tsoodził* (Mount Taylor), as early as 1748, but they, and later the Jesuits, had little success in gaining more than a few converts. Some, however, did attain the coveted martyr's crown in the attempt. Years later a small Catholic church served the Navajos with indifferent success during the captivity at Fort Sumner.

ST. MICHAEL MISSION
In 1896, Mother (now Saint) Katharine Drexel of Philadelphia, founder of the Sisters of the Blessed Sacrament for Indians and Colored People, purchased

Marie Girdner and Old Wagon.

a 160-acre tract of land in Arizona, eight miles below Fort Defiance and just
south of the Navajo Reservation. (Katharine Drexel's father, Francis Drexel,
was partner with J. P. Morgan and others in an international banking empire.)

Soon afterward, in October 1898, a trio of Franciscan friars—Anselm Weber,
OFM; Juvenal Schnorbus, OFM; and Placidus Buerger, OFM—occupied a stone
building originally built as a trading post at nearby *ts'ohootso* and established
a small mission. Mother Katharine's selection of the site for the school was just
above the mission, and in December of 1902, St. Michael Indian School was
established to teach Navajo children the Four Rs: Reading, 'Riting, 'Rithmetic,
and Religion. A post office was approved and designated St. Michaels, Territory
of Arizona, with John Walker as postmaster.

The early Franciscan friars were often American citizens but mostly of German
origin, and English was their second language. Early reports were published in
German, and Navajo students leaned to speak English with a German accent and
to sing German Christmas carols. Father Weber served as superior at St. Michael
until his death in 1921, and with two other Franciscan missionaries, Berard Haile
and Leopold Ostermann, made tremendous contributions in spreading Christianity
and translating portions of Scripture into the Navajo language.

Other missionaries followed, and Catholic churches were established on the
Navajo Reservation at Chinle in 1905 and Lukachukai in 1910. In their work
with the tribes, Catholics were somewhat tolerant of native culture, especially
among the pueblos, and chose to incorporate some of the native rituals into
Christian celebrations rather than condemn them all as "heathen," an approach
to conversion that goes back to Pope Gregory the Great, who, as early as the
year 601, wrote a letter of instructions for Bishop Augustine regarding the pagan
English. His words have come down to us in *An Ecclesiastical History of the
English Nation* (c. 731), by the Venerable Bede:

> If the people are allowed some worldly pleasures, they will more easily
> consent to come to desire the joys of the spirit. For there is no doubt that
> it is impossible to efface everything at once from their obdurate minds,
> because he who endeavors to ascend the highest place, rises by degrees
> or steps and not by leaps.
>
> Thus the Lord made himself known to the people of Israel in Egypt.
> He allowed them to use the sacrifices which they were wont to offer the
> devil in his own worship, permitting the sacrifices formerly offered to
> the devil to be offered thence forward to God, and not to idols, and thus
> would no longer be the same sacrifices.

The Protestants, however, took a more conservative approach to Navajo
religious practices. They accepted the concept of *hôzhô* in all relations between

men as admirable, but Irvy Goossen, in *Getting Acquainted with the Navajo Field* advised:

> You are not going there to change the age-old customs of the Navajo tribe. Many of their ways are good even in this modern age. They have been proven to be good for them. You are not going there to make white folks out of them. You are going there to teach the Christian way of life.
>
> The Christian way has nothing to do with running water, bathrooms in the house, or how many times a month you take a bath. A Navajo Christian can pray to the Lord as well in his dirt-floored hogan as you can in your living room with a soft rug.
>
> Because they have to haul their water, sometimes many miles, they are not able to use water as freely as you are used to.

Protestants were strongly opposed to the many religious rites they considered pagan—particularly witchcraft and the myriad superstitions about curses and evil spirits that were associated with death. This made it extremely difficult to present their message of the death and resurrection of Jesus that made salvation and eternal life possible for all mankind.

Traditional Navajos' fear of any contact at all with death made it necessary for them to destroy all possessions of the deceased, even the hogan he died in, and no Navajo ever wanted to be present at any funeral or burial services. Even using the timber of the hogan as firewood for cooking could cause illness, or even death, as could any wood struck by lightning.

This dread of any contact with the dead also led to the practice, which became familiar to me and my family, of calling on a missionary or trader to perform that duty, as white people did not seem to be affected by *ch'įįdii* (evil spirits, or ghosts).

QUAKER PEACE POLICY

In 1868 the new Ulysses S. Grant administration moved to correct the rampant graft and corruption that had developed in the administration of Indian affairs by creating a Board of Indian Commissioners to administer the "Quaker Peace Policy," which proposed joint supervision of Indian agencies through churches to "Christianize and civilize the Indians."

Missionaries were to be recommended by denominations, and assignments of Quakers, Protestants, and Catholics were made to the various tribes. The Navajo Reservation was allocated to Presbyterians, who were to provide education for the Navajos, with all instruction given in English. A few Episcopalian missionaries were also established on the Navajo Reservation before the turn of the century, when the Presbyterian Board of Foreign Mission church at Fort Defiance was established.

One of the many visitors to the Mission.

Early attempts to establish schools on the Reservation, however, met with very little success until 1901, when a party of Presbyterian ministers and laymen explored the southern edge of the Reservation from Flagstaff to Fort Defiance for a suitable place for a Presbyterian mission. They chose a site in Ganado, near the Hubbell Trading Post, and Charles and Alice Bierkemper were sent to "evangelize, educate and medicate the Navajos."

Lorenzo Hubbell, although raised a Catholic, welcomed the pioneer Presbyterians to Ganado, provided a place for them to live, and made a free horse and wagon available for their use. Charles Bierkemper, not only a minister but also a stonemason, started the first stone "Old Manse" that served as living quarters, meeting room, and classroom for the day school for children started by Alice Bierkemper, and by 1906 a medical doctor completed the original pioneer missionary staff.

The Mennonites were working in Tuba City by 1892, the Gospel Missionary Union was established at Moenkopi by 1896, and the Protestant Episcopal Church founded the Good Shepherd Hospital at Fort Defiance in 1897. Soon a number of other denominations were active on the Navajo Reservation, including the Baptists at Two Gray Hills, a nondenominational "mission to the Navajos" at *tolchaco,* and the Methodist Faith Mission at Aneth in southern Utah.

In 1888 a Methodist Church had been erected in Gallup, and by 1891, a Methodist mission at Fort Defiance. In that same year Mary Eldridge and Mary Raymond arrived by stagecoach at Henry Hull's trading post below the Hogback Mesa, on the edge of the Navajo Reservation, representing the Women's Society of the Methodist Episcopal Church, and immediately set up a tent nearby. They started a ministry riding out to visit Navajo camps along the San Juan River, usually on horses and sometimes even on burros.

This mission was soon moved, and a small adobe building was constructed at Jewett, a small settlement just below where the Animas and La Plata Rivers ran into the San Juan below Farmington. After years of effort by many, it slowly developed into a school, with dormitories—one for boys and one for girls—and an industrial-farm complex. A small cottage hospital was built not far above the mission.

Then in October of 1911, after a great rain, a tremendous flood of the combined three rivers roared through the San Juan Valley. At one place it ran forty feet deep and half a mile wide. The water devastated the entire valley, and the mission complex as well as fifty other houses and miles of railroad track were completely swept away. Although the original mission was a total loss, the Women's Society of the Methodist Church selected a new site just west of the small town of Farmington and, with the people of the area, built an entirely new mission and school on the high ground well above all rivers. Later the Navajo Methodist Mission High School was established there.

In 1900 another Christian Reformed mission was established at *tóatchi,* a branch station of the Fort Defiance Agency, which was developed, first by the Reverend L. P. Brink, followed by Mark Bouma.

In 1898 Ethel Sawyer was sent out to the Tuba City area to work with the Navajos, where she was soon joined by Ginny June Johnson, and they actually lived in the camps to evangelize that part of the Navajo Reservation.

THE MORMONS

You recognize as word of God
what Brigham bids you do.
To stay or go—at home, abroad,
is all the same *to you.*
> —ELIZA R. SNOW, "To Franklin D. Richards,
> One of the Twelve Apostles," in *The Latter-Day Saints'*
> *Millennial Star,* Vol. 16 (Liverpool, 1854)

The Mormons, or Church of Jesus Christ of Latter-day Saints (LDS), led by Brigham Young and based in Utah, was committed to spreading the Mormon faith to the area south of the San Juan River by establishing stakes, or divisions, of the Mormon Church, each organized to constitute a church in itself. In this way some two dozen small agricultural settlements were established in the Little Colorado Basin, and by the late 1870s a group of nine families were settled around the Moenkopi Wash in what is now northern Arizona. This movement of the Mormons south from Utah and across the San Juan at Lees Ferry inevitably brought them in contact with Navajos moving west from the Chuska Mountain region, and there were incidents of conflict over the years.

BUCKSKIN APOSTLE

Jacob Hamblin, a native of Ohio, converted to the LDS in 1842, emigrated west, and eventually established a small farm along the fertile Moenkopi Wash, where he gained the support of *Tuvi* or Tuba, a Hopi chief who had become a Mormon convert in the 1870s.

Hamblin, sometimes called the "Buckskin Apostle," had extensive experience with both the Hopis and the Navajos. He had served as a scout for Kit Carson in the 1865 expedition against the Navajos, and as a guide for John Wesley Powell's expedition through the Grand Canyon in 1869. His relations with the Hopi people were somewhat better than those with the Navajos.

For years the Navajos, during the summer months, maintained small farms in the Moenkopi Wash area, as did the Hopis, both growing corn, melons, and peaches, and this had caused a continuing struggle for farmland and for water between the two vastly different tribes. The Hopis resented any intrusion by

A Navajo visitor to the Sweetwater Trading Post,
dressed to impress.

the Navajos and stubbornly resisted any attempt to change their ancient way of life. Frequent clashes of culture resulted in some ill will, but the two tribes coexisted, the Navajos calling the Hopis *kiis'aanii* and the Hopi referring to Navajos usually as *dacabimo,* but sometimes as *tsamewa* or "bastards."

In 1878 the Mormons laid out a town site area just north of Moenkopi and named it "Tuba City" in honor of the Hopi chief. But the Navajos called the place *to' naneesdizi,* or "mixed water," an appropriate name for an area where water rights were certainly becoming very mixed, with the Hopis, Navajos, and Mormons all attempting to irrigate their small fields.

The Mormon presence at Tuba City, however, was definitively resolved when it was ruled they had built on Indian land, and therefore they could not secure title to their property. In 1903 the U.S. government paid the settlers $45,000 for their improvements and added the Moenkopi Wash area to the Navajo Reservation, and the Mormon families dispersed to other Mormon communities. Many moved to the new Mormon settlements at Fruitland and Kirtland, on the San Juan River above Shiprock, just bordering the Navajo Reservation.

Relations between Catholics, Mormons, and Protestants were always very competitive, occasionally vituperative, but relatively peaceful.

To the Navajos, religious beliefs were the center of their life, and they had most beliefs in common. However, Christians seemed to have a number of different religions, so the Navajos found it hard to distinguish between Catholics, Mormons, and Protestants, who didn't seem to agree with each other's faiths nor, for that matter, with each other.

The Navajos found a way to distinguish among all these differences in belief: Catholics wore robes and were therefore *'éé' neishoodii* or "long coats." Protestants wore short coats, *'éé' 'ádaalts'íísígíí,* which became their name, and Mormons wore no coats at all but could be identified as *gáamalii,* the Navajo pronunciation of Mormon.

One day at Sweetwater an old Navajo was relating something he had heard, and the trader, Ace Palmer, questioned him, "Who told you that?" The old man replied, "I didn't know the man." Mr. Palmer persisted, "Well, was he a white man?" and the old man declared, "Maybe white man, maybe *gáamalii,* I don't know!"

In *Indians I Have Known,* Byron Cummings, one of the founding fathers of Southwestern archaeology, tells of a similar incident in 1908. Johnny Benow, a renegade Ute, when questioned about a dispute with a rancher near Monticello, Utah, protested: "Me no kill nobody. No kill Indian, no kill white man, and me no kill no Mormon."

One outspoken secular trader, John Kerley of Moenkopi Wash Trading Post, did not improve matters, however, when he tried, unsuccessfully, to persuade the Franciscans to establish a mission there, as "Tuba needed a more liberal religious leader who smoked and would not condemn drinking, picnics, card parties, and picture shows." He didn't explain why anyone would oppose picnics.

The Clan Holcomb

HORACE A. HOLCOMB

My grandfather, Horace A. Holcomb, was the patriarch of the family and never abandoned his role as head of the Mission. A tall, spare man with a neat white beard, he had a ramrod-straight bearing and the stern gaze of a retired cavalry colonel, although I never saw him on a horse. Always neatly dressed in black, even in the vastness of the Reservation outback, he wore a three-piece dark suit with a hard collar and conservative tie every Sunday and whenever visitors were expected.

He was born November 13, 1852, in Dryden, Michigan, and in his younger years worked on the family farm. At a time when attending high school was considered a higher education, Horace A. Holcomb went from his farm home to Oberlin College in Ohio, where he studied for three years. He married Mary Webster in 1878, and for some time they taught school together and also operated a dairy in Michigan.

Ten years later, at the age of thirty-six, he entered the first class of the new Moody Bible Institute in Chicago, completed his education, and was ordained in the Congregational Church in 1890, just before his fifth child, Ruth, was born. He then served as a minister for several parishes in Michigan and Kansas and was pastor of a Presbyterian church in Auburn, Kansas, when he resigned and joined the Gospel Missionary Union in 1894.

The Gospel Missionary Union had been founded by George S. Fisher, the son of missionaries to the Caribbean. He had resigned from the YMCA in 1892 to promote foreign missions and find young men and women to take the Gospel to West Africa.

H. A. Holcomb had his heart set on being a missionary to Africa but was assigned to "Home Missions" and worked as an evangelist in Nebraska and northern Minnesota, serving small farmers, men in the lumber camps and sawmills, and the railroad crews building the famous "Soo Line." In Nebraska Grandfather lived for a time in a sod house and reported: "A little 'soddie' with only two rooms makes rather close quarters for a family of seven, especially as the cold weather comes."

The next year, at the age of fifty-seven, Grandfather was finally appointed by the Gospel Missionary Union to serve in the Soudan (now Mali) in West

H. A. Holcomb and his original covered wagon.

Africa but was asked to first take a short "temporary assignment" to the Navajo Indians in northern Arizona Territory, as he already had a limited experience with Native Americans, gained by working with the Ojibway Indians in upper Minnesota and over the line in Canada.

Grandfather really wanted to go to Africa but faithfully accepted this assignment. He left his wife and youngest daughter Mary in Akeley, Minnesota, and went to Arizona, where he joined his older daughter, Clara, who was already working with the Navajos for the Gospel Missionary Union.

MARY DORATHY WEBSTER HOLCOMB

Grandmother never forgot that she was a Webster and the direct descendant of John and Agnes Webster of Warwickshire, England, who came to America and settled in Suckiaug, the Indian name for what is now Hartford, Connecticut, where John Webster became governor in 1636, according to a history of the Webster family published in 1915 by William Holcomb Webster.

Grandmother was more adventurous, however, than all the Websters between her and those illustrious ancestors. They left the comforts of Europe for the wilderness of New England and then took almost 300 years to move from Connecticut to Michigan, whereas after Mary Dorathy (a family spelling of the name) married Horace Holcomb she was constantly on the move for her entire life.

Mary was born in 1857 in Michigan, received a good education, and was a teacher when she married Horace Holcomb. Then he went into the ministry,

Mary and H. A. Holcomb.

and Mary faithfully followed her husband to Kansas, Nebraska, Indiana, Illinois, Minnesota, and finally to the Navajo Indian Reservation in the Territory of Arizona. During the many moves she became a mother—six times. Two of these children were lost. Firstborn Grace lived only a few months, and the first son, Harold Alwyn, drowned in a river accident in Minnesota when he was in his early twenties.

When her husband was appointed to the Navajo Reservation in 1909, Mary became responsible for the work at Akeley and remained there alone with her youngest child, ten-year-old Mary Ellen, who was to become my mother. Mary was not inexperienced in missionary work, for as the children had grown older, she had occasionally accompanied her husband on his circuits. He wrote of one visit she made with him to the Ojibway Indians: "We enter their little wigwams and Mrs. Holcomb sits down with them, shows them a picture card, and turns it over and tries to apply it to their lives."

After Grandfather left for Arizona, Mary's reports to the Gospel Missionary Union indicate that "Mrs. Holcomb" had a very busy schedule. First there was an extensive visitation list of ladies in Akeley whom she called on regularly, and she also counseled with the sick and terminally ill in that area and conducted a weekly mothers' prayer meeting in her home.

Mary also made regular trips to Pine River, arranged for the use of a schoolhouse, conducted weekly services, organized a Sunday school for children, and held prayer meetings in her home. She found time to write reports and a number of religious articles that were published in the official Gospel Missionary Union bulletin, the *Gospel Messenger*.

In November of 1911, after over a year of waiting, Mary Holcomb received word from her husband that she should come to Arizona. She disposed of the small place in Akeley that had belonged to my Uncle Harold, packed and shipped all their personal belongings, and prepared to make the long train ride to the Territory of Arizona with her eleven-year-old youngest daughter, Mary.

CLARA ELIZABETH HOLCOMB

Aunt Clara, who was seventeen years older than my mother, was also a product of the Gospel Missionary Union of Kansas City, which she had joined in 1902. During her training days she had shown an aptitude for languages and became interested in translating the Bible for missionaries working with people without a written language of their own.

Clara was particularly interested in African languages, as the "Dark Continent" was the mission field where she expected to be assigned. At that time a young man named George C. Reed was also training at the Gospel Missionary Union to be a missionary to Africa, and he and Clara made plans to go together and share in translating the New Testament.

George Reed went to French Equatorial Africa as planned and became a pioneer in that field, translating sections of the Bible into Berber in Morocco as early as 1919. He made an expedition with George Fischer up the Niger River where they preached in the city of Timbuctoo (now spelled Timbuktu), ancient stronghold of Islamic learning, and became the first Protestant missionaries to return—alive.

Clara, however, was assigned to Home Missions, probably considered a more proper field for a single young woman, and she worked for several years in Kansas. She had her first exposure to Indians in Black Hawk, Colorado. She was called back to the Gospel Missionary Union headquarters in Kansas City for a short time before being assigned in 1909 to the Navajos at Tuba City in Arizona Territory. She never went overseas, but lived the rest of her life on the Navajo Reservation.

She never saw George Reed again, but over the years, they kept up a regular correspondence and shared the joys and the disappointments of missionary life in their widely separated fields. She always had a small framed picture of George Reed on the nightstand beside her Bible, and after dinner she often read us portions of his long letters from Africa, describing his visits to exotic places with names like Bamako and Timbuctoo. These letters fired my young imagination, and I determined to go to the "Dark Continent" as soon as possible, although I was not destined to accomplish this goal for over a half-century.

Clara Holcomb left Kansas City accompanied by George Brown, another missionary sent west by the Gospel Missionary Union, and arrived in Flagstaff, Arizona, in the winter of 1909. There she found a party of Navajos loading a wagon with freight for the Red Lake Trading Post, deep in the Reservation beyond Tuba City.

The team departed about noon but were immediately delayed when the freight wagon became mired in mud while still in Flagstaff. Then the wagon was damaged while being hauled out of the mud hole, and it was nearly dark before the journey actually got under way around the snow-covered San Francisco Peaks.

The primitive track to the north followed the old "Mormon Road" established when the LDS were attempting to colonize the area around the Little Colorado River. A new iron bridge was under construction but not completed when the little party arrived, so they had to ford the river near Cameron. Progress was extremely difficult, and they didn't reach Tuba City until evening on the fourth day, after ninety hard winter miles on the road.

7 Kin Łigaaí

The small Hopi village of Moenkopi, just south of Tuba City, was built by Hopi farmers from Old Oraibi, who had been farming in the valley since the 1300s, on the site of ancient Anasazi ruins from the Great Pueblo Period.

Peaceful villagers, the Hopi planted their corn, melons, and peaches and followed their traditions and complicated ancient religion, including the Snake Dance, for centuries. Then in 1868 they were suddenly completely surrounded by the greater Navajo Reservation, created when the Long Walk brought the Navajos back from *hwééldi,* which started a continuing struggle for farmland and for water between the two very different tribes.

Founded by Mormon pioneers, Tuba City was the headquarters of the Western Navajo Agency of the Bureau of Indian Affairs (BIA). When the Holcombs arrived it was a small town consisting mostly of government offices, a boarding school, a hospital, and a Babbitt Brothers trading post. It was the center of activities for that entire part of the Navajo Reservation.

The Gospel Missionary Union station was a small white building under a line of tall Lombardy pine trees near Moenkopi. It was appropriately called *kin łigaaí,* or "white house," by the Navajos, but the missionaries called it the Mission House. The old house had originally been occupied by a family that left in the Mormon exodus a decade earlier, and no one seemed to know who had occupied the place since or what they did, but soon after moving in, the missionaries found a door in the floor and a stairway leading into a room below, where they uncovered equipment showing that at some time someone had been printing counterfeit money down there. Not a very auspicious start for a Christian mission to the Indians.

When Aunt Clara finally arrived at *kin łigaaí,* she joined Emma Johnson, who had been working with the Gospel Missionary Union on the Navajo Reservation for several years. Although assigned to Moenkopi, Emma Johnson and Clara Holcomb actually worked out in Navajo camps in the surrounding area and developed an extensive itinerary of outreach. This meant making extended trips into the field with pack burros and establishing base camps near one Navajo outfit, then visiting all the camps to a radius of fifteen or more miles. ("Outfit" was a common Reservation term for a family or group of relatives living together.) In this way they were able to see most of the Navajos living within each area, particularly the women and children who almost never ventured as far from home as *kin łigaaí*.

Aunt Clara wrote of one extended stay she had with Emma Johnson at a Navajo camp soon after she arrived:

> Our camp was on the sunny side of the canyon and the huts were built on a shelf of rock. We were given a place in the south side of our neighbor's hogan to spread our sheepskins and if we had stretched our feet out straight in front of us they would have been in the open fire which was nearly in the middle of the rock floor.
>
> Between us and the fire we set up an oven grate on small rocks, and by raking fresh coals under it from time to time, as we cooked, we had a very good "stove."
>
> Some of the days were very cold, and we found it necessary to turn around to warm our backs and cool our faces. As we had no thermometer we did not know that the temperature was down to 15 degrees below zero, and we were fairly comfortable most of the time.

She went on to describe their hosts:

> The people of this camp—except the son-in-law, in whose hut we lived—are very covetous, and if we had been disposed to whatever they asked, we would have been out of food, dishes, bedding, etc. long before it was time to return home.
>
> They assumed that they were poor and we were rich; but they had a fair-sized flock of sheep, and drove up eighty or ninety horses and colts one day, which were perhaps half their herd. Aside from their begging and stealing, these people were friendly and from a language standpoint, we have never had a better place to camp.

Aunt Clara knew she had to learn the complex and difficult Navajo language if she was ever to communicate with these people. She continued:

> Our fifteen-year-old hostess was exceptionally good in giving us the full conjugation of verbs of which we had only one or two forms. Some of the people were careless, others gave good attention; but we could not see that their interest was anything beyond courtesy, yet God has told us to preach the Word, and we may pray and hope.
>
> Early in February we made arrangements with the same friend who had brought us to camp to take us home. We set out about noon on the 5th, with some bedding etc. on the animals we rode, while the most of

our goods were packed on an extra burro. We camped for the night at Indalkit and reached home late the next afternoon, just six weeks from the time we had left.

This was a relatively short camp trip for the two indomitable missionary women, but many trips lasted for three or four months, and the two sometimes even moved with the Navajos as they drove their herds in search of pasture. They eventually acquired a tent and thereafter often set up their own place to live in a Navajo camp. This gave them a degree of privacy but sometimes posed problems, especially during bad weather.

In her report of January 1910 Clara described how one new year was brought in with their unwilling attendance at a Navajo healing ceremony:

New Year's evening a heavy wind storm came up. The ground was quite muddy from melting snow, and the strain of the wind on the tent pulled up several of the stakes and soon it came down. There was nothing else to do then, but move our belongings into the hogan.

That night it snowed and froze and it was ten days before the ground thawed enough to allow us to drive the missing stakes and put up the tent again. Thus we were living in the hogan during an entire six days of a "Sing."

During some of the performances we were asked to leave the hut for a couple of hours. With the monotonous noise of the singing and shaking of their rattles kept up—with some intermissions—from nine in the morning until nine, twelve or even three o'clock at night, we found it hard to study, pray or even sleep.

Now that our tent is up again, it seems quite a palace to us, and we do not want to exchange it for a much finer place, with the service of Jesus excluded.

H. A. Holcomb arrived in Arizona Territory in 1910 and from Flagstaff rode horseback out around the foothills of San Francisco Peaks (*dook'o'osłííd*), sacred mountain of both the Navajos and the Hopis, and set out across a desert entirely different from anything he had ever seen in his former parish in the Land of a Thousand Lakes. He reported on his arrival:

After our ninety miles on horseback, it did some good to come in sight of our little oasis home. The mesas, like great fortresses, hem us in three directions. On two sides they come quite near the mission house.

Here and there at the foot of mesas a little stream of water gushes out, and until it spends itself in the sands, it makes the desert rejoice and bloom.

H. A. and Clara Holcomb during the very early days of the Mission.

Surely we are among our people. Their little hogans are on every side, from daylight until dark they come and go, and we hear their weird snatches of "Happy song" but they are not happy in the Lord, for they know Him not.

Grandfather Holcomb was a veteran of field visitation work and enjoyed the vigorous outdoor life it required, but he did not speak Navajo. So his responsibilities were largely administrative, and in 1911 he was put in charge of the Mission at *kin ligaaí* and regularly sent a "Navajo Mission Report" back to the Gospel Missionary Union in Kansas City. One early report mentioned many visitors and very few days without callers at the Mission House. Later he reported 1,600 visitors over the year "of sufficient age to understand some Bible teaching."

On a very few occasions H. A. Holcomb was able to help in actual field work and very formally reported one incident back to the Gospel Missionary Union: "On December 14th Misses Johnson and Holcomb moved out, hoping to spend the winter among the Navajos who live northwest of here. The place where they are stopping is some twenty-six miles distance. Mr. Holcomb accompanied them, helped them in getting settled, and dragged up a pile of wood for them, returning home after an absence of four days."

Once established at *kin ligaaí,* H. A. Holcomb sent for his wife, Mary Dorathy, and his daughter, eleven-year-old Mary Ellen, to join him, and when they took the train to leave on December 1, 1911, they were very excited to be "leaving the United States to live in the Territory of Arizona!" However, their life "abroad" was very short, as two months later, in February of 1912, Arizona became the forty-eighth state.

Mary Holcomb was soon out riding out with the younger ladies to visit the surrounding hogans, and her description of one of her first camps is interesting:

Miss Johnson and I mounted our ponies and rode westward a little more than a mile.

Here we found a large "shade" containing fifteen persons, twelve of whom were old enough to understand something of what was said. Just at the left of the door sheepskins were spread for us to sit upon.

Next to us sat the old grandmother, both blind and deaf and bent nearly double with age, busily spinning yarn for a blanket. Just beyond her several young men were lounging on blankets and sheepskins, next was a young woman weaving a rug, and opposite us two mothers and their little children. In the center of the room were the dishes and cooking utensils.

The Gospel Missionary Union had started an extensive orchard of apples, peaches, and pears, along with a vineyard and an alfalfa patch, and H. A. Holcomb was delighted to indulge his lifelong passion for making things grow and often wrote of his fine harvests of grapes, vegetables, and fine fruit. He was especially proud of his apricots; they were unusual in that area and he gave them to Navajo visitors to the Mission.

When Mother arrived at *kin ligaai* there were very few white people on the Navajo Reservation, and for her entire first year she did not see another white girl her own age and felt the loneliness very keenly. However, she did have frequent contact with Navajos, both adults and children, and soon became known as *ch'ikééh ts'ósí,* or Slender Girl, by the Navajos. Grandfather was of course known as *daga lagai,* or White Beard.

I know little about the Holcomb years at *kin ligaai* except for the stories Mother told of her early days as a young girl on the Reservation. One story was of how they acquired a large Anasazi pottery jug that she still had. Fruit was sometimes used as a medium of exchange at that time, and an Indian man had brought the jug to *kin ligaai* and traded it for a bucket of peaches. Navajos had a morbid fear of anything pertaining to the dead and would not touch anything associated with the ancient ones, so I assume the enterprising Indian was a Hopi. In any case he was probably satisfied that he had gotten the best of the bargain.

Mother's favorite episode of the time was in 1913, when Theodore Roosevelt came across from Ganado with Lorenzo Hubbell to see the snake dances at the Hopi villages, and he stopped overnight in Tuba City and stayed with the trader, Sam Preston. When the word spread that Roosevelt was at the trading post, almost everyone in the area, including a few children, rushed up to see the former president.

The elder Holcombs did not go up to the trading post to see Roosevelt, but Mother did and, as the shy mission kid, not as well dressed as the other youngsters, she hung back as everyone crowded about the seated visitor. Teddy Roosevelt noticed her in the back and called her up front, patted her head, and said, "Young lady, you go home and tell your mother that I said you are a good girl." Mother never tired of relating this adventure.

Mother also had a sensational version of the violent *taddytin* affair. The son of a Navajo policeman, *taddytin* was something of a renegade and troublemaker and lived east of Tuba City. His refusal to send his children to boarding school at Tuba City brought him to the attention of Walter Runke, Agent of the Western District of the Reservation, and Runke had the unenviable responsibility of bringing the fellow to justice.

Taddytin was a big man, so Runke sent two *bilagáana* Indian Service employees—Robinson, the Indian Service farmer at Kayenta, and Wilson, a policeman stationed at Tuba City—to the *taddytin* camp at *nitsin* canyon to arrest the young troublemaker and bring him to Tuba City.

The posse had no trouble locating their man, but he refused to leave his hogan peacefully. After a lengthy negotiation they moved to arrest him, and he shoved a cocked gun into the stomach of Robinson and pulled the trigger. However, his cartridges were too small for his gun, and he had wrapped them in cotton to keep them in place, so the weapon jammed and didn't fire, but Wilson shot in response and killed *taddytin.*

Several years later the BIA decided that Agent Runke was responsible for the whole affair and brought him to court, and the ensuing trial dragged on and on, becoming a subject of conversation in the small community. Eventually Runke was acquitted, but in 1920 he resigned as agent and later served as the postmaster at Flagstaff.

Another of Mother's stories told of the morning when Grandfather Holcomb was in Tuba City on business and, upon concluding his business, set out to walk the three miles back to the Mission. Just then his friend spotted a Navajo in a wagon going toward Moenkopi, hailed the man and, speaking in Navajo, arranged a ride to the *kin ligaaí* turnoff. The young man nodded assent, Grandfather gratefully climbed aboard, and off they went.

For some time they rode in silence, and Grandfather, who was familiar with Greek and Latin but had never learned to speak Navajo, came to the conclusion that his host did not speak much English. As they rode down the hill, he began a message for the young man, speaking slowly and distinctly and using simple words and gestures to make his points clear.

The young man listened intently and politely nodded his head but answered not a word, and Grandfather completed his talk. Feeling that he had failed to reach the young man, he rode on in silence until they reached the turnoff to *kin ligaaí,* and he indicated in sign language that it was his stop. Then, just as Grandfather was getting out of the wagon, the Navajo casually inquired, "Mr. Holcomb, where did you attend theological seminary?"

After a few years Emma Johnson retired from her work with the Navajos at *kin ligaaí* and returned to Kansas City, and soon after her departure Clara Holcomb was forced by ill health also to leave the Reservation for Oakland, California. At first the only work she could find was hand-dipping chocolate in a candy factory, but in 1914 she was employed by Western Book and Tract Company, owned by H. A. Ironside.

When it came time for high school, it became necessary for young Mary Holcomb also to leave *kin ligaaí,* and in 1916 she went to school in Flagstaff. There she remembered seeing Glen Girdner, just before he left to serve in the army, but he did not recognize her when they met several years later at the Girdner ranch on Oak Creek, south of Flagstaff.

At *kin ligaaí* the Mission staff dwindled, and Grandfather Holcomb became very discouraged with the slow progress of the Mission and reported to the Gospel Missionary Union:

My wife and I are here alone, and we two sit down to our little table with no one else around it, the first time for over thirty years. On two sides of our oasis are the mesas near by, on the others distant mountains with sandy wastes and rock between, with here and there a stunted brush.

A white man seldom comes this way, but many of our Indians do. Most of these who come have heard the Gospel many times and we feel if we can say but a few words even, perhaps the Spirit will bring to their remembrance other things they have heard. A few days ago an old woman came walking over the frozen sand to see us and was so lame from walking she could hardly move about for several days.

She is rather a welcome guest, as she is very cheerful and also quite grateful. This last is a flower that seldom wastes its fragrance on this desert air.

He closed his report with the cry, "Oh, that God would turn some of these to Himself, so that we might see a company of true Christians here about us!" This was the last Holcomb report from Moenkopi, as the Gospel Missionary Union reorganized its goals and reduced its Home Mission efforts to focus on overseas work, particularly in West Africa, and the small station at *kin łigaaí* was closed.

TWENTY YEARS LATER

In the 1930s Dad, my brother Danny, and I had occasion to drive to Oak Creek, and Dad decided that rather than go the roundabout way through Shiprock we should try the direct route across the Reservation, following an old military road through Marsh Pass west of Kayenta and on to Tuba City. It was a shorter way than the route through Gallup, New Mexico, but an almost impossible road through sandstone canyons, precipitous wash crossings, sand hills, and high rocky ridges, including the formidable Comb Ridge.

Near Red Lake Trading Post we met a carload of men, a professorial-looking older man and four younger men, all out trying to push a loaded car through an extensive sand patch. They were probably one of the archaeological expeditions from an eastern university exploring the Anasazi ruins in the western canyons at that time. We made another stop near Marsh Pass at a place where Dad had heard that there were many garnets. Danny and I searched around a few anthills there and indeed found a handful of the tiny, dark red semiprecious stones, which I still have.

When we finally arrived at Tuba City I was surprised to find that it looked more like a small Midwestern town than a Western outpost in Indian country. The main street was lined with tall Lombardy poplars, and there were the three large sandstone buildings of the old boarding school, a hospital, and other buildings that once had been dormitories, classrooms, workshops, cafeteria, laundry, and

Navajo on the rim trail above *tsegi hoch cho* canyon.

bakery. BIA agency offices, the houses of other government officials, and a few shops made up most of the rest of the town. One non-government, distinctive, octagonal building, the original Babbitt Trading Post, stood out from the rest.

Moenkopi, just south of Tuba City, remained a small Hopi village, and although we searched we couldn't find a trace of *kin ligaaí,* the old Gospel Missionary Union mission site, and saw only an open field and a few trees still standing.

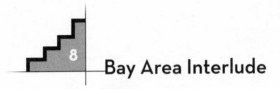

Bay Area Interlude

After the mission at Moenkopi closed, Grandfather Holcomb worked for a time with the Mennonites in the Tuba City area, but then he learned of the new Indian school that Harry Ironside had started in Oakland, California. In 1915 he and Grandmother also moved to the Bay Area to assist Dr. Ironside in the new missionary training school, which consisted of two Hopis, one Navajo, and one Hualapai.

In the summer of 1917, Mary Holcomb followed her sister and parents to Oakland and enrolled in Oakland Technical High School as "Marie Holcomb," a singularly independent act at the time—but the new name stuck.

For a time Mother stayed in the home of H. A. Ironside, who was a great fundamentalist evangelist, in the tradition of Dwight L. Moody before him and Billy Graham who came decades later.

Ironside was also a prolific writer and, over the years, wrote over eighty books, pamphlets, and dissertations on biblical subjects such as "Notes on Jeremiah," "Notes on Nehemiah and Esther," and his best-known work, "Holiness, the False and the True." Years later he conducted the funeral service of the renowned evangelist Billy Sunday.

At that time Marie Holcomb was very slim, and Ironside often teased her about being "so skinny." One morning she heard him next door putting on his shoes and grunting with the effort. At breakfast when he again remarked that she was so skinny because she didn't eat anything, she retorted, "At least I don't have to groan when I put on my shoes in the morning!"

A stout bald man, Ironside had an office in an upper story of a building in Oakland, and during Mother's stay with his family he decided to have his name painted on his office windows. A local painter was employed and industriously spaced the name on the three panes of windows, carefully painting "HAIR ON SIDE." Everyone was amused except the good Harry Ironside.

THE PLYMOUTH BRETHREN
Soon after joining Harry Ironside in Oakland, the Holcombs became involved with the Oakland Assembly of Plymouth Brethren, a very fundamentalist group that had broken away from the Church of England in the 1820s, about the

The Holcombs in Oakland, California, 1918. Mary is sitting in front, and behind her are Clara, Marie, and H.A.

same time John Wesley was organizing the Methodists. The name "Plymouth Brethren" came from the port city of England, and the denomination spread rapidly, first through southern England and then parts of Ireland before reaching North America thirty years later.

Some twenty years after I left Immanuel Mission, Jeffrey L. Staley arrived as a seven-year-old boy with his missionary parents and grew up there as I did. Years later he described the Plymouth Brethren in *Reading with a Passion*.

The Plymouth Brethren, he wrote, are organized with "no particular focus of assemblies and no organizational headquarters with evangelical local churches—autonomous but not independent." Their "central teaching is that of the Bible and weekly celebration of the Lord's Supper with the Breaking of Bread, and governance is by plural leadership."

By adopting this fresh start without authority, precedent, or guidance beyond the letter of Holy Scripture, they discarded eighteen centuries of the Church, and in some ways the lay-led Plymouth Brethren beliefs resemble those of the Quakers. They were considered by some to be authoritarian and sectarian in their views that drew a circle to include all children of God and exclude all others. As Staley wrote, "The name Immanuel means 'God With Us'…and for the mission staff God could only be found with us on that ten acres of fenced desert, and nowhere else within a fifty-mile radius."

While they were in Oakland, Grandfather and Aunt Clara retained a burning interest in continuing their Navajo work, and Ironside encouraged them to

Clara and a friend on Ocean Beach in San Francisco,
with Cliff House in the background.

consider starting a mission in the Four Corners area. In addition to his active evangelical activities in the Bay Area, Ironside was very interested in promoting missions to the Indians and played a very important role in finding dedicated people to open two small mission outposts in Arizona—one in Valentine, established by the Andersons, and Immanuel Bible Chapel in Winslow, started by Carl Armerding and his sister Minnie.

However, there was nothing in the remote Four Corners area of the Reservation. Under Ironside's influence, and after much prayerful consideration, Grandfather Holcomb and Aunt Clara felt called to return to the Navajos and establish their own mission in that northern part of the Reservation where there was very little missionary activity.

Grandfather had the "know-how" and Clara knew the language, but Mary, the frail mother, would require care. Grandmother Mary Holcomb was in rapidly failing health and very reluctant to leave civilization again for what she knew, from years of experience, was a very primitive pioneer life back on the Navajo Reservation. Mother, meanwhile, was part of an active group of young people and, for the first time in her life, was included in religious activities and social functions with people of her own generation.

Parties, picnics, and outings to the beaches and Sutro Cliff House were new to her, and the ferry trips across the bay to wartime San Francisco were a favorite activity. Some of her most exciting memories were of the exuberant celebrations in the streets when the news of Armistice and the end of World War I reached the West Coast.

Mother had a special friend during her time in Oakland, Louise Fauscutt, and they had many adventures and good times together. They remained close friends long after both left the Bay Area, Mother for Arizona and Louise for San Diego, where she married Ralph Barker, brother of Florence Barker, a key player in the early days of Immanuel Mission.

Another member of Mother's group of young people was R. Stanley Dollar, who had worked in his father's steamship business office since he was thirteen. His father, Robert Dollar, a native of Scotland, had originally been in the lumber business, but then became involved in shipping and started a steamship company in 1902. By 1918 the Dollar Line had become a fleet of ships plying the Pacific with a very distinctive dollar sign painted on their funnels, and he went on to establish a near monopoly on the Pacific Coast. One ship, named the "Stanley Dollar," was to serve until World War II, when it was sunk by a German U-Boat.

Knowing Stanley Dollar, young Marie Holcomb became fascinated with ships, shipping, and ocean travel, and years later when I was in my early teens she suggested a career at sea, perhaps as ship's purser, would be ideal. She knew the Dollar Line probably had such openings. Stanley had succeeded his father as head of Dollar Line in 1932 and now headed the largest fleet of passenger and cargo liners operating under the U.S. flag.

Being paid to wander the seven seas certainly appealed to me, but, alas, the Dollar Steamship Line experienced financial difficulties, and in 1938 it was taken over and became a part of the American President Line. There would be no life for me on the bounding main; however, I was destined to cross the oceans many times.

During her later days on the Navajo Reservation, Mother retained many memories of the Oakland days and told us many stories of wartime San Francisco. One cold night she was returning on the ferry across the bay to Oakland after a day on the beach. Near the Cliff House there was suddenly a yell and a splash. The passengers all rushed to crowd the port rail and saw a struggling man in the wake of the ferry, shouting and frantically trying to swim.

The captain called an emergency stop and within minutes the crew dragged the dripping man back aboard, and an exchange between the captain and the wet, shivering man followed:

"What the devil were you trying to do?"
"Commit suicide."
"Kill yourself? So what made you start swimming?"
"Cold water!"

Mother graduated from Oakland Tech in June 1919 and soon found employment with a medical laboratory. She remained in the area for a short time, but when Grandfather Holcomb and Aunt Clara decided to return to the Navajo Reservation, family duties prevailed, and Marie very regretfully ended her career. In October 1920 she moved with her mother to Arizona to live with her brother, Lee Holcomb, on a ranch on the west side of Oak Creek, which he had leased from the Girdner family.

9   Oak Creek Days

Grandfather James P. Girdner and Grandmother Nola Girdner were living in Piedmont, Kansas, when they decided to move "Out West" with their four young children, whose names were Glen, Dale, Stanley, and Eva. In the early fall of 1907 Grandfather auctioned off the farm, house, and wagon, along with all the livestock, equipment, and furniture, and deposited the money in the local bank. Unfortunately the bank soon failed in the Panic of 1907, and the Girdner family was suddenly not only homeless but also without money.

However, J. P. Girdner was a very persuasive man and managed to arrange a night meeting with a bank official behind the bank and then withdrew his money, so he was able to purchase six tickets on the Atchison, Topeka and Santa Fe Railway to Arizona Territory. The *Elk County Citizen* of December 18, 1907, noted the event with a brief: "The Girdner family left. Sorry to lose them, but since they must go, we wish them success."

The Girdner family, unused to the constant motion of a long train ride, became a little ill, and Grandfather decided to make a short stop in Las Vegas, New Mexico, where he put them in a hotel to recuperate while he checked for any new opportunities in that area. He decided to continue on to Arizona, so they re-boarded the train and moved on as far as the small Arizona town of Ash Fork, where they switched trains, first to the railroad that ran from Ash Fork to Phoenix.

Then, at a place called Junction, they boarded a passenger coach attached to the "Peavine," a narrow-gauge string of freight cars that took coke to the smelter furnace at Jerome and copper matte back to civilization.

Aboard the Peavine, Grandfather Girdner was seated with a little man with a beard, about seventy years old, who introduced himself as Clark and said he was from Montana and on his way to Jerome to look after some mining interests. Grandfather, also a small man with a beard, said he was from Kansas and was also headed for the Verde Valley, where he hoped to find a place where he could start a new life for his family. The farmer and the miner soon became engaged in earnest conversation about the future of Arizona.

Grandfather was greatly encouraged by Clark's enthusiastic predictions for Arizona Territory, and they took a mutual liking to each other and passed the

Oak Creek.

time in animated conversation until they arrived in Jerome and parted ways, never to meet again.

Soon after this, Dad decided to change his middle name, "Hansel," which had been suggested back in Kansas by a family friend who loved the gloomy tales of the Brothers Grimm. Grandfather Girdner, impressed by his dynamic little traveling companion, suggested that his eldest son be renamed Glen Clark Girdner, and Dad readily agreed.

Eventually the family learned that Jerome, then one of the largest towns in Arizona Territory, was supported by the United Verde Copper Mine. The mine was owned by Senator William A. Clark, reputed to be the richest man in America, who took away a personal total of $60,000,000 from the "Glory Hole" under Cleopatra Hill in Jerome, and who also happened to be Grandfather's good companion on that train trip to Jerome. In fact, Clark also owned the train that they were riding.

Perched over the Verde Valley, high on Mingus Mountain, Jerome was a tough place, teeming with hard-rock miners from all around Europe and known as the "wickedest town in Arizona Territory." Ten-year-old Glen realized from the twenty-three saloons, the gambling, the drug and alcohol abuse, and the prostitution, brawling, and occasional murders, that he was no longer in Kansas.

Surprisingly, the only story I remember Dad telling me of this time was about how a local physician, Dr. Hawkins, traded his doctor's buggy for the first automobile in Jerome, and a pack of young boys chased the sputtering car as it labored up one of Jerome's precipitous streets—and passed it on the hill. Dad probably thought I was too young for many stories about frontier Jerome, even when I was about the same age as he had been in 1910.

It is interesting how the other members of the family remembered Jerome: Grandmother discreetly spoke only of the smell of the sulfur, coal, and cigar smoke. Eight-year-old Dale remembered it as a "wild mountain town where the majority of the population consisted of single men," and seven-year-old Stanley was horrified to see blood one morning in the dust just outside their flimsy house and later described the town as "Hell on earth," but never in the presence of his mother. Three-year-old Eva only remembered that the streets were full of burros.

LOOKING FOR A HOME

Grandfather Girdner found a temporary home in Jerome for his family and contracted with a Mexican man who owned eight burros to pack about 200 pounds of wood up the steep hill, where they cut it up with a bucksaw for firewood to ward off the chill January winds blowing down off Mingus Mountain.

He then located and bought a high-wheeled Bain wagon and a team and looked for a place to live, somewhere in the Verde Valley below the teeming mining town, and eventually he found it. It was a homestead on Oak Creek just above its junction with the Verde River, and he paid $600 for a 49-acre ranch.

Grandmother Girdner was not impressed by the small claim and described it as "a ditch, a fence, and a lot of mesquite bushes," but, curiously, the ditch was the most important part of the bargain, as it included water rights for irrigation, an activity completely unknown to J. P. Girdner, the farmer from Kansas.

The ranch had been the homestead of Captain Andrew Jackson, nephew of the legendary Stonewall Jackson. He had also served in the Confederate Army as captain of Company B, 19th Virginia Cavalry. Captain Jackson had moved west to Arizona in 1876 and had taken a homestead that was mostly a rocky hill above some good bottom land on Oak Creek.

However, Captain Jackson was more of a horse and stock trader than a farmer, and he often left his wife, Margaret Ann, on the ranch alone to tend to the chores. Later she told of seeing and hearing yelling Apaches ride by on the hills above, but they never approached the small cabin on Oak Creek. After Captain Jackson died, his widow married David Dumas and moved to a place in Sedona on Oak Creek under Court House Rock. By the time the Girdners arrived on the scene, the little ranch was accessed by horseback or wagon over a single dirt track, lined with large cottonwood trees.

Grandmother called the road "Shady Vale Lane," probably in memory of her childhood home among the green trees and valleys of Lockhart lands in faraway Tennessee, but it is now known as the Old Pump House Road, probably in honor of a pump installed years later by Uncle Stanley Girdner.

At first the family lived in a one-room tent-house with an 18 x 24–foot floor of rough lumber hauled by Grandfather Girdner in his wagon from Jerome, and supported by posts set in tomato cans filled with kerosene to keep out all unwelcome little guests. Grandmother's father, Patrick Robert Kennon Lockhart, who was a carpenter, among his many other trades, came out to the wilderness of Arizona Territory to help design and build a two-story frame building. In 1910 the Girdners moved into the house that was to be home for nearly a century.

After Grandfather acquired a few horses and the beginnings of a cattle herd, he registered the Girdner "four bar cross" brand that always reminded me of the British Union Jack. Over the years Grandfather and his three young sons dug ditches, ploughed, and planted, and soon had the beginnings of a thriving small farm. In addition to the basic pioneer foods of corn, squash, beans, sweet potatoes, black-eyed peas, peanuts, and melons, they grew alfalfa, and they planted orchards, primarily of apples and peaches, but they also cultivated apricots, pears, plums, some berries, and my favorite, a particularly delicious fig.

ROAD TO JEROME

There wasn't much money in circulation at that time, but there was a market for produce in Jerome. The trip up Mingus Mountain, 2,000 feet higher than Shady Vale Ranch, was something like an expedition for the family.

Road through Oak Creek Canyon.

Grandfather would cut enough hay to cover the bottom of the wagon and then put roasting ears, cantaloupes, and other produce in season on the hay and start the long round trip to the city on the hill. In the cold months he would make the same journey with pork and beef. Usually Grandfather made the trip to Jerome alone, and in the early years he had a number of adventures in that wild little mining town.

One morning, as he arrived in town before sunrise, he spotted two melons on the edge of the main street bordering a saloon. He stopped his team and as he approached the curb he realized they were actually two heads lying there in the dark. He hastened back to his wagon and completed his business without a word to anyone, and when he departed the town the "melons" were gone. He watched the paper for days and even discreetly asked a few questions but never learned anything more about the incident.

Aunt Eva told of a less dramatic trip to the city on the hill. She and Grandmother Girdner helped load the wagon, then climbed aboard, and they were on their way. About sundown they camped at the foot of the mountain. Next morning, Grandmother washed Eva and dressed her in her best dress before they drove up into town. Uncle Stanley later gave his version of trips up the hill:

> Our dad would start to Jerome about four in the morning. To make it easier on the horses, the kids would walk. Very often we'd have to stop and fix the road. I don't think we ever went anywhere without road building tools—picks, chains, and sometimes dynamite. We'd get to Jerome late in the evening. We'd sleep in our camp beds right by the wagon.
>
> In those days burros would wander all over town. One of us would have to stay up all night just to fight the burros away. The next day we'd sell off the cantaloupes and roasting ears and whatever else we'd brought.

Eva also recalled that her three brothers, Glen, Dale, and Stanley, went to school in a wooden shack located on the edge of the ranch, but by the time she attended school it was in the new two-room Red Schoolhouse built on the hill about a mile above the Girdner place. This school was eventually attended by four generations of Girdner youngsters.

Dad later wrote that he first became interested in the Navajo people at this early time and felt somewhat concerned that they had no Bible and writing: "The New Testament in Navajo language—may be the result of my work someday." He later added the comment, "A big ambition! I doubt if I knew one word in Navajo at that time."

NORTHERN ARIZONA NORMAL SCHOOL

After finishing at the Red Schoolhouse, Dad worked on the Gates Ranch for a very short time and then started school in Flagstaff in 1915. At that time very few students in Arizona remained long in school, but Dad, and later Aunt Eva, both attended Northern Arizona Normal School, now Northern Arizona University, and she later rode as the Grand Marshal of the Flagstaff Parade.

Dr. Rudolph Harin Heinrich Blome was the president of the school when Dad attended, and as the second president of Northern Arizona Normal, Dr. Blome had played an active role in developing the college. However, he was a native of Hanover, Germany, and, although he had been raised in the United States, he had returned to Germany to study for his PhD at the University of Jena.

After the outbreak of World War I, Dr. Blome came under attack by some townspeople who violently objected to an "enemy agent" being in charge of the education of young Americans. The student body rallied to their president's defense, and Dad was part of a group of young men that invaded a meeting of the town fathers one night in support of the president and capped their protest with a hearty "three cheers for Dr. Blome!"

One of the town zealots then stood and huffily declared, "I never cared much for this modern rah, rah, rah stuff—let's have a real American cheer for our country!" and led his fellow patriots in an awkward but loud "Hip, hip, hurray!"

PRIVATE GLEN C. GIRDNER

With most of the young men in his class, Dad left Flagstaff in 1918 for military service. He later learned that Dr. Blome had resigned his position and continued in Arizona education for a few years but died in 1923. Sixty years later, a beautiful old Georgian-style building built on the campus of Northern Arizona University during this time was renamed the Blome Building, in honor of the man they ran out of town during World War I.

Grandmother Girdner, a sturdy pioneer woman who had received a good education before she came west, held very strong religious convictions, including an opposition to war. She supported President Woodrow Wilson when he ran for re-election under the slogan "He Kept Us Out of War," but much to her disgust, soon after Wilson was re-elected, the United States entered the great conflict in Europe and Dad was drafted into the army.

Grandmother believed in direct action and immediately wrote to both Arizona senators and went to Phoenix to see George W. P. Hunt, Arizona's first governor, in an effort to keep her son out of the foreign conflict, and eventually succeeded in having him classified as a conscientious objector. Her son, however, did not share her deep convictions and wrote of the time: "Feelings were all running high. Germany had torpedoed some of our ships and we were pretty mad and ready to stomp our feet when President Woodrow Wilson at last agreed we couldn't sit back and let that kind of thing go on any longer, we were at war."

Dad was part of a group from Arizona that reported for duty in 1918, with the 3rd Division of the U.S. Army at Camp Pike, Arkansas. Located about eight miles out of Little Rock and named after Zebulon Pike, intrepid discoverer of Pike's Peak, the camp consisted of about 32,000 troops, of whom 11,000 were in a strictly segregated black contingent, and he later told many stories about incidents in both groups.

Soon after he arrived at Camp Pike, Dad found that the large purple "C.O." (for "conscientious objector") stamped on his record did not endear him to his sergeants, but eventually hard work and attention to the business of being a soldier enabled him to overcome the unfortunate start to his military career, and he was actually tapped for officer candidate school just before the war ended. In January 1919 he and his buddies were shipped back to Arizona on a "very slow train."

The veteran of a few months in the army was welcomed back to Oak Creek, where for a short time he proudly wore his uniform on occasion, until the day a woman from the neighboring farm, Mrs. Petschauer, exclaimed, "Oh, I see you are wearing your union suit."

For those born after 1930, this was then a common term for a one-piece version of men's underwear, usually called "BVDs." When anyone pressed for an explanation, this term was said to be an abbreviation for "buttoned vey down."

HORSE AND BUGGY MAILMAN

Soon after returning home from the war, the young veteran Glen Girdner worked for a short time at the post office in Jerome. He then signed a four-year contract to carry the U.S. mail from Cornville to Indian Gardens in lower Oak Creek Canyon, seven miles above Sedona, riding a horse and leading a pack mule. Sometimes he drove a buggy.

He was scheduled for a sixty-four-mile round trip twice a week, but Dad called it his "try weekly" trip, as he often encountered inclement weather, scorching hot in summer and cold in winter. Creek crossings during high water were even more of a problem. The Cornville Bridge had not been completed then, and there were only three fords on all of that part of lower Oak Creek.

When Oak Creek was running bank to bank, Dad would throw the bag of incoming mail across the flood to the rancher waiting on the other side. He later described this as the first "airmail" in all of Arizona. Midwinter was the worst season for carrying the mail, as ice would melt during the day and run down into Oak Creek, which would be at high tide in the late afternoon when Dad arrived in the Sedona area.

When he was unable to ford the raging water, his only alternative was to camp for the night in a cornfield on the west side of the creek, build a fire, and cook his supper in a Dutch oven. Tying his mules to a tree to prevent an unscheduled midnight departure, he would crawl into a fodder shock—his private motel for the night. Next morning the creek would usually be frozen, and he would be able to cross and head on up the canyon to the post office at Indian Gardens. This resulted in a very long trip up to the canyon and then back to Cornville on the next day.

One day he managed to cross the creek but found the track so muddy that the mules slowed down almost to a stop. He tried to speed them up by swinging a mailbag around his head and shouting. This worked, but one day he discovered one particular mailbag happened to have a small hole in the corner, and he was startled when a small box shot out and flew under the wheels of the buggy. He stopped and leaped out, only to find a sample tube of toothpaste smeared completely around one muddy wheel. That day some of the mail went through—a hole in the bag.

On another very windy day, two cowboys were waiting on their horses for their mail when one carelessly dropped a piece of paper that was caught by a gust of wind and blown under the buggy. This spooked the mules, and they bolted so fast they tore off the front wheels and dragged them bouncing off across Grasshopper Flat. The cowboys found this hilarious but rode laughing and shouting after the runaway mules, roped them, and then came back to help Dad put his buggy back together. Dad didn't think it was that funny…but all in a day's work.

THE MAILMAN AND THE TEACHER

Marie Holcomb moved with her mother to Oak Creek in October of 1920 to take a teaching position in a one-room grade school. She and her ailing mother lived in an old farmhouse on a ranch that her older brother, Lee Holcomb, was leasing from the Girdner family.

This was the same ranch that was later occupied by Uncle Don and Aunt Sue Lockhart, with their children Vivian and Kennon. Even later, when Uncle Dale Girdner's house on the home ranch burned, he moved into the old place. He eventually retired from ranching and, after adding a number of pioneer and cowboy items such as saddles, cowboy gear, chaps, and hats, turned the ranch into a showplace he called "Geronimo's Hideout." Apaches had roamed Oak Creek for years, but I doubt Geronimo ever set eyes on that ranch.

Marie Holcomb only had a two-year contract, as it was assumed by the Oak Creek school board that a new teacher would be married before that time was completed, since cowboys rode down from as far as Sedona and up from Camp Verde to court the single young women teachers. True to this story line, the young rancher–mail carrier Glen Girdner started courting Marie Holcomb after New Year's of 1921, although it was under difficult circumstances as she was living with her aged mother and a very large older brother.

Dad wrote of the time: "I was twenty-three and had taken a contract to carry mail from Cornville to Sedona on horseback, and had two more years to finish. I soon recognized the remarkable personality of Marie-Slender-Maiden and a new thing began—a love that grew for forty-one years."

10 The Quest

Go ye unto all the world and preach the gospel to every creature.
—MARK 16:15

As mentioned earlier, after World War I ended, Grandfather Holcomb and Aunt Clara, after a number of meetings with Dr. Ironside to discuss plans for bringing the Word to the Navajos, had been encouraged to leave California, move back to Arizona, and establish a mission.

They made the decision to return to the Navajo Reservation but went first to Oak Creek to visit Mary and Marie at Lee Holcomb's leased ranch. Then, in early 1921, they left the ranch and drove to Chinle to look for a mission site, both there and in the Lukachukai area. Carl Armerding joined the Holcombs, and together they embarked on what Dad described as "a scouting expedition that required many months of searching by horse and buggy."

Using Chinle as a base, they searched there and also around the Lukachukai Mountains, but all did not work out smoothly, and many prospects were checked out but abandoned. Several times they returned to Lee's ranch home on Oak Creek for reconnoitering and rest.

NELSON AND ALICE GORMAN
During their time in Chinle, the Holcombs stayed with Alice and Nelson Gorman. Alice was a Christian woman from a prominent Navajo family, one of the nineteen children of *peshlakai atsidii,* one of the first Navajos to establish a reputation for working silver, who had gained wide recognition by displaying his work at the World's Fair in Chicago in 1893.

Alice had been educated off the Reservation at Grand Junction, Colorado, and was active with the Presbyterian mission at Chinle. She was instrumental in establishing a congregation that met in hogans or her home, and sometimes at the trading post. Eventually she was able to build a church, with the Reverend A. K. Locker as the first pastor. Over the years, Alice Gorman also translated over thirty hymns into Navajo.

Nelson Gorman's sister.

At the time the Holcombs were in Chinle, Alice Gorman's husband Nelson, had cattle operations near the Black Mountain and operated one of the first of the very few Navajo-owned trading posts on the Reservation. As a nomadic people, the Navajos had their own view of property rights and did not traditionally accumulate excess personal material goods that would encumber their constant moving about in search of game and booty. Anything acquired by one was shared with all members of their extended family—the clan.

This was especially true of food, which only came sporadically. Usually when someone in the group made a kill, it was shared equally with other members of the clan. A Navajo trader with a store of food and other goods was therefore expected to provide for any clan relative in need—making any profit almost impossible.

"ERIN GO BRAGH"

The first question asked of a Navajo child bound for boarding school was always, "What's your name?" And the answer was usually a long Navajo name or clan association that the confused official could not reduce to writing. Faced with the task of providing a "proper" Anglo name, an army register was often a convenient source of names for these officials.

One day a new group of young Indians arrived from Chinle, bound for boarding school, and were lined up to register. The official in charge consulted this handy army list and wrote "Gorman, Howard" for the first boy in line. For the second boy in line he assigned the next name on the roster—"Gorman, Nelson." Thus, two unrelated families were ever after Gorman, a name almost impossible for Navajos to pronounce, and which came out more like *"gáamalii."*

Nelson and Alice Gorman had a teenage son, Carl, who was reluctantly attending the boarding school at Rehoboth, New Mexico, at that time, but was later to play a very active role in the famed Code Talkers operation of World War II. After the war, Carl Gorman became very successful as a Navajo artist. He also developed a taste for classical music, and it was said he would listen to Caruso singing *Rigoletto* on the Victrola while he painted in his San Francisco studio. Carl Gorman often exhibited with his son, R. C. Gorman, who later became extremely popular as a Navajo artist in his own right and for many years had a studio in Santa Fe, New Mexico.

NORTH TO SHIPROCK

After an unsuccessful quest for their mission in the southern part of the Navajo Reservation, the Holcombs moved up to the far northwest corner of New Mexico and worked out of Shiprock, a small village that had been founded in 1903 by the BIA agent at that time, William T. Shelton, known to the Navajos as *naat'ánii nééz* or "Tall Boss."

During the early 1920s, Shiprock became the headquarters for the Northern Navajo Agency, and in addition to the BIA and superintendent's offices featured a hospital and the regional boarding school, with a complex of school buildings: boys' dormitory, girls' dormitory, kitchen and dining room for students, and housing for a number of employees. I particularly remember, from my own visits there years later, flowers and extensive grass lawns that did not exist on my part of the Reservation. An extension of the Northern Area Agency was located down on the irrigated bottomlands of the San Juan River and included barns, stables, shops, warehouses, and a jail.

The commercial part of Shiprock was small, consisting only of three trading posts, one garage, one gas station, and a tiny post office operated by the formidable Mrs. Evans, whose husband ran his garage nearby. And on the hill just above Shiprock stood a lonely Presbyterian mission, served by the Reverend Charles Campbell.

An unimproved road ran north from Gallup to Shiprock, crossing over 100 desert miles of New Mexico along the edge of the Reservation, and then continued forty-five more miles to Cortez, Colorado. A branch road ran east along the San Juan Valley through the extensive farming and fruit-growing Mormon settlements of Kirtland and Fruitland, on to Farmington and Aztec, New Mexico, and eventually to Durango, Colorado.

Another primitive track, now known as Highway 160, went meandering westward for over 250 impossible miles across the desert, canyons, and mesas of the Navajo Reservation, back into Arizona, past Kayenta and Tuba City, and on to today's Highway 89, which runs south from Utah to Flagstaff, and then to Oak Creek.

BEYOND THE FOUR CORNERS

The Holcombs made Shiprock their base for an extensive search of this northeast corner of the Reservation, and Grandfather, with Carl Armerding, made three trips on horseback across the San Juan to "spy out the land" of the vast Four Corners area.

Today the Four Corners National Monument and Tribal Park serves hundreds of tourists who pay a fee to enter. Colorful flags snap in the wind, and a bronze disk marks the exact spot where visitors may take pictures while standing in the four states of Arizona, New Mexico, Colorado, and Utah, all at the same time.

A visitor center, picnic tables, and restrooms are available now, but for years this place had no water. Surrounding the park are dozens of pickup trucks parked behind tables, stalls, and booths, where Navajos sell all kinds of jewelry, souvenirs, road maps, beads, and the delicious Navajo frybread with all its calories. Most prices are negotiable, and the place has been described as a combination of an outdoor mall and a flea market.

In the early 1920s, however, it was an empty windswept plain on the edge of the Colorado Plateau, nearly inaccessible by automobile and one of the most

Our good friend Bob Martin, later vice-president
of the Navajo Tribal Council.

remote places in the United States. A single stone, placed in 1912, indicated the spot where the two new states of New Mexico and Arizona joined the two older states of Colorado and Utah. The journalist and humorist Ernie Pyle visited this site in 1939, and Richard Meltzer quotes his reaction in *Ernie Pyle in the American Southwest.*

After sitting on the lone stone marker, Pyle wrote: "It made my rather scant bottom repose in four states simultaneously. I don't care how big your bottom is, you can't do better than that."

"THIS IS THE PLACE"

Grandfather and Carl Armerding rode beyond the Four Corners to a red pinnacle known as Boundary Butte, as it was on the boundary of the original Navajo Reservation. There they turned their horses south and rode another twenty trackless miles to Walker Creek. It was named for Lieutenant L. G. Walker, who led a small exploratory military detachment from Fort Defiance to the San Juan River and back in 1859. Grandfather and Carl found, among the mesas around Walker Creek, a lonely little abandoned rock trading post. Grandfather stopped and, like Brigham Young before him, announced: "This is the place!"

By inquiring around, they learned that the little rock building was owned by a Navajo trader named Bob Martin, who had moved to Red Mesa, so they turned their horses around and headed north again.

BOB MARTIN

A big full-blooded Navajo, Robert Bowman Martin had attended Hampton Normal and Agriculture Institute in Virginia some twenty years earlier and spoke English well. In addition to being a trading post owner and dealer in sheep, he had also worked as a farmer, served as an interpreter, and later was to become a member of Navajo Tribal Council when it was organized. Bob Martin had been the Navajo interpreter for General Hugh L. Scott in the settlement of the "Last Indian War," a series of skirmishes in 1915 between a band of hostile Utes, under a Paiute named Posey, and the *bilagáana* settlers and Mormons for the border lands above the San Juan River near Bluff, Utah.

According to Navajo custom, Grandfather Holcomb and Carl Armerding had a long conversation with Martin before bringing up their plans to establish a mission. Then another long talk brought about a very satisfactory deal: they could take possession of the old trading post on Walker Creek for the price of $400, and Grandfather had found his Mission.

Grandfather also found a lifelong friend in Bob Martin, who visited Immanuel Mission many times over the years, sometimes with members of his family. One summer day when I was a child, we visited Martin and his wife, *esenapa,* and their family when they had a temporary camp in the Carrizo Mountains a few miles above the Mission.

The Martins had a daughter, Ruth, who was a couple of years older than I was, and three sons, Robert, Fred, and Geronimo. There were also two younger girls—Susan and a baby I only remember as a baby. About the only other thing I remember of that visit was that it was the only Navajo camp on the Reservation where I ever saw a flock of chickens.

In April of 1922, after another short visit back to Oak Creek, Grandfather and Aunt Clara made the long wagon trip to the site of the new Mission and moved into the former trading post. It was a little two-room rock building, with a flat beamed roof and clay floors, not over 10 x 30 feet in dimension. Most importantly, however, there was a very small spring of fresh water located about 200 feet to the north of the old building.

PERMISSION FOR A MISSION

Before either a trading post or a mission could be established on the Reservation at that time, permission to build had to be obtained from the local Navajos, and after that petition was passed, it was submitted to the Bureau of Indian Affairs for official approval. So, following Navajo custom, the Holcombs put up a *chaha'oh,* or shade, and in the summer of 1922 invited the entire community to a feast.

They served a typical meal of bread, beans, apples, and candy, with coffee in scalding-hot tin cups. Then, after the big feed, and due time for discussion, the idea of a mission was brought up. The idea was initially well received until *ch'ah lapaiae,* Brown Hat, a forceful old man with considerable influence in the area, loudly denounced the proposal and urged the gathered Navajos to reject any effort to ever allow a *bilagáana* mission in their country. Several other Navajos then followed his lead in opposition, and the meeting dragged on.

Navajo discussions were not resolved by a vote in which the majority prevailed, but by continuing discussion until everyone present agreed, so meetings could continue for hours, or even days, as everyone was allowed to talk without interruption. Any call for a vote to force a decision would be regarded with suspicion, especially if it was made by a white man pushing for immediate action. Haste would only result in more discussion. Finally this meeting ended without approval by the Navajos.

The dedicated Holcombs, however, decided to continue their effort to bring the Gospel to the Navajos here at *dik'óózh ta* (meaning "Among the Greasewood"), as the old trading post site was known, with or without official approval, and the Navajos began to visit Immanuel Mission in increasingly large numbers. In March of 1923 the Holcombs recorded 216 visitors to the new unofficial mission. Initial refusal to accept the idea of a mission was not unusual with the Navajos. For example, the application for the Presbyterian mission that became the famed Sage Memorial Hospital at Ganado was turned down twice before approval was finally obtained.

11   The Great Migration

A
t the end of the 1922 school year Marie Holcomb and her mother Mary, who had just celebrated her sixty-fifth birthday and had already experienced a decade of Reservation life, left the banks of Oak Creek and took the long, hard journey to the desolate Navajo country, first by train and then by wagon. By July the Holcomb family was again reunited, but back at the ranch on Oak Creek, Glen Girdner was not too happy about being left behind.

MUDDY ROAD TO SHIPROCK

As soon as Dad finished his contract with the U.S. Postal Service in the fall of 1922, he straightaway left Oak Creek for the Four Corners and the girl who had left him behind. The train trip to Gallup was uneventful, and he was able to arrange further transportation to Shiprock, but Mother Nature intervened and the weather turned ugly.

Cold wind and rain continued until the flatlands of eastern Navajoland were covered with lakes of mud and shallow pools of very cold water. The dirt road that ran along the eastern border of the Reservation had been "improved" but lacked culverts or bridges across arroyos, and those usually dry "washes" were now filled bank to bank with torrents of muddy water.

After several days the rain finally slackened, and a group of travelers decided they could wait no longer in Gallup and put together a convoy of trucks equipped with foul-weather gear, chains, shovels, tow lines, and drinking water. The lead truck would plunge in and churn ahead until it mired down and could go no further, while all the other wayfarers watched from the bank.

When the lead truck stalled, everyone waded in and pushed and shoveled until they got it out on the far side, then attached a tow chain, and waded back. Through endless repeating of this drill the tired, muddy little convoy finally struggled into Shiprock, leaving behind 100 miles of well-churned mud.

Dad immediately began looking for some way to negotiate the remaining fifty miles from Shiprock to Immanuel Mission. He found that Asael "Ace" Palmer, the trader at Sweetwater, was in town for supplies and caught a ride with him, arriving at Immanuel Mission exhausted and disheveled, but in less than two weeks he had accomplished his mission, and 'a 'tééd ts 'ósí, Slender Maiden, agreed to be his bride.

THE BEST-LAID PLANS OF MICE AND MEN

Plans were made for Marie Holcomb and Glen Girdner to be married at Immanuel Mission with Marie's father, the Reverend H. A. Holcomb, officiating. But first there was the matter of a marriage certificate, and the two set out, again with cooperative trader Ace Palmer, and drove to Aztec, the San Juan County seat, a town just beyond Farmington.

Once arrived at Aztec they learned to their dismay that a license issued in New Mexico would not be valid outside the state, and if they wanted to be married in Arizona they would have to apply for a license in St. Johns, the county seat of Apache County, a round trip of over 300 miles. Dad was not interested in repeating his expedition of just a few weeks before, so they decided they should get married at once, took the New Mexico license, and off they went in search of someone to perform the ceremony.

They finally located a surprised Methodist minister, the Reverend W. L. Massegee, at his home, and, with the minister's wife and one other lady, Mrs. Frank Wood, as the only witnesses, Marie Holcomb and Glen Girdner were married. The date was December 7, 1922.

Next day, Dad and his bride were picked up by Mr. Palmer, who found the whole episode hilarious and continued to kid them as they bounced back over the rough Reservation roads. They, in turn, laughed with him when on every jounce of the truck he flew up and crushed the crown of his brand-new Stetson on the roof of his truck.

Grandfather Holcomb did not find the situation that funny, and some Navajos were disappointed that the white man's ceremony they had expected to observe would not take place at Immanuel Mission, but Dad was welcomed into the family. After a few days, and after careful prayer and consideration, the family decided that the new Mission was not yet able to support six missionaries, so Mother and Dad would seek employment off the Reservation until the new Mission was organized and authorized by the local Navajos and the Bureau of Indian Affairs. Dad moved to Albuquerque on January 12, 1923, later followed by Mother.

FLORENCE BARKER

Meanwhile, the Holcombs had recently been joined by a woman in her thirties, Miss Florence Barker, who had trained as a nurse at St. Joseph's Hospital in Denver. After eight years of practical experience in Wyoming, she was working in California when she, too, came into contact with Dr. H. A. Ironside, the great promoter of missions to the Navajos.

Ironside's fervor soon made Florence Barker interested in missionary work, and when she learned of the need for a nurse at the fledgling Immanuel Mission to the Navajos she contacted Aunt Clara by mail. Aunt Clara was delighted with the prospect

Newlyweds Marie and Glen Girdner, just after they
returned to Immanuel Mission in 1922.

Clara Holcomb, Florence Barker, and H. A. and Mary Holcomb.

of a nurse at the Mission and immediately wrote and invited her to join them in Arizona.

Arrangements were made, and in late October 1922, Florence traveled by train to Gallup, and then by auto stage to Shiprock, where she was met by Grandfather Holcomb and Aunt Clara, who had come the fifty-seven miles from the Mission with a wagon and team to pick her up. After two days on the "road" and Florence Barker's first night in a hogan, the dirty and exhausted party finally arrived at Immanuel Mission and were thankful for the hot dinner awaiting them.

Florence Barker's large trunk of basic medicines and supplies was delivered to Immanuel Mission by Ace Palmer several weeks later, when he arrived with Mother and Dad on their return from their wedding adventure, and Florence was even more delighted with the seven letters that had been waiting for her in the Shiprock post office.

Free medical attention at the Mission soon became an attractive alternative to expensive native ceremonies, as Aunt Florence immediately set about treating the local people for a wide variety of complaints: coughs, colds, fever, headaches, bruises, small injuries, broken bones, boils, cuts, and many unidentified ailments.

Later, during a flu epidemic she treated twenty-two people on one desperate day, and in March of her first year she served seventy patients.

An early patient was a somewhat disheveled Brown Hat. The cantankerous old Navajo who had so strenuously opposed the Mission came in for repairs one afternoon after his horse had "spread him on the ground."

On another memorable day, a young man whom Florence called "Sir Lancelot" brought in his favorite horse with a bad barbed-wire gash on its shoulder and asked her to sew it up. Three Navajos threw and tied the animal near the hitching post, and Florence Barker took her medicine kit outdoors, arranged the various instruments on a towel, sutured the wound, and everyone was happy—except the horse.

On one of her first nights at Immanuel Mission she wrote in her journal: "Since the Indians have found out that I am a 'mixer of medicine' they have had all kinds of aches and pains, one lad did have a severe cold and I doctored him up. I'll have to give bead pills to some of these Indians; if they can get something for nothing they are happy! I've seen some white folks with the same ailing, though."

Another poignant entry in her journal added: "Oh, it's a cold night to sleep out in this tent, but just think of the Indians, sleeping out on the ground near their flocks of sheep!"

JOHN CURLEY

About a month after the arrival of Florence Barker at Immanuel Mission, they were joined by John Curley, an educated young Navajo man from Ganado whom they had known in Oakland. Curley had also been encouraged by the evangelist Dr. Ironside to go back to the Navajo Reservation and take the Word to his own people as a missionary. Curley arrived in December of 1922 and immediately began his own independent hogan visitation.

At first Curley was very helpful in giving Aunt Clara and Florence Barker help in learning the difficult Navajo language, but he only remained about four months at Immanuel Mission before he abruptly packed up one day and, Navajo-style, rode off without explanation, never to be seen again at the Mission.

It was planting time at home, so he returned to the family farm near Ganado where he was needed. He later became active with the Presbyterian effort at Ganado and worked in translation of English to Navajo with Fred Mitchell. Dad described him as a "willing camp worker."

12 Two Women on Horseback

fter Mother and Dad left for Albuquerque, Clara Holcomb and Florence Barker assumed the responsibility for all outreach work, and these two dauntless women carried the message, riding on horseback to the far-flung Navajo camps scattered among the mesas and canyons of the enormous area around Immanuel Mission.

Aunt Clara had a white pony that she called John Mark, and Florence Barker soon acquired a beautiful black stallion that she named Lael, or "Belonging to God" in Hebrew.

The dedication of these two women, no longer young, in riding the winding sandy Reservation trails on horseback is hard to imagine, but Florence Barker carefully kept a journal recording not only the details of every day's activity and the Navajos she dealt with during her time at Immanuel Mission, but also her own personal thoughts, prayers, and concerns about what she observed on the many trips she and Clara made out to the canyon country.

An entry in her 1923 journal relates the story of one of these trips:

The "singing woman" [Aunt Clara] and I were riding thru the beautiful canyon east of our Mission. Why did the Navajos have to call it "Good for nothing Rocks?" At the head of this canyon we followed a rough trail which led to the hogans we had planned to visit that summer day.

The Navahos were real friendly; in fact they were always asking us to come and see them. If they moved to fresh pastures and built another hogan, they would tell us in much detail how to find their new home, so we could visit them.

I had brought various medicines, which I carried in my saddlebags. The medicines and treatments were readily received by most of the Navahos. Of course they had their medicine men, but found the white man's medicine helped.

The Navajo hosts invited their guests to sit with them:

Florence Barker on Lael.

We were offered sheep skins on which to sit and we placed the blanket we had in our saddles on the sheep skins and then settled down. The Navaho women never suffered knee cramps. We asked permission to sing some hymns and tell of God's word. All were quiet and listened politely. Of course the small children would dart in and out behind the blanket that was hung up for a door. Yes, the babies would cry too—but not for long—we had grown used to such interruptions.

The Lord Jesus, the forgiveness of sins, and the hope of eternal life were carefully explained by the "singing woman." When the story was finished there would be a short silence.

Then if the man of the family was present, he would speak out in a soft, dignified voice and say, "Yes, it is a good story, but it is the white man's story. The Navaho has his own story."

Quickly the "singing woman" would reply, "But in the Navaho story there is no Savior." Almost in a sad tone the Navaho man would repeat, "Yes, Savior gone."

They mounted their horses and turned toward the Mission. Later, Florence Barker wrote:

Our hearts were heavy—the miles seemed so long and the trail so rough. The sun was casting long shadows, evening was coming upon us. As [I] rode along on my big black horse I sent a heart-cry up through the canyon walls toward the blue of [the] Heavens. "Oh God, can you ever save a Navaho—can you, dear Lord?"

Years passed. Later I transferred into the Government Field Nursing Service and I worked among many other tribes of Indians. Then a day came, when an invitation was received to attend a meeting of Wycliffe Translators. Many Christian leaders and others were present.

They were to be given the first copies of the New Testament translated into the Navaho language. How thrilled and happily expectant these Navahos were to have God's word in their own tongue. How eager they were to learn to read it too and, as I looked over this group of Christian Navahos, [I] felt rebuked of the Lord. "Oh ye of little faith." "Yes," I prayed, "Dear God forgive me."

She felt that her question was answered:

The answer has at long last come. You can save the Navahos, hundreds, yea thousands of them, they have your Holy Word translated into Navaho. It is wonderful! The Navahos now know and believe the

Florence camps with the horses.

Gospel story is for them too, not just for the white man—and they have the Savior—for them He is not gone anymore.

BERNHEIMER EXPEDITION

Charles Bernheimer, a wealthy New York businessman, sponsored several expeditions to the Navajo Mountain area of the Reservation and wrote a book entitled *Rainbow Bridge: Circling Navajo Mountain and Explorations of the "Bad Lands" of Southern Utah and Northern Arizona*. Here Bernheimer described an incident that occurred during his 1923 expedition, led by Earl Morris. He wrote, with some original spelling of names:

> We camped at sundown on a bleak windy spot on the North Slope of the Carrizo Mountain and next morning found us at a lonely trading post called To-Thla-Kan, in charge of one of Wetherill's friends. He lived there with a charming little family—three of the finest young children I have ever met. No one could give information about the canyons which we intended to penetrate. We were especially eager to know whether they held ruins about which Morris had heard reports.
>
> We went to the home of the Reverend Mr. Hookum, ten miles off the main road as we had heard of an Indian living near there who could direct us. Miss Hookum and Miss Baker, a trained nurse, two bright and fearless young women, gave us directions.

Clara Holcomb in the canyon country.

TWO CAMERAS IN THE CANYONS

From an early age I remember the Kodak camera about half the size of a shoebox that Aunt Clara always took on her field trips to Navajo camps, which she began before I was born.

She often went to the *tsegi* ("canyon") country south of Immanuel Mission, a vast network of canyons and side canyons with dozens of small mud Anasazi ruins built high in little coves, sheltered by cliffs above, and often invisible from the canyon floor, since they blend with the red sandstone walls. Many of these ruins were accessible only by small hand-pecked holes in the almost-sheer cliffs and appeared untouched for centuries.

Aunt Florence, as I always called her, also had a similar camera, and now I wonder at the perseverance of those two women in packing such cumbersome equipment around on horseback through that very rough back country.

Over a period of two years, however, Clara Holcomb and Florence Barker made hundreds of priceless photographs of the *tsegi* as well as of early-day Navajo camps and of any Navajo who would stand still long enough to be photographed—and even some who wouldn't. On one occasion, two ancient Navajo men wrapped themselves in their blankets and dropped to the ground and were recorded for all time as a couple of unidentified bundles.

After the film was exposed it was carefully unloaded and mailed to the Fox studios in San Antonio, Texas, to be developed and returned several weeks to a month later. What an occasion on the day the mailbag arrived and was unlocked to find the little red and tan packets, addressed to Clara E. Holcomb, and each bearing a one-cent and a two-cent postage stamp! Everyone would gather around to carefully examine each picture and identify every person represented, then try to determine exactly where each was taken in all the canyons and mesas surrounding Immanuel Mission.

Aunt Clara sorted the black and white photos and painstakingly mounted each one in a large brown canvas album, with each pictured Navajo carefully identified, in order to create a permanent record for us to identify any Navajo who returned to visit Immanuel Mission. These volumes are now permanently lodged at the Northern Arizona University Cline Library Digital Archives.

Many books have been written and thousands of pictures taken of Anasazi ruins over the years, and I could write pages of description, but Aunt Clara's very plain albums with their succinct one-sentence descriptions for each photograph, tell the story far better than any prose I could compose:

"A cliff dwelling, like a porch under overhanging rock"
"Not easy of access. Secure from invasion"
"Brick red rocks, with ribbons of white rock"
"Old castle occupied many hundreds of years ago" (correction added later: "thousand years ago.")

The large catalog proved to be immensely interesting to visiting Navajos: they would ask for the *naaltsoos bikáá 'e'el'íígi* and eagerly examine and discuss every picture in detail, shouting with surprise and delight at any familiar face, commenting on the person, his horse, and every piece of equipment shown, and all the while laughing, joking, and telling stories about every Navajo represented.

Occasionally, however, at the end of the day when the albums were stored away, some faces were scratched out to prevent identification, probably by someone who feared his picture might be recognized by evil spirits that would cause him problems in the future.

Glen and Marie with newborn Alwin in Albuquerque.

13 Albuquerque Days

EARLY DUKE CITY

In the early 1920s, Albuquerque was actually two separate towns. The first was settled by a group of pioneers who came down from Santa Fe in 1706. For over two centuries Albuquerque remained a small, quiet village of descendents of the original pioneers, living around the San Felipe de Neri Church, and the traditional old lifestyle continued uninterrupted.

Then, in 1880, the Atchison, Topeka and Santa Fe Railway reached New Mexico, and a division point was planned for Bernalillo, but that peaceful little village just upriver from Albuquerque didn't like the prospect of noisy trains with switch engines chugging around, and large noisy machine shops with hundreds of outsiders rushing about in their peaceful town, so they chose to stay with their convenient stagecoach service.

The Atchison, Topeka and Santa Fe moved downriver a few miles, selected a site above the old village of Albuquerque, and began laying track. They built first a depot and then a roundhouse, and then acres of railroad shops and small wooden buildings began to spring up to house the new railroad employees and service activities.

By the time Dad arrived, the combined Albuquerques made up a respectable settlement of over 15,000 people, and he soon found a job on a crew laying grey streak marble for the ground floor of the nine-story First National Bank building on Central Avenue. It remained the tallest building in town for over forty years, and the new National Bank became a first stop on Dad's mail route when he was reappointed as mail carrier of the United States Postal Service. He was assigned a route that started at the bustling Santa Fe depot and the Alvarado Hotel and continued down Central Avenue through the tiny business district of New Town, with its small grouping of professional and business offices, shops, and homes of the new Anglos.

"Anglo" was the name applied to anyone from "Back East." According to a favorite story of the time, someone once asked a black porter at the station, "Who will be your next governor?" He replied, "I don't know, they haven't told us Anglos yet."

The big event of the day in Albuquerque was the moment when the Chicago to Los Angeles train came roaring into the station. Then the broad platform swarmed with passengers getting off to take a welcome break from the long, weary hours of rolling through the "Great American Desert" and exercise their pets, find something to eat, and maybe do a little shopping.

Movie actors, statesmen, and celebrities from Albert Einstein to Rudolph Valentino (and his big dog) rubbed elbows with common travelers from all walks of life who crowded around the row of silent Pueblo Indians sitting along the station wall with pottery, jewelry, and rugs displayed on blankets before them. Behind the passive Indians and through cool porches and Spanish–Moorish arches, the most magnificent waterhole of their trip awaited, the Fred Harvey Alvarado Hotel. Here passengers were greeted by smiling Harvey Girls in crisp uniforms. The Harvey Girls seated them at oak tables with hammered copper tops and linen tablecloths, already set for dinner, and presented long menus for their selections.

The menus listed not only steaks and roasts and broiled trout but also a variety of vegetables, salads, desserts—and even fresh milk! It was all served in less than half an hour, before the "All aboard!" called them back to their train: their "first real meal since leaving civilization."

Usually, if they had a few minutes before their train pulled out, visitors could visit the Indian Building next door to the Alvarado. Designed by Mary Colter, the first professional woman architect in the Southwest, it housed a fascinating museum of Indian artifacts and featured a Hopi altar, ancient rugs, baskets, and antique Spanish items. Cases and shelves were loaded with quality silverwork, carvings, Navajo rugs, Chimayo blankets, and gorgeous pieces of petrified wood—all just waiting to be taken Back East as souvenirs of the Indian Country.

One of the first buildings below the railroad station was the just-completed six-story Sunshine Building, housing a number of offices, including the law offices of legendary Elfego Baca, folk hero and gun-toting attorney, now fifty-eight years old and still deep in New Mexico politics.

Farther down Central was a business operated by a man from Italy who regularly received *Il Popolo d'Italia* with the masthead: "Revolution Is an Idea That Has Found Bayonets." This was a Fascist newspaper founded and published by a man named Benito Mussolini, who had just taken over as dictator in Italy. Dad said he took a deep breath of clean, free Albuquerque air when he came out of that dank little shop. Dad's route ended at the western edge of New Town, where the magnificent Franciscan Hotel in the new "Pueblo Expressionist" style was under construction.

Beyond the hotel stretched two miles of open desert that could be crossed by walking or by riding a horse car pulled by a tired old mule to Old Town Albuquerque. Mother joined Dad as soon as he obtained full employment with the Postal Service, and they rented an apartment also occupied by Carl Armerding and joined the Albuquerque Assembly of Plymouth Brethren where Carl was active.

Mother soon became acquainted with the cleaning lady who lived in Old Town. One day this woman confided to Mother that her nephew had a source for fresh veal and she might be able to get Mother a few steaks for a good price. Mother, a new bride on the limited budget of a mailman's salary, jumped at the opportunity to put meat on her table and entrusted the woman with a few coins. When the steaks were delivered, Mother was pleased with her find, the meat was tender and delicious, and the price was certainly right.

A few days later, however, Maria again came to Mother and confidentially told her steaks would no longer be available as her nephew had been arrested for bootlegging young burro meat and asked her to not tell anyone. Mother was willing to agree this secret would stay just between the two of them.

HOT TAMALES

Tamale vendors from Old Town regularly walked the streets hawking their wares, and one evening, shortly before I was born, Mother heard the familiar "Hot tamales—hot tamales!" in the street below and felt a sudden craving for Mexican food. Dad hustled down to get some for her, but when he arrived on the street he saw the man almost a block away and moving rapidly down the street.

Dad ran after him, shouting, "Hey, wait! I'll take some." The vendor, glancing over his shoulder, replied, "All sold out," and continued on his way, still shouting, "Hot tamales—hot tamales!"

1508 NORTH FOURTH STREET

Soon afterward, the young Girdner couple moved about six blocks away to a little house out in the country on 4th Street, where I was born on October 10, 1923. The attending physician was Dr. Lassiter, partner with Dr. Lovelace in the small practice now known as the Lovelace Clinics.

Several members of the Assembly gave my folks small gifts of money to celebrate my arrival, and they opened an account in for me in a local bank and faithfully deposited my money, thus launching me on a life of thrift. Unfortunately, the bank failed and I lost my money. Maybe that was when I acquired a lifelong distrust of banks.

FIRE AT THE MISSION

Mother and Dad kept in regular contact with progress at Immanuel Mission, usually by mail, as the Holcombs seldom ventured far from home, and in June of 1923, they had received news of disastrous events. Florence Barker wrote:

> I was just getting dinner ready when a bad sandstorm hit us. I heard Charlie and Con call from the backyard and as I opened the door to see what they wanted, a mass of flame angrily greeted me! Our shade, made

of cedar boughs and serving as a back porch, was burning. I slammed the door shut and screamed for Clara. She came and we ran through Mr. Holcomb's room to the shade. Clara ripped open a curtain and the heat flamed on her face. We saw that it was hopeless to do anything and we just had to let the fire burn. Our beds, nearly all our bedding, my trunk, suitcase: everything is gone!

She continued with her story:

We ran back into the house telling the Indians who were there to bring water in buckets, [so] we might be able to keep the fire from spreading to the roof of the house since it would have to do so against the terrific wind. For a while we threw water up on the roof but it too began to burn.

Charlie wisely told us that it was no use; we'd better carry things out, for the roof was going to burn entirely. We took his advice and began carrying everything out; we hardly knew what to pick up first, it was like a confused dream. The back door soon burned out and the wind tore through, carrying the surface burns from the tar but they didn't amount to much.

We worked for about an hour carrying our belongings out of the house and had just finished when the burning boards began dropping from the roof and it was unsafe to enter the house.

Although homeless, the missionaries felt lucky to escape:

Only one who knows and has witnessed a sandstorm realizes what it meant to carry all our belongings outside. After we could do no more we sat down, bathed our faces in water and had a time of prayer, thanking God for keeping us from harm and for letting us save as much as we did.

Our greatest loss was in the backyard. Everything burned; our wagon, saddles, bridles, harness, the new cooler, the tent and all the things stored there. Our grain, the woodpile, chickens and chicken house, our scales, alfalfa and Leal's shade are gone. We had several shades in the backyard with various things stored under them and that is what caused so much damage—the whole backyard was on fire at one time.

We are so thankful that none of our animals were tied in the back as they sometimes are. I felt badly to lose my trunk and so many personal things, but I would have felt worse to have lost Lael.

Florence Barker ended her chronicle with the comment: "We had hoped we wouldn't have to sleep in our tent through another winter, but we never thought of disposing of it by burning it!"

Marie and Glen Girdner.

The next day Con rode over to Sweetwater to inform them of the disaster at Immanuel Mission, and about six that evening Ace Palmer arrived with his truck to rescue the missionaries and their remaining belongings and take them to Sweetwater, where they rented a two-room shack, actually a small storeroom, beside the trading post. It was so crowded that Clara and Florence slept on camp cots outdoors, where it was much cooler.

The Mission family lived in their temporary refugee camp at Sweetwater for seven weeks before a new roof was completed on the old trading post, and during all this time Ace Palmer and his wife Lois (Foutz) Palmer provided the assistance and encouragement that made it possible for them to move back to Immanuel Mission in August.

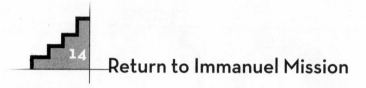

14 Return to Immanuel Mission

LEGAL AT LAST

At the end of January 1924, discussions of the petition to establish Immanuel Mission culminated in yet another meeting. At the time, Florence Barker was spending a few days with Hazel Fairfield in Tsegi Canyon when Ray, who was Hazel's brother and one of the camp boys, rode into camp with a message. Later Aunt Florence wrote in her journal:

> I was having a lovely time with Hazel but was anxious to know what the superintendent was going to do about the signatures for our petition. Ray saddled my horse and soon I was off. It was a glorious day for a ride and Lael is a grand horse, full of pep. What a beautiful country to ride through.
>
> When I arrived I found the little house crowded with people. Not only Superintendent [A. H.] Kneale and his Navajo interpreter Deshna, and the Reverend Campbell, Presbyterian missionary in Shiprock but also a number of Navajos were also waiting. Brown Hat had not yet arrived so I started to prepare a meal for the group.

Acting as Kneale's interpreter, Deshna Claw Cheschillie or "Curley Left Hand," had been educated at Fort Lewis Boarding School in Colorado and was to serve as Chairman of the Navajo Tribal Council from 1928 to 1932. Aunt Florence went on:

> The superintendent talked kindly to Brown Hat, asking why he had not gone to Shiprock. Brown Hat answered with the plea that his wife was sick and Mr. Kneale then told him to wait until she was stronger, then come to Shiprock and then told Brown Hat that we Immanuel Mission folks were his friends and he felt badly that we didn't have a permanent mission site.
>
> He would like to have Brown Hat sign a petition to the government to grant some land. Brown Hat was one of the headmen, [and] had been called to see what he thought of the situation, for he wanted to

get the signatures of the Indians. Brown Hat talked about everything else, trying to hedge the subject. The superintendent let Brown Hat talk himself out and then put the question squarely to him. Would he sign?

We mission folks were sure praying. I was out in the kitchen grinding meat for dinner. But I could hear all that was going on and was listening and praying.

Would he sign the petition? It was tense for a moment and the old man was silent. Mr. Deshna told Brown Hat that if he would put his thumb down he would sign right after. "*T'aa'ako* [That's all right]," Brown Hat said and, before he could change his mind, Mr. Kneale had the petition and ink pad in front of the old man.

The turning point had arrived. Aunt Florence then wrote:

We almost held our breath while Brown Hat's prints were put down. God has brought to pass that which we had barely hoped for. Brown Hat had boasted that he never signs any paper, much less sign this one.

"The heart of the king is in the hand of the Lord and He turneth it wheresoever He will." Our prayers that have ascended to the throne of grace for two years have been answered.

After a dinner that included biscuits, a pot of coffee, and some apples, Superintendent Kneale's party left Immanuel Mission and, after a stop at Sweetwater Trading Post to get ten more signatures (thumbprints) on the petition, returned to Shiprock.

The temporary Mission that had been in operation for two years was now officially sanctioned by the Navajos and by the Department of the Interior, and ten acres of land were allocated to establish a Mission. However, as all Reservation land was under government control, no part could be privately owned, nor could any buildings or improvements built at the Mission be removed or sold.

Grandfather named the new institution Immanuel Mission, "God with us," as a fitting name for a faith mission with no sponsor, which was entirely supported by volunteer contributions from a number of Plymouth Brethren Assemblies in cities across the United States from Boston to San Diego. It was truly a faith mission as government funds were never accepted, nor was any money requested from any Navajo or group of Navajos, either then or over the years to come.

THE LORD WILL SUPPLY

Superintendent Kneale continued to visit the Mission during those early days. In his memoir *Indian Agent,* he quoted a conversation he had with Aunt Clara. As

Alwin's first walk through the woods with Marie and Glen.

there were three denominations of Protestants operating in the Northern District of the Navajo Reservation, he asked her whom she represented. She replied, "We represent no organization."

Kneale then asked the source of their funds and supplies and she explained: "When we feel the need of anything, we take the matter to the Lord and it is in His hands." Superintendent Kneale persisted, "And do you always receive the things you feel essential?" and she replied, "Not always, but when we fail to do so, we know that the things we asked for are not necessary to the prosecution of His work, otherwise we always receive them."

Superintendent Kneale then wrote: "As I looked around their miserable habitation, I thought I could detect several items that might easily be considered essential and, before leaving, remarked, 'Miss Clara, Delco lighting would prove a great convenience, wouldn't it?'"

Miss Clara was forced to admit that possibly it would. When I told her I had friends in New York who would gladly present them with this convenience, she inquired, "Are your friends Christians?" "I am not altogether sure they are professed Christians," I replied, "but I do know they would consider it a privilege and an honor to present you with a lighting plant. I have reference to the organization known as the Elks."

But Miss Clara would have nothing to do with it. She said, "If the Lord wished us to have a lighting plant, He would provide it. We could not accept anything from your friends in New York."

SUPERINTENDENT KNEALE

In 1899 Albert H. Kneale joined the United States Indian Service at the Pine Ridge Indian Agency of the Sioux in South Dakota. Over the next quarter of a century he served at a number of agencies, the Cheyenne and Arapaho School in Oklahoma, the Shoshone School at Wind River in Wyoming, the Crow Boarding School on the Little Big Horn in Montana, and finally as Superintendent and Special Disbursing Agent of the Winnebago and Omaha Indian Reservations in Nebraska.

In 1913 Kneale was appointed Supervisor at Large, reporting directly to the Commissioner of Indian Affairs. He then served at Sioux Standing Rock Reservation in North Dakota for a short time before a nine-year stint as Superintendent of the Uinta and Ouray Reservation in Utah. He was assigned the Northern Navajo Reservation in 1923 and arrived in New Mexico about the same the time that I did.

NEW CAR AND NEW HORIZONS

Mother and Dad were closely watching developments on the petition for a mission, and when the news finally arrived that it was signed and approved, they immediately began preparations to return to the Reservation as planned. Dad gave up his postal service appointment, and they packed all their worldly possessions and hired a truck to ship them to their new home at Immanuel Mission, back across the line in Arizona.

The Assembly at Albuquerque had established an automobile fund for the Mission, and a number of other Assemblies also contributed to this fund, so after adding the savings Mother and Dad had accumulated during the ten-month stay in Albuquerque, they were able to purchase a new Model T Ford for less than $500.

Black, of course, the new vehicle had a canvas top and the new heavy-duty Ruxtel axle that was Dad's pride. It had four speeds forward, and he boasted that it was "the best car I ever drove in sand dune country." He was also proud of the new foot control added by his brother Stanley, so that this Model T was never driven with the "stiff, clumsy hand-operated accelerator."

In June 1924 Mother, Dad, and their eight-month-old son set off for Immanuel Mission in their shiny, brand-new car. Mother was driving and approaching Laguna Pueblo when an Indian, who apparently had even less driving experience than Mother, ran into our fine new automobile, and the happy homecoming was delayed while the right front wheel was temporarily repaired with a crowbar.

Eventually, we arrived at Immanuel Mission with our slightly used Ford and moved into the small rock trading post with the four missionaries already in residence. Aunt Florence wrote soon after that the confusion of seven people in a two-room rock shack "sort of got on everyone's nerves."

The three newcomers occupied a small space put up where the tent had stood on the northwest side of the old trading post before the fire. The walls were rough stone and lumber, the floor was packed earth, and overhead large wooden vigas held up a new flat roof. I had a crib, Mother and Dad shared a small bed and, with all our earthly possessions stacked around us, we had a cozy nest in the wilderness.

During summer, activities were mostly outdoors, but as winter approached and cold winds came sweeping across the Colorado Plateau, we were forced into the main room of the old house. There stood the kitchen stove, the only source of heat for the entire building, and the main room became the center of all activity—cooking, eating, and meeting with visiting Navajos, who often stayed overnight, sleeping by the stove in the same area.

Outside of bed, there was very little privacy for anyone.

15 Night of the Big Wind

t was at this point on the night of December 16, 1924 that a fierce sandstorm blew the roof off our house and sent me off to stay in the nearby hogan with Con and Grace. After leaving me there, Dad started back to the roofless trading post but on the way stopped to sit and rest for a moment. A little later he realized he had temporarily lost consciousness and had been sitting for some time, and he got to his feet and made it back to the house, where he found everyone was now wrapped in all the clothes they could find.

Aunt Florence was able to patch up his bleeding scalp while everyone else wandered around trying to assess the damage by the feeble light of a flashlight and soon found the heavy timber ridgepole of the roof had crashed down on the stove and turned it over, spilling a dust of ashes, partially burned wood, and a few glowing embers across the dirt floor. They were eternally grateful that the fire in the stove had died down earlier in the night and the entire Mission was not burning again.

There was little that could be done in that dark, cold, and windy night, so they all gathered in the roofless living room for prayer and to work out a plan of action. They decided the only available shelter from the windstorm was a small brush-topped hogan out in the cow pen that had recently been converted into a shelter for the livestock. The family gathered all the blankets and quilts they could find and packed out to the barn, where they drove the unfortunate cows out to face the elements, cleaned off sleeping space on the sandy floor, and huddled down together on the hard earth floor for a long wait until dawn. In the morning they finished cleaning out the stable and started moving clothing, food, stove, cooking utensils, and books down to the temporary shelter from the subzero weather, where they arranged a very primitive camp life.

While clearing away the wreckage in what had been our room, Mother and Dad found one forty-pound rock that had crashed into my bed, doing substantial damage to my crib but fortunately not to me. The roof had blown off in two sections; one crashed in the back yard and the other smashed into the new Ford. The ridgepole of the house damaged one side and jammed the radiator, but Dad was able to patch it up enough to get it running.

Grace and Con.

Dad and Mother then started a long trip through the snow to Farmington to purchase building materials for rebuilding the roof, leaving a small baby and a grandmother suffering from dementia in the care of three beleaguered middle-aged missionaries in a brush hut out in a cow pen, covered by snow.

A Navajo boy was sent to recruit some help to repair the roof, and four Navajos named Constellations (or Con), Charlie, Father of Twins, and Ray immediately set to the task of repairing the roof. They started by constructing a temporary shelter at the house, as the temperature had fallen to more than 10 degrees below zero, and by the time Dad and Mother returned from Farmington everyone was clearing away rubble. The work crew had salvaged some boards and part of the roofing paper and began replacing the roof. They completed the job in about a week, cleared out the snow, set up the stove, and started a fire.

After six nights in the cowshed, seven cold and unkempt missionaries crawled out of their hut and began to move their quilts and clothing back into the repaired rock house. But first Aunt Florence insisted she should take a photograph for the record.

Dad was more concerned with the present business of getting out of the miserable cold than with history and objected to being photographed. Years later he told me, "Just to get things moving on, I took off my hat and turned toward her camera with a sheepish grin." The black and white photo shows a motley group of refugees standing beside a snow-covered brush hut, all wearing tight smiles for the camera, and one sullen-looking fellow grimacing in the foreground.

Moving out of the cow barn after the big wind; Mary, H. A., Marie, Clara, and Glen.

Aunt Florence commented after the move: "Oh, it was grand to be warm again. One who has never been without a roof doesn't know what he has missed! I have never appreciated a roof so much as I do now. When we moved back into the house we were still terribly crowded and everything was in much confusion, piled up 'mistakenly' as our Navajos would say, but at least we were warm."

Hazel Fairfield came over to help, and after the workmen were given a dinner of beans, squash, biscuits, coffee, apples, and candy, they left us as possibly the first Christian family in modern history to celebrate Christmas in a stable.

16 Building in the Desert

With nine people, including a baby, and a grandmother becoming less and less responsible, all crowded in one small rock house, Dad soon tired of living in a commune, even with a new roof. He realized that more space had to be the first item on his agenda.

NEW ROCK HOUSE

As the new member of the team at Immanuel Mission, he was responsible for providing this living space, and so in the summer of 1925, he and two Navajos cleared a temporary road to the nearby mesa. Then with picks and shovels they quarried blocks of stone from a ledge and hauled them down to the Mission by wagon. Dad, a man named Franklin, *tsar god,* Con, and Jack completed a three-room rock house in a few months, and the Girdner family moved out of the commune and into what Florence Barker called "the first real house in this desert country."

As the rock house neared completion, Grandfather Holcomb put together another crew of Navajos and started digging a basement for a much larger building nearby. For this excavation, in addition to picks and shovels they were able to use a two-horse Fresno scraper that scooped dirt much faster than men could dig with shovels alone. Cold weather delayed the construction, and the basement was temporarily roofed over, but when the rock house was nearly completed, Dad, who was familiar with the Pueblo style of adobe construction from his Albuquerque days, began to work with George Hadaka and a couple of other helpers, experimenting with mud for an adobe brick that did not crack when it dried. After considerable trial and error they found a suitable mix, and Dad commented, "We learned a few things."

Before they could even begin their monumental building project, however, they had to construct two mud mills. These were powered by two weary horses that walked endless rounds pulling a pole and paddle contraption that slowly mixed mud, which was then cast into a mold to form adobe bricks. The bricks were laid out in rows to dry in the hot desert sun, and, for the first time since coming to the Reservation, the missionaries prayed for no rain.

BIG ADOBE HOUSE

Dad proudly counted 43,000 adobe bricks that he and his team had produced that summer. He decided he must have found the right formula for durable adobe, and in fact the building made of those adobe bricks was still standing nearly a century later, in spite of occasional thunderstorms and frequent violent sandstorms.

A foundation for the main adobe building was laid and as soon as Dad completed the rock building in August of 1925, he recruited six Navajo men, including Roy Scott and George Hadaka, to work with him to build a new adobe "Mission House." None of these men spoke English, and Dad was very new at Navajo, but they were somehow able to communicate enough for him to train them in his newfound art of laying adobe, and they went to work. Dad commented on their progress: "I was on my own and learned to work with Navajos who knew no English. I made some funny mistakes but the people very seriously corrected me and then we all laughed together."

Sometimes Dad would set me up on the wall so I could supervise the entire project. As I was a two-year-old, I have only a few memories of all this activity, but I do recall one occasion when Mother took me into the basement, and I looked up and saw men standing on scaffolding and nailing up boards for the main floor of the room above. Another vague memory is of Dad carrying me around that project in a large bucket.

A number of volunteers came out to the Reservation during this time to help with the construction of the main building. One of them, Dad's youngest brother Stanley, came up from Oak Creek for the summer and took an active part in the early phases of the building.

UNCLE STANLEY

A young man in his twenties, Stanley Girdner, in addition to his long hours of construction of the new building, also had a number of exciting adventures during his stay at Immanuel Mission. With a friend who was also with him, he succeeded in climbing the sheer rock of *tsé sa'an,* the first and probably the only white men to scale that forbidding great red round rock mesa standing several miles south of the Mission.

Stanley didn't know a word of Navajo when he came to the Reservation but soon developed a great relationship with the Navajo construction crew. One day he persuaded about half a dozen men to stand in a circle around his Ford and hold hands. He then motioned for the man at the far end of the loop to put his hand on the fender, and when he did, Uncle Stanley took the hand of the Navajo at the other end and then reached in and grabbed the spark plug, sending a jolt of electricity around the circle.

The surprised men jumped around, shouting and laughing, and everyone enjoyed the practical joke except one older man who angrily strode off, probably convinced the new *bilagáana* was trying to bewitch him.

JAKE MORGAN

Jacob Cassimere Morgan, an educated Christian Navajo man, drew up the original plan for the adobe building and then, in September of 1926, came back to the Mission, hammer in hand, and put up the framework for the roof. One of the first Navajos on the Reservation to own an automobile, Morgan had his own transportation.

As a boy, Morgan had attended school at Fort Defiance, and then went to the Hampton Agriculture Institute in Virginia, where he completed carpentry training. After graduating in 1900, he returned to Hampton for another two years to study business. For twenty years after returning to the Reservation, Morgan worked in several positions with the Bureau of Indian Affairs, operated a trading post, and even served as a school band director at Crownpoint Boarding School. He also was considered one of the best cornet players in the Southwest.

Morgan was eventually ordained by the Christian Reformed Church and was active in Grand Junction, Colorado, for a time before going back to Hampton to translate Scripture into the Navajo language. By 1925 he was assisting the Reverend L. P. Brink in starting a mission school in Farmington. When the first Navajo Council was created in 1923, Jake Morgan represented the Shiprock District and later became the fifth Tribal Chairman, serving from 1932 to 1936. He came into contact with Superintendent Kneale during this time, but ironically, these two men who had been so instrumental in the founding of Immanuel Mission became bitter political rivals.

ALL'S WELL THAT ENDS WELL

By November of 1926 Aunt Clara and Aunt Florence were able to move their bedroom into the kitchen area of the new adobe building and some privacy was now possible, but actual livable space was still very limited, and Grandfather and Grandmother remained in the old rock trading post for six more months.

We celebrated Christmas of 1926 with a big family dinner in the new house, followed by coffee, buns, beans, apples, and candy in the old rock building. An extraordinarily heavy snow had fallen before just before Christmas that year, and snow lasted until the next spring, but the adobe house was completed, and Dad proudly wrote: "We had finished the first two buildings of the Mission at the place where stood the ghost of Martin's trading post sold to the Mission. It was 1927."

The old rock trading post was converted into several rooms. One served as a room for Navajos staying overnight at Immanuel Mission, and another temporarily became an enclosed rabbit run. In time the old trading post building

Uncertain method of transportation
(Glen carrying Alwin in a bucket).

was again modified as needed for other activities. After we replaced the Ford Model T with a new Model A in the late 1920s, the old car was stored for years in the back of what was now the garage and served as an entertainment center for the youngsters.

The big room became our workshop, with a workbench high enough to accommodate a tall Grandfather; however, a small boy needed a box to bring him up to a working level. On the wall behind the bench was an extensive tool-board that featured dozens of common and special tools. In addition to a large vice, mounted on the bench, there were hammers, mallets, saws, a miter box, drills, wrenches, and rolls of wire.

At one end of the workshop we stored road repair equipment and garden and field implements: shovels, hoes, picks, mattocks, axes, hatchets, a posthole auger, wire cutters, wire stretchers, crowbars, sledge hammers, sickles, and one large scythe—a relic of Grandfather's dairy farming days in a far greener country. Lumber and building supplies were also stored in this area, as were wooden boxes and lugs, bushel baskets, twine, gunny sacks, rolls of wire for fencing, pipe and fittings, nails, bolts, and nuts. Missing from all this inventory was any kind of garden hose. All trees and plants were watered by bucket, with waste water from the kitchens.

Along an outside wall not far from this room a small grist hand mill was attached to a post for Navajos to use for grinding corn and their treasured Arbuckle's coffee beans, and this mill proved to be the favorite feature of Immanuel Mission to visiting Navajos.

WORK NAVAJO-STYLE

Early in the building program we learned that few Navajos considered work to be full-time, as did the *bilagáana,* but instead considered it temporary and for extra funds. When a clan member needed help or a sing was to be held, a Navajo felt obligated to attend, even though he knew that a sing could last for as long as nine days and nights. This was his private business, and he did not see the need to inform anyone before leaving the job.

Historically the Navajos had been free to move around in search of whatever they needed to sustain life, and most did not have much and shared what they had with the group. Now hunting, gathering, and raiding were limited, and only sheep required daily attention, but people could work if necessary to satisfy a specific need. Not full time, however, as a regular income would only encourage other clan members to look to you for support.

Navajo men had become skilled as silversmiths, weavers, and sometimes farmers, but few were mechanics or other technical workers. All was to be changed forever by World War II, when some Navajos left the Reservation to join the armed forces, and many others went to work at the munitions depots at

Pause in the construction of the Rock House.

Fort Wingate, just east of Gallup, and Bellemont, just west of Flagstaff. But that was after my time on the Navajo Reservation and not part of this story.

BUILDING FOR THE AGES
During one of the remodeling projects I "helped" Dad close an interior doorway to make the corner room a place for Navajo families to stay on overnight visits. When we finished, Dad stood back to appraise our rather rough stonework and speculated, "Some archaeologist will probably uncover this site in about a thousand years and, on examining this they will write that an 'inferior tribe overran an older civilization and tried to modify the fine craftsmanship of the superior culture with a crude attempt at masonry.'"

The final building, constructed much later, was a cattle barn to replace the historical old house of Big Wind fame, and I wonder if Dad was thinking of another possible windstorm when he built that barn with great big stone blocks. The cows entered this barn from the corral through a large door and stood between two stanchions while they were being milked. A small side door led into the back area, where bales of hay and large 100-pound sacks of grain and other feed were stored. The evening milking is one of my most treasured memories, sitting on a couple of feed sacks in that snug little barn with a kerosene lantern casting flickering shadows while Dad milked our two cows and recounted stories of his life at the Four Bar Cross Ranch, at Northern Arizona Normal School, and in the army.

All too soon I found myself to be the one sitting on the three-legged stool under a cow, usually alone with only the cow to talk to.

Frontier Medicine

WALK IN BEAUTY

"Walking in beauty" is a common definition of the Navajo concept of *hôzhô,* or being in harmony, which is the fundamental theme of their religion and their philosophy of life. It went far beyond the religion of most *bilagáana* in that it applied to all phases of their everyday life. They believed many problems and all illnesses were caused by being out of balance with the universe and could only be resolved by returning to an alignment with beauty by using the mind's capacity to heal itself. To some extent this is not inconsistent with the *bilagáana* belief of "mind over matter" in resolving personal problems.

TABOOS

Even though Navajos lived in crowded hogans with little or no opportunity for segregation or quarantine of those with contagious diseases, they knew little about organic diseases and therefore didn't worry much about exposure or contagion, as they had no concept of viruses, germs, or bacteria.

They were convinced that sickness indicated a lack of balance in life caused by some unfortunate recent event, or possibly an episode that took place even decades before, and the everyday life of the Navajo was burdened by a whole system of taboos, curses, and witchcraft. Even talking about sickness could be dangerous, and on several occasions the missionaries were held responsible for an illness because they had "come to our camp and talked to us about death."

To deal with an illness, it was necessary to find and remove the cause of the sickness and discover what taboo had been broken that caused the problem. Then, to restore the harmony and the proper balance of the patient, a person was required who knew how to diagnose the cause and recommend the proper ceremony to restore health. This person could be a stargazer or more often, a *ndilniihii,* or "listener."

The *ndilniihii,* often a woman, first engaged in long discussions to identify clues from incidents of past behavior by the patient that might have broken a taboo. She would then sprinkle sacred pollen and pray until her hand began to tremble and indicate what caused the illness and what ceremony was required to correct it. An herbal treatment might then be used but, even if effective, complete harmony could only be restored by someone who knew the required ceremony. A medicine man who knew this appropriate ritual was then consulted and arrangements were made for a "sing" to restore harmony.

HATAAÍII

Medicine men called *hataałii* played a basic role in everyday Navajo life and were held in high esteem, but it took years for a man to carefully memorize exactly the rituals of chants, prayers, and sandpainting required for restoring harmony, and any mistake could completely void the ceremony.

A ceremony could also be ineffective if it was not paid for, and therefore a "sing" could mean financial disaster for a Navajo family of moderate means, as payment in cash, jewelry, goods, or livestock was always expensive. A sing could take all the resources of a family as, in addition to the considerable fee for a medicine man and any assistants required, the ceremony was also a social occasion and would attract a number of clansmen and friends who would have to be properly fed, usually for several days. Some ceremonies took days to perform, and the *yeibichai,* a winter ceremonial, required nine days and nights to be completed.

In his book *Sagebrush Lawyer,* A. T. Hannett, a mayor of Gallup in the early 1920s, recalled one wild midnight ride. First, a meeting of a number of officials hosted by his brother, Dr. J. W. Hannett, was interrupted when the McKinley County sheriff suddenly appeared, accompanied by a very agitated Navajo man seeking immediate help for a very sick child.

The doctor and his guests immediately drove out in several cars over rough Reservation roads to the campsite where many Navajos were attending a healing ceremony. Dr. Hannett gave the infant emergency medical attention and then learned that the medicine man had already collected nine sheep a day, a flock of twenty-seven sheep, for his three days of unsuccessful singing.

Infant diarrhea and enteritis were very common. Tuberculosis, then called consumption, was also extremely prevalent on the Navajo Reservation, at a rate nine times the national average. After infant mortality, tuberculosis was the major cause of death on the Reservation. Trachoma-infected eyes were also a common problem, but there was very little that could be done for this dread disease. Surgery was drastic, with only indifferent results, and trachoma remained prevalent on the Reservation until the new sulfanilamide was produced, years after we had all left Immanuel Mission.

BILAGÁANA MEDICINE

Medical care on the Navajo Reservation was originally the sole responsibility of the U.S. Army, and "field matrons" were working on the Reservation as early as 1891. Then in 1912 the Bureau of Indian Affairs established a hospital in the

Shiprock District to serve a huge area, with a population that was even more widely dispersed than the Reservation average, estimated at that time to be fewer than two Navajos per square mile.

Florence Barker gained wide recognition in our area as a woman who could provide relief and comfort for many injuries and ills, and very soon after she arrived at Immanuel Mission, Navajos began coming to see her in flocks with their multiple cuts, scrapes, and bruises.

However, *bilagáana* medicine, for the Navajo, was considered only a temporary treatment of symptoms, and a return to complete harmony of body, mind, and spirit could only be attained through complete cleansing of the mind through traditional ceremonies. Many Navajos, on leaving the hospital, would immediately arrange a sing to resolve the inner conflict brought on by the hospital stay and restore harmony with the world around them.

Florence Barker's favorite cure-all for small cuts was iodine, but I agreed with the Navajos and much preferred mercurochrome, as it made a beautiful red display of the wound—and didn't sting as much as a swab of brown iodine. Often a Navajo would request *agháhwiizídí,* or laxative, but as I had a violent distaste for the standard remedy, castor oil, I would do almost anything to avoid taking that treatment.

One morning I was watching Aunt Florence dispensing medicine when a Navajo man came in and asked for something for his stomach. Aunt Florence immediately diagnosed the problem, and, to my horror, got out the large bottle of castor oil and poured a shot glass full and handed it to her patient. I watched with an overwhelming sympathy for the poor man as he slowly took the glass, looked warily at the thick yellowish liquid contents, and sniffed cautiously before downing the oily potion in one long draught.

Then, to my amazement, he smacked his lips, handed the glass back to Aunt Florence and asked for another round. I couldn't believe he polished that one off too, asked for a third, and then wanted a bottle of the wonderful stuff to take home. His delight with castor oil did not improve my taste for the stuff, even when Mother tried to disguise it in orange juice—that only gave me a distaste for oranges. Other remedies were fig syrup or Epsom salts, but neither would fly for me.

On another occasion a young man asked for salve for an abrasion on his arm, and as he and his companion were eating at a small table Aunt Florence put some yellow salve on a small plate and placed it at his elbow. His "friend" called his attention to this by exclaiming, "Look, the nice woman brought you *mandagyíiya!*" (or butter, adapted from the Spanish word *mantequilla*). He spread it on his bread and ate it, but when Aunt Florence returned to the room soon after, the fellow had completed his lunch yet didn't seem to appreciate her generosity very much.

Alwin and Florence at Sweetwater Trading Post
with Navajo visitors.

Several emergency situations tested our amateur medical staff. Mother was home alone one day when a man was brought in with a rattlesnake bite. This was really traumatic as Navajos had a terrible fear of any contact with snakes. The very word *na'ashǫ'íí* was considered a curse.

Mother had an anti-venom kit she had never opened, and she was hesitant to experiment, but the victim and his companions were nearly hysterical, expecting him to die immediately, so she got out the kit and read the instructions. The prescribed procedure was to apply a tourniquet above the bite, make several cuts, and suck out the venom before injecting a shot. Mother followed instructions, and the man survived the ordeal—and so did Mother. However, Marie Girdner never again volunteered to treat a snake bite.

Everyone at the Mission was almost daily exposed to whatever the current infection was, and each of us children had a turn with every malady of the day— whooping cough, measles, chicken pox, and common colds—but beyond the discomfort and inconvenience at the time, there were no visible lasting problems for the younger children of our family. I, however, contracted polio when I was four years old, with temporary traumatic results—and also tuberculosis, although that was not detected until thirty years later.

For some reason Aunt Florence had a small supply of strychnine that she kept in her medicine chest. I do not know why she had it or how she used the deadly alkaloid but do remember my strict instructions: "Don't even touch that bottle." Many things that are now considered extremely dangerous were handled daily at the Mission, usually with caution but with little fear. Grandfather kept cyanide, dynamite, and caps rather casually stored in the shop, and mercury was not considered particularly harmful. For a time I had a little drop of the stuff in a small can that I carried around to entertain Navajo boys by dividing it and then rolling it back together again.

THE RELUCTANT DENTIST

Occasionally Dad was drafted to perform emergency dental work when a suffering Navajo came to Immanuel Mission for first aid. There were two pairs of dental forceps in the Mission medicine chest, and Dad would seat the patient on a sturdy kitchen chair, recruit a couple of men to hold him, choose an instrument, and grimly set about extracting the tooth.

I will never forget watching a particularly long, difficult episode when I was about six years old. Two husky young fellows tried to keep a struggling middle-aged man on the stool as Dad pried and twisted his instrument to remove the offending tooth. He finally extracted the stubborn molar and dropped it in a pan.

The two "friends" relaxed their grip and the patient jerked loose, rolled off the stool, and threw himself on the dirt floor, yelling and threshing around with dust and blood on his face. Such episodes gave this small boy a profound dread of any dental procedure, and it was years before I was able to venture into any such activity without a premonition that something terrible was about to occur.

KEES

A slender sixteen-year-old Navajo sheepherder, *kees* lived with his family several miles east of the Mission. One hot afternoon *kees* and his younger brother were out with the family herd a few days after a government work crew completed a flood-control project in an arroyo nearby. A dynamite cap had been inadvertently dropped near the site and left behind when they completed their project.

Curious, *kees* picked it up to examine it, noticed some kind of dark powder substance in the bottom of the little metal tube, and with a piece of wire was scraping the lethal little object when it suddenly exploded in his hand, blowing off parts of three fingers and tearing his neck and face.

Seeing all the blood, the younger brother ran to their burro grazing nearby, removed a dirty old flour sack that served as hobbles to keep the animal from straying, and returned to stop the flow of blood and bind up the wound. The boys decided to not tell anyone about the accident, but when they returned to the camp that evening the family immediately saw the cloth bandage and then became alarmed when *kees* fainted soon after.

The father quickly rounded up horses, and he and the younger brother escorted *kees* to the Mission, arriving just as we were finishing supper. That night was one of the very few times we ever skipped evening prayers, as all attention was immediately turned to the injured young Navajo.

Mother removed the bloody, filthy, makeshift bandage, cleaned the wounds, treated them with iodine, and covered them with clean cloth. To our amazement, *kees* never spoke nor changed expression during the entire ordeal, but he did register some trepidation when he learned he would have to go to faraway Shiprock for further treatment at the hospital.

The younger brother was sent home with the horses. Dad bundled *kees* and his father into our automobile and set off in the middle of the night for the trip of over fifty miles of rough Reservation roads to the government hospital at Shiprock, and the rest of us went to bed. Dad returned late the next afternoon and reported a successful delivery to the hospital, but we heard nothing more about *kees* for nearly a month. Then one day he turned up at the Mission, proudly displaying his repaired hand. Parts of three fingers were missing, but he considered himself a battle-scarred veteran.

Some emergency trips to the hospital were not as successful as this expedition, and Navajos were usually hesitant to undertake the long, hard journey as it entailed considerable traveling, first on horseback to the Mission or a trading post, and then by automobile to Shiprock, where they would be far beyond the support of their extended families.

Dad started for Shiprock one cold night with an older man with an advanced case of what we thought was pneumonia, but when he arrived at a place called Red Wash at about midnight he found the notoriously tricky crossing a raging stream of muddy red water. He waited several hours for the water to subside, then cautiously crossed and had churned halfway up Blue Hill when he became completely mired in the sticky blue-black clay.

After carefully covering the man in the back seat with a blanket, Dad trudged back down the hill, waded the cold muddy water of Red Wash, and walked on through the snow and slush to Beclabito Trading Post. Hugh Foutz immediately drove him back to rescue the stranded patient in the stuck car on Blue Hill. The Navajo was still breathing but died before they could dig the car out and drive back to Beclabito. This episode only served to confirm the deep Navajo suspicion of hospitals, and they reasoned that if so many people died at the hospital the place must certainly be full of evil spirits.

Bilagáana medical treatment was gradually accepted, and as the years passed, old medicine men and old chants were lost. The value of ceremonies for problems other than diseases and injuries was still valued. As one tribal official, himself a medicine man, once observed, "We cannot cure tuberculosis but we can heal disease of the mind and the heart."

18 When the Queen Came to Shiprock

Queen Marie of Romania, known as the "Modern Queen" for her many diplomatic activities, often represented her little country in other nations, and in 1926 her tour of the United States included a stop in Shiprock to see the "Red Indians." At the time we were visiting the Palmers in Fruitland, and both Mother and Mrs. Palmer became excited by the royal visit and determined to go down to Shiprock and attend the royal reception.

Neither Dad nor Ace Palmer was too impressed by royalty and certainly didn't want to make the trip, so Mrs. Palmer drafted her brother to act as chauffer. Mother was uneasy about the brother's driving abilities, but Mrs. Palmer assured her he was a very deliberate man and an excellent driver, so Mother reluctantly agreed, and that evening the three of them set off in our car for the journey down to the Navajo Agency in Shiprock.

Most Model T Fords of that time were operated by a steering wheel, two hand-controlled levers for spark and gas, and a foot brake. To get the car going and to speed up, the driver pulled the gas lever down, and he pressed the brake with his foot to slow up or stop. But our car had been specially modified by Uncle Stanley, replacing the hand accelerator with a foot-operated one. When they were ready to leave, Brother carefully pulled out of the driveway and slowly set off down the road to Shiprock, and Mother began to relax.

Soon, however, he started picking up speed and within just a few minutes they were roaring down the road at the terrific speed of nearly thirty miles an hour, overtaking all other traffic, skidding around corners, and bouncing through ruts at a bone-cracking pace. He would jam on the brakes, sending up a cloud of dust for no apparent reason, then jerk back to speed and race on down the road. They were among the very first guests to arrive at the Agency.

When they returned to the car after the reception, Lois Palmer asked her brother why he was driving so fast, and all he could say was that the car just started speeding and he couldn't slow down. After Mother explained the foot pedal arrangement, the trip home was uneventful but slow.

All was peaceful as they drove back up to the Palmers' house in Fruitland, but only until they opened the door and found that Dad and Ace Palmer had enjoyed an evening of conversation but had not paid much attention to the two small boys.

Bill Palmer and I had also enjoyed the evening. We discovered a big basket of fresh eggs on the kitchen counter and proceeded with an engineering project of our own: stacking a few dishes on the counter, we added a large bread board and made a splendid slide. Bill then climbed up on a chair and rolled the eggs down the slide while I stood at the bottom and caught them as they came down. Well, most of them.

On the morning after this incident we accompanied the Palmer family to Sunday services at the Mormon church, and I was surprised to discover that the first hymn we sang was one of my favorites, as were many others in the hymn book, and I then found I was familiar with much of the ritual that followed.

19 Getting There Was Half the Fun

For a long time after Grandfather Holcomb and Aunt Clara came to Immanuel Mission their only transportation was by horsepower—riding on a horse or driving a wagon pulled by a team of horses. In fact, Grandfather never learned to drive anything but a team. During my early years I rode with either Grandfather or Dad in the old box wagon to many places within about a nine-mile radius of the Mission, usually on wood-gathering trips for the firewood that provided all our heating for so many years. However, I only drove the team on very rare occasions and then only for very short distances.

RUNAWAY WAGON

Years later, Grandfather started out one day to gather a load of wood, and I rode with him up front while my younger brother, Danny, sat in back, with his legs hanging off the back of the box. When we came to the pipe-iron gate to the fence, Grandfather handed me the reins, got out, opened the gate, and then, to my surprise, called to me, "Drive the wagon through." I cautiously drove through the gate and stopped and looked back as Grandfather closed the gate and started for the wagon.

Just then something suddenly spooked the horses, and they jumped and started running up the road. We pounded along, Dan hanging on for dear life while bouncing about a foot straight up with every jolt of the wagon.

Grandfather was running along behind the wagon, shouting at the top of his voice, "Pull them in! Pull them in!" But I couldn't stop them until they ran into a great thicket of greasewood and cactus. I eventually learned to handle a team quite well, but Dan would never again ride in any wagon I was driving.

MODEL T FORD

The car Dad and Mother brought back to the Mission in 1924 was a fine black new Model T Ford with side curtains and isinglass windows that snapped right on in case of a change in the weather (made of mica, small isinglass peepholes were inserted in oiled-canvas side curtains to save on the use of glass, and provided limited visibility). Of course they didn't provide much protection from wind or cold, and when winter came we had to bundle up in coats and blankets and placed hot bricks wrapped in paper under our feet.

Reservation travel: H. A. and Clara.

This was effective for perhaps an hour, and then on a long journey we were soon rolling along with only muffled conversation and covered up to our eyes with coats and blankets. When we ventured a few chattering words we blew out clouds of steam with every sentence.

THE LONG ROAD TO TOWN

Although the trip from Immanuel Mission to *tsé bit'a'í* ("rock with wings," or Shiprock) was little more than fifty miles, it was almost always an expedition, and during the early days the old original "road" to town usually made the round trip a two-day experience. It could sometimes take the best part of a week when rains flooded the arroyos or snow blocked the passes.

The first major obstacle was only a few miles east of Immanuel Mission, at *tsé tah,* "among the rocks," a well-named tangle of hills and rocks and sand on the track through the foothills of the Carrizo Mountains. Sandstorms often blew enormous loads of sand onto a Reservation road overnight and created great dunes that would literally stop an unsuspecting motorist in his tracks. When this happened it was time to climb out of the car and pull out the shovel, standard equipment on all trips, and start moving sand off the track. If this proved to be futile it was time to start looking for another way around the dune, and the trip became a little longer. On the return trip, a day or two later, the sand dune might have shifted to cover the new route.

Farther on, the road wound down a long, steep hill on a dug way just wide enough for one vehicle, then crossed a permanent sand dune area and a wide rocky wash before coming down to Teec Nos Pos Trading Post, about halfway to town. The temperamental Red Wash and always-muddy Blue Hill were still ahead.

Washes were tricky. Snowmelt and sudden rain could come down from the mountains in an awesome rush of water. I have seen a flood come down a dry wash with a crest of four feet of foaming, muddy water. Brush and dead trees would be carried along for miles. It was impossible to cross such a wash, and the procedure was to stop a safe distance back on the bank above the flood and just wait for the water to run off.

A delay like this would frustrate a white man, and he would fidget in the stationary car or impatiently walk up and down the bank. A Navajo man, however, would quietly find a place to sit and then just doze and "let his soul catch up."

Often a Navajo, a trader, or a missionary would discover a stranded pilgrim in the desert, hung up on a high center or mired in sand, and sometimes they would have to rescue an unwary motorist who had become tired of waiting and ventured into an arroyo running with a flood from a local thunderstorm. Even then there was usually nothing that could be done to save the car, and I have seen several unfortunate vehicles that had been covered by a flood and the next morning showed only a little windshield and perhaps a patch of roof above the sand in an arroyo channel.

EARLY NEW MEXICO ROADS

In 1929 there were only 281 miles of hard surface out of over 4,000 miles of roads in the entire state of New Mexico. The well-traveled road from Albuquerque to the capital city of Santa Fe featured "La Bajada," famous for its ascent from the valley of the Rio Grande up to the plateau of the Sangre de Cristo Mountains, and it was so very precipitous that the New Mexico Highway Department posted a sign: "This road is not fool proof but safe for a sane driver. Use low gear. Safe speed 10 mph." Even the storied U.S. Route 66 was not completely paved from Chicago to Los Angles until 1937, just before I left the Navajo Reservation.

In a very unflattering statement Dennis Riordan, an early superintendent of the Northern District, once described the Navajo Reservation as the "most worthless land that ever laid outdoors," and roads in the area at that time actually were not much more than a track across that desert that indicated where a previous driver of a wagon or occasional automobile had once gone that way.

In time, wind and erosion as well as infrequent traffic deepened these tracks and they became fairly well defined parallel sandy ruts with grass and bushes growing in the high space between the tracks. These "high centers" could tear off the bottom of a low-riding car and were navigational hazards for newer cars designed with the lower carriage for comfort on city streets. Most trucks and lighter cars with higher carriage, such the Model T and later Model A Fords, had enough clearance to negotiate these primitive routes. But not one road was hard-surfaced at that time, and only two roads even crossed our part of the Navajo Country.

One, Highway 666, ran from Gallup to Shiprock in New Mexico along the eastern edge of the Reservation, and the other road, now Navajo Highway 164, wound its way from Shiprock to Teec Nos Pos in Arizona, then on past Mexican Water and through Marsh Pass, Kayenta, and Tuba City, finally reaching what is now Highway 89 on the western edge of the Reservation at Cameron. Just before Sweetwater, a track turned off this main road and ran around the end of a mesa to Immanuel Mission, where all semblance of a road ended at our front gate.

Dad wrote of Reservation travel:

Every kind of car carried a shovel and water and most carried an extra gallon of gasoline and some carried oil. Marie sometimes drove while I pushed. When we could go no farther the only way out was to shovel away the loose surface sand before a new start could begin.

I want to say here that in all my driving on Reservation roads of that day, I never drove a car that could get through sand dunes like that Model T with the Ruxtel axle!

This unsolicited commercial could have substantially helped the Mission budget if only it had come to the attention of the Ford Motor Company.

Tire problems were also expected on any trip, and we seldom traveled to Shiprock without experiencing one or more flat tires. When this happened we would have to get out, jack up the car, remove the wheel, take off the tire, and remove the inner tube to locate the puncture. Next we cleaned the inner tube with an abrasive and applied a patch to the tube before it was stuffed back in the tire and bolted to the wheel. The tire was then laboriously pumped up by a hand pump before the jack could be removed and the engine started. Sometimes this required cranking by hand.

Eventually a more permanent patch became available, the Shaler 5 Minute Vulcanizer: "A match is all that is required." This was a kit that featured a G-shaped device, a patch, and combustible material in a small metal box that clamped over the puncture. When lighted it produced a flash of intense heat and with the pressure of the clamp, sealed the patch to the inner tube. There were round patches for punctures and oblong patches for cuts.

Popular in the 1920s, this process was not new, having been developed in the previous century by Charles Goodyear. It provided a longer-lasting repair than the adhesive patch but did not eliminate the lengthy process of getting the tire off the wheel and then back on the car.

The new Model T Ford. H. A., Marie, and Clara, 1924.

ADVENTURES IN A MODEL T FORD

Dad also wrote: "Both Clara and Florence learned to drive in this sandy country and later traveled some of the poorest roads in Arizona." He went on to report that Aunt Florence had turned the car over once—but quickly added: "It wasn't her fault." This was one of Dad's classic understatements, and a longer version of that incident appears in the Florence Barker journal: "Before Thanksgiving," she wrote, "I drove in to Farmington with Constellations [also known as Con], and three little girls who were to enter school."

The car gave her trouble immediately:

> Something went wrong with the auto and we had a terribly hard time making it up the hills. Then it ran out of water because a pipe leaked and the engine overheated and we had no power.
>
> The bolt that holds the steering wheel in place broke and several times the wheel came off while the auto was going up steep hills. It's a wonder we didn't have an accident. I had also broken my glasses the day before so it was a great strain to drive without them.
>
> When we finally arrived in Farmington I was dead tired and ached all over from nervous strain. I put the car in a garage and had it fixed while I did some shopping. Then I picked up the car and drove to Shiprock and the next day I started for the mission expecting to arrive in the afternoon after an easy trip.

However, this was not to be. "A few miles out of Shiprock the auto's gas control stuck," she wrote. "I stooped to loosen it but it was caught and when I straightened up again the car was going at a terrific speed off the road, hurtling into a canyon!" She continued:

A bridge crossed the canyon but I was headed into the canyon instead of over the bridge. I managed to turn the car, though I don't remember how.

The Lord's hand must have turned the wheel. The car was going at such a furious speed that when I turned the wheels, it flipped over. The auto stopped about four feet from the brink of the canyon. There was a loud snap as the wheels broke, but otherwise the car seemed to turn over quite easily.

A Navajo on horseback chanced by, and Aunt Florence sent a message to the BIA Agency at Shiprock asking for help. Superintendent Albert Kneale and the head of the Indian school came to the rescue and managed to get the car turned right side up, and they returned to Shiprock, where she had dinner with Superintendent Kneale and his wife, Etta.

Superintendent Kneale then contacted the garage but found there were no wheels available in Shiprock. He did locate some old wheels at the agency, and a mechanic worked until four in the afternoon to get the car repaired, and Aunt Florence finally set out again on the fifty-mile trip to Immanuel Mission.

I had hoped to have no more trouble with the auto, but every once in a while something would go wrong," she wrote. "The fan belt would not stay on and the engine overheated. Then the carburetor acted up and the car seemed to have no power. I would have never have made it except for my faithful Indian. He pushed the auto up many hills!

About eight miles from the Mission, Constellations suggested a shortcut, which proved to be a good trail for a pony but a very bad road for an automobile, and they were soon stuck again in sand. They worked for over two hours trying to get the car out of the sand and up a small hill, and finally unloaded everything and carried it up the hill, then got the auto up and reloaded, and Aunt Florence continued her story:

I had visions of getting to bed before long, for I was very tired. The nervous strain was awful, especially after the accident. I started the engine, pushed down … and it wouldn't budge! By that time it was midnight so I gave up and gave my Indian a sheepskin and he curled up on the ground while I rolled up in a blanket on the front seat.

On the road to Rock Point.

Aunt Florence couldn't sleep, and about four in the morning she crawled out of her blanket and made the long walk to the Mission in the dark, arriving just before dawn.

In the morning, Dad walked out to the car, carrying breakfast for Constellations, who hadn't eaten since the morning before, and finally got the car running again and drove back to Immanuel Mission. Aunt Florence concluded her story with:

> Later, when the Indian started home, I gave him a nice wool muffler and candy for his children and he was pleased. He still wonders whether I know how to drive a car or not, and I wonder too. I had wanted to travel alone, for the experience. I got experience all right—enough to last me a long time!

NEW MODEL A

We acquired a little four-door Model A Ford in the late 20s and marveled at the luxury of an enclosed space that protected the passengers from the elements, but I was particularly impressed by the little round thermometer mounted on the hood.

My brother, Danny, and I were also delighted with the horn's distinctive "ah-HOO-gah" that distinguished the Model A from all other cars of the time. Much to the distress of Mother and Aunt Clara, we entertained each other by blowing it constantly, until Dad finally warned us that we were running down the battery and pointed out that we didn't want to get stranded way out there at the Mission.

Unfortunately, the beautiful green finish soon had a white mark from a side window to the back of the car. A Navajo man had persuaded Dad one evening to take him over to *tó atin* mesa to get a horse that had strayed from his camp a few days before. I was allowed to accompany Dad, Yellowhair (the Navajo man who lived with us), and the other Navajo as we drove to the camp where his horse was being held. They decided to lead the animal back by automobile.

A long rope was tied to the horse, and the Navajo sat in the back seat with Yellowhair and held the rope as we led the horse back to Immanuel Mission at about the slowest speed the little Ford would go without stalling, but almost at a run for the poor Reservation pony. The Navajo was very grateful, but after he and his horse left we discovered the friction of the rope had rubbed the paint off to create a new design on our splendid new car. That mark remained on the little green car for the rest of its time at the Mission.

SPLENDID GIFT FROM LOS ANGELES

After thousands of miles of Reservation roads and a long, eventful trip to California that we were to make in 1929, the little Model A began to show signs of wear, and breakdowns and engine failures became more frequent, although Dad was an accomplished "shade tree mechanic" and could fix almost everything with the rudimentary tools and materials on hand. Still, in time major problems developed, and the repair bills at the garage in Farmington became more costly, and one day the garage owner called Dad's attention to the amount carried on our repair bill and remarked, "Your ship is getting pretty high on the reef!"

Our prayers began to mention the lack of funds to pay the Mission's outstanding bills, and then one day in the summer of 1935, we had a surprise when a well-dressed man driving a dusty but new Chevrolet arrived at Immanuel Mission as we were sitting down to dinner. We all went out to greet our visitor, and Dad recognized him as Mr. Buchanan of the Plymouth Brethren Assembly we had visited in Los Angeles in 1929.

After introductions and greetings, we invited Mr. Buchanan in to join us at dinner, but he turned and opened the door of the new car, drew out a sheaf of papers, and turned back to us, saying, "I will eat no bread nor drink water until I have delivered my message." He then gave a short prayer and handed Aunt Clara the papers and the keys to the new car.

Aunt Clara thanked Mr. Buchanan graciously, handed the keys to Dad, and we all went in to dinner. After a few days driving our new automobile, Clara dubbed our beautiful new vehicle *lapaiae* or "Brown"— probably for its light tan color and not in honor of our old antagonist, Brown Hat.

20 | Clemenceau Days

EPIDEMIC

In the mid-1920s a crippling epidemic had swept Arizona, and even though we lived in a remote mission on a reservation, I was somehow exposed to the disease. I came down with infantile paralysis, a viral infectious disease of the central nervous system now more commonly known as polio.

It was a day's journey each way to the nearest medical facility, and after a preliminary diagnosis it was pretty much up to Mother to see me through. The prevailing medical wisdom at the time was splinting and casting to immobilize the body. This led to the development of the iron lung, which gained wide attention when a number of patients were completely immobilized for years, but this procedure was not available to a small boy far away on the Navajo Reservation. Mother began a therapy that closely resembled the "Sister Kenny Method."

Sister Elizabeth Kenny was a nurse in Australia. Neither Catholic nor a nun, she got her title as a military rank given nurses in the Australian Medical Corps, and after World War I she was working as a traveling nurse in Queensland with aborigines, or bushmen, under primitive conditions not too unlike those on our own Navajo Reservation.

Like Mother, she had very little formal training in medicine and no medical assistance available, so she experimented with a procedure of massage that was aimed at keeping the muscles of the limbs mobile. She also frequently used hot-tub therapy for her small patients. As Sister Kenny described her therapy some years later: "I used what little I had, hot water, blankets, and prayers to a Healing God. I rubbed their little bodies and soothed their fears with the loving word of God."

Mother independently developed exactly the same therapy and clothed me in wool and massaged me for hours. I was too young to remember anything about that period at the Mission, but now I reflect on that lonesome young woman in her twenties, expecting her second child in a few months, while her first son was desperately ill with something that no one knew anything about. Like Sister Kenny, she, too, maintained a constant vigil of prayer, I know.

After a few months I had passed through the critical phase of my illness and had some use of my arms and legs, although I didn't resume walking for some time. Since Mother was also expecting their second child, after much prayerful

Alwin with new brother Danny, who arrived during the family's time at Oak Creek.

discussion, it was decided that Dad and Mother should move back to civilization for a short period of medical attention. Perhaps Dad could also earn some much-needed funds for the Mission.

Dad, Mother, and I left the Reservation in June of 1927 and moved back to Oak Creek in what Aunt Florence described as "a car falling apart." I only vaguely remember what was taking place but was happy to be on the ranch, where I enjoyed the attention and all the other benefits of being the only grandchild in the entire Girdner family. Then everything changed!

LITTLE NEWCOMER

All I remember of the event that changed my life forever is being taken up to the house on the hill and lifted up to see a red little newcomer in bed with Mother. I was not impressed by the squalling little fellow and wondering why he was getting so much attention from all the grownups standing around and excitedly commenting about Daniel E. Girdner, the wonderful new baby.

UVX

Soon after Danny arrived, Dad secured a reappointment to the Postal Service in Clemenceau, a new town off Oak Creek but not far from the ranch, and our new family moved into a little four-room frame "company house" near the post office in the back of the UVX Commissary.

The United Verde Extension Gold, Silver and Copper Mining Company, locally called the "UVX," had developed a mine from a deposit of ore discovered in 1914 in the Verde Valley just below Jerome. Copper ore from the 2.5-mile-long "Josephine Tunnel" at the 1,300-foot level of this new mine was hauled south by a standard-gauge trolley, to where it was smelted in a 480-foot stack smelter, then the tallest structure in Arizona and fifty feet higher than the rival Clarkdale stack. For forty years, smoking smelter stacks dominated the entire Verde Valley.

RAWHIDE JIMMY

James Stewart Douglas Jr., known as "Rawhide Jimmy" to distinguish him from other men named Douglas, was the founder of the UVX in the Verde Valley. He had been in France during World War I, as director of the warehouse division of the American Red Cross, and became a friend and admirer of Premier Georges Clemenceau of France, then a man in his seventies.

When Douglas returned to Arizona he named the little town that had grown up around his smelter "Clemenceau." I remember a bust of the ferocious little Frenchman that stood on a pedestal in the lobby of the Bank of Clemenceau, which was also controlled by Douglas, and Clemenceau's picture appeared on all the checks. Clemenceau was pleased with the honor and gave a valuable vase to the little copper town with a name no one could pronounce.

An episode I would rather forget occurred one evening when I went with Mother and Uncle Lee Holcomb to pick Dad up at the post office at the rear of the UVX commissary. As we were leaving the post office we walked past a number of open barrels of dry foods in the grocery section when I spotted a barrel of dried dates—my favorite fruit.

I insisted I wanted some of the delicious fruit, but Mother was equally insistent that I wouldn't like them. I kept protesting until finally Mother selected one date and handed it to me. I gulped it down and was even more convinced it was just what I wanted, so Dad bought a small sack of them and handed it to me.

We went on to Uncle Lee's car, parked out on Darling Street, and as soon as I was seated in the back seat I pulled open my sack of hard-earned goodies and popped a couple of dried dates in my mouth. They were dry but not sweet, just very salty with a strong, strange flavor, and I realized that, as usual, Mother knew best—they were not dates but dried shrimp. Uncle Lee was the only one who would eat them.

Periodically during our time in Clemenceau, we drove up the precipitous road to the copper town of Jerome. It was then a thriving mining town of 15,000 residents, and the third-largest "city" in Arizona, built on the edge of the largest copper mine in the world. Pat Savage described it elegantly in "Jerome, Ghost City in the Sky":

Skyscrapers? Ha! Unpainted, one and two story wooden shacks on two-by-four stilts as bare as a stripper's torso at the conclusion of her act, with skirting of old boards and rusty tin resembling a tipsy charwoman's garb, clung by toehold and scratch of fingernail to the almost unscaleable cliffs.

I was treated in this strange, fascinating city at the new United Verde hospital, which had just been completed that year and was described by the local press as "the most modern and well equipped hospital in Arizona, possibly in the Western States."

I remember very little of either the doctors or the hospital other than one session when a particularly vile liquid medicine was prescribed for me, but I detested the stuff. The doctor and Dad tried to stir my interest in the nasty black liquid by telling me it contained iron, but with little success. If that was iron, it must be badly rusted—and I still didn't like it. I was never convinced it could possibly help me, and even if it did help, I still detested the stuff.

A more agreeable trip up the hill was the time our proud parents arranged to take their two young sons to a photographer's studio. In a formal portrait for posterity, I was posed leaning on a table with baby Danny lying beside me. This was a necessary arrangement as I had not yet regained enough strength to stand alone without some support.

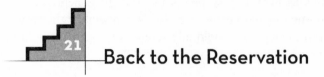

Back to the Reservation

I n April of 1928 we returned to Immanuel Mission, and I gradually regained the use of my legs and was soon able to engage in an active outdoor life. During all this period in my life everyone in the family treated me as a normal boy. No one ever said or did anything that might suggest that I could not move like a normal boy, and I was not given special privileges because of my handicap.

Many changes had taken place during the ten months we had been away from Immanuel Mission. Yellowhair, a middle-aged Navajo man at that time, had come to the Mission soon after the Girdner family left for Oak Creek, and Florence Barker had left in August for a three-month vacation in California. She then decided to accept an appointment to work as a field nurse with the Supai Tribe, who lived at the bottom of the Grand Canyon.

I do not remember much of Aunt Florence, as she left Immanuel Mission before my fifth birthday. Evidently we had a good relationship. Many years later I found references in her journal to her experiences with the Girdner family, and in one she mentioned a trip Mother and I had taken: "Marie and Alwin returned from Albuquerque. I missed the little fellow very much. He and I are great pals." In his manuscript Dad notes Aunt Florence's departure with this tribute: "After five years at the mission, as long as she lived, she gave out the Gospel Message."

Aunt Florence was to work with Indians for the rest of her life, first with the Supai in the Grand Canyon area, and then later for many years with the Acoma in New Mexico. When she retired, she took a cottage on the Southwest Missionary Conference grounds in Flagstaff, and I last saw her in 1963.

Alwin posing by the gasoline pump for irrigating.

22 Yellowhair

itsii' łitso, a Navajo man of about fifty, was living at Immanuel Mission when we returned from our great adventures in Clemenceau. Little did we know then that he would remain at the Mission years after every one of the Girdner family had long departed the Navajo Reservation. Dad wrote about Yellowhair's arrival, and I will let him tell the story of this gentle Navajo man.

A PORTRAIT OF YELLOWHAIR FROM GLEN C. GIRDNER'S MANUSCRIPT
Now let me tell you about this man known as Yellowhair. He was not a chief, nor a medicine man, or head man, or a great warrior, so his name will have to stand alone with none of these distinguishing titles. It was the year our Danny was born that this remarkable oldish man first visited us. We had finished the first two buildings of the Mission at *dak osh tah,* where stood the ghost of Martin's Trading Post. This was in 1927.

However, his tall erect bearing, his large frame with no fat on it, his wrinkled face, and one ear split so badly that he could never wear turquoise ear stones; all made me remember him after that first time. He was a *bit ah ni,* there may be a legend about this old clan but I have never heard it.

On the day he came to the Mission he stopped and waited outside the gate before he came in. The well-mannered Navajo visitor always gave his hosts a little time to tidy up a bit before he entered. Perfect Navajo manners!

After some scattered comments he warmed into conversation and at long last Yellowhair came out with the thing that was worrying him. I'll try to quote him in English as nearly as I can [as Yellowhair spoke only in Navajo]:

> I've come from *teec nos pos,* from the missionary's house. As you know I have been living there with the missionary and his wife and in time I began to understand the missionary's teaching and I think it is good teaching. I believe as he does. I am as he is. I believe it is true that all this *keyah* (country) was made by some Great One as they believe. I am as they are.

He held both hands out in front, palms down and near together and closing all fingers except the two forefingers, which he moved close together, side by side. "Just alike." (Sign language.) Yellowhair went on:

These Sunday people (missionaries) are old now. They will have to go back to live among their own white people. This is good. It is right that they should spend their old age among their own. But I will be alone, no place to live, even here in the land where I was born and among my own race.

I am not welcome to live with my very own *bit ah ni.* The mother of my children has been dead for a long time. My children have their own families now, and I don't know where they are: probably among the white people I don't know. This makes me feel bad and bothers me so. I am alone. It is not good for a man to live alone. One would suppose I would be welcome to live as a part of some family, or some relative's home, but I am not welcome. I could be a help to them. I'm not lazy. I can work. But no one wants me. I am alone and have nothing. Even right here among my very own clan brothers and sisters I'm an outcast; all alone in this great country. I think the same things over and over.

It is useless to think about it this way. Yes, it is really utter vanity to think this way. I am just trying in vain to think sensibly about it. Yet I have not given up hope. I think, just maybe, you folks can help me. I can do many of the tasks you are doing every day. I don't ask for money for my work. Maybe in turn you would give me a home and these clothes will wear out some day. I will go now. Think about it my brothers, my sisters.

And he was gone.

Well, the missionaries did think about it. His talk about being alone was understood. Other Navajos told us about Yellowhair's younger life and said he had been rejected by the Navajos. The traditional taboo of marriage of two of the same clan was strong. Navajos just don't do that. In-breeding, as livestock [breeders] call it, is rare.

Yellowhair had married a girl of his own clan (perhaps a rather close relative) and Navajos believe that a violation of that taboo will cause a twisted mind, even insanity. We, at the Mission, had heard before that Yellowhair had suffered a severe fever at one time and was left with a lowered mentality.

Personally, I could not feel that his thinking was too badly damaged. Some, yes, but that misfortune gave the Navajos who had known him before a chance to say *joakon* ("There now: See.").

Yellowhair.

It was true that the missionaries were wasting time on many chores and their work was plainly hampered. They decided to try out his idea. The plan worked out very well, all were happy, and Yellowhair spent the rest of his life at the Mission … over thirty years.

Yellowhair soon learned to bake delicious homestyle bread and even won a first prize at the Indian Fair at Shiprock, New Mexico, and from him we learned to speak a little better Navajo as we could talk to him in Navajo only. He became quite fond of our four children. Helen and Ronald were born into the family during those years.

When Alwin and "Danny" were about nine and six, we decided to let each have a "project" and they were both all for it. At Farmington, New Mexico, we bought for one boy a baby pig, and for the other boy, baby turkeys. They were to care for their "babies" and receive the profits when the parents sold them in the fall of the year.

There were troubles, however. The pig escaped one night and was gone. Well, I was confident we could track it and find it, provided a coyote had not already found it. I had done a little tracking before of strayed milk cows and strayed horses. I had tracked Mission saddle horses several miles and found where someone had "borrowed" them, and I thought that in an hour I would have the pig again. I was wrong. When the trail reached hard and rocky ground I gave up completely.

Back at the Mission, Yellowhair told me that he had walked in another direction to Hosteen Black Goat's camp and they told him some bad news. It seems that in the early morning their dogs had seen a strange animal and had mangled it badly before Hosteen Black Goat could stop them. While he was tying up the dogs, the *bisoodi yazhi* (little pig) had run back among the rocks and escaped.

After the midday meal Yellowhair and I set out for the rocks to try to pick up the trail if possible. Maybe the piggy was still alive. We both walked back and forth in the sandy flat to the north and west of the rocks thinking the pig might have left for easier going in the sandy flat. It would have been a waste of time to wander around among the ledges and rocks as high as our heads, and besides, solid sandstone could show no tracks.

Well, we separated and each looked for tracks and didn't find any. Yellowhair came over to me and suggested we look together over some of the area I had covered. I thought, "Oh sure," (but I didn't say it) "you'll pick up the trail and see my tracks crossing it, where I couldn't even see it, and the big laugh will be on me."

Sure enough, that is just what he did. He didn't laugh at me—just started out in a long swinging gait up the slope toward Sweetwater Trading Post, four or five miles away. "There—see? There go the tracks," he would say, pointing his bony finger at something at his side, swinging it back and forth as he walked briskly along. All I could say was, "Yeah."

I didn't see any tracks, nor could I see that the ground had been touched by anything heavier than the wind, and nobody knows how many moons it was since any rain. Once or twice I did see a few consecutive tracks in a stretch of soft sand.

Well, to see his tracks, I watched intently for some moved pebbles or some slight impression on the ground and growled silently that he was walking by faith and not by sight. Maybe he could smell a slight pig smell in the air but it certainly wasn't by sight! … But he was!

When we reached the road leading from the Mission to Sweetwater Trading Post, I began to see a few tracks. No blood showed. Suddenly Yellowhair stood still, listened and said in almost a whisper, "There." A few steps from the road between two clumps of *tlo aziihi* (Mormon tea), lay the pig, still and completely relaxed. Maybe asleep. He was asleep.

Fortunately no coyote had found him. One ham was pretty badly torn. We gently carried him home in a gunny sack and he was soon O.K. He never tried to run away again.

I never bragged about my tracking abilities again. I do brag about Yellowhair's. I couldn't BELIEVE it. If he had been a white man I might have slapped him on the back and roared, "Good work, ol' boy!" but such complete lack of dignity would never do.

That evening, however, at supper I did break down and say to the family something like this, *"doo la oo hosteen hoii yaa da"* where he could hear me. "He sure is a smart man." I just had to say something. And so ends one of the true stories of Yellowhair of the *bit ah ni.*

YELLOWHAIR AT THE MISSION

Dad mentions Yellowhair's clan but only as an "old clan that probably had a legend." The *bit ah ni,* "Folded Arms Clan," listed indeed was an old clan, and later Yellowhair told us a little about the origin of the name, explaining that the word for "wing" was *at'a* and that in the early days his clan during cold weather would go about with their arms folded beneath their blankets, thus giving them the appearance of a bird with wings. I am not sure of his father's clan but remember it as *tábąąha',* the "Water's Edge Clan," and I know his family originally lived in the San Juan River region.

Yellowhair soon became "family" and Mother always addressed him as *shináàhai* or "older brother," but usually we referred to him as "Uncle," as among the Navajo the mother's uncle was the most important man in the Navajo family.

Yellowhair relieved Dad and Grandfather at the woodpile and chopped wood almost every day, especially during cold weather. He discouraged any attempts to intrude on his domain, although he didn't object when I was assigned the chore of carrying armloads of chopped wood into the large wood boxes in the

Tsé sa' an (Sitting Rock) and *tse ghize* mesas, just south of the Mission.

houses, as that took no skill. Filling the wood box was one task I never learned to appreciate but, as Danny grew older, he provided considerable assistance and we eventually acquired a little red wagon that greatly expedited our fueling efforts.

THE GOOD SHEPHERD

Yellowhair's favorite chore was tending our cows, and he soon took complete charge of that activity. We had at the Mission a fine pair of old German field glasses that dated back to World War I, and Dad would occasionally let me use them. Yellowhair soon had custody of the field glasses, and he watched every movement of his herd during the day. He was very reluctant to let me use them just to stand carelessly on the front deck and look around.

However, I sometimes got to use them, and I particularly remember one late afternoon when I stood on the porch watching for Dad, who had walked out beyond the prominent butte called *tsé sa'an* (Sitting Rock) to help bury a young woman who had died the night before in one of the camps in the *tsegi*. Finally, just before sunset, I saw a flash between the rocks and by watching carefully saw it was the last rays of sunshine reflecting off the shovel Dad was carrying over his shoulder.

When talking with me, Yellowhair often launched into the Navajo tales of Changing Woman and First Man and went into graphic detail with his accounts of the misadventures of White Shell and the bloody deeds of the Warrior Twins.

To me his low, monotonous tales in Navajo were hard to follow as he recounted all the interminable details. It all seemed obscure and hard to believe, and I was generally uninterested in his stories. He probably considered my lack of interest to be impolite, as he listened to our lengthy discussions of Bible stories and faithfully followed the precepts of our Christian faith as he understood them.

COFFEE-COLORED SHIRT TALE

The summer before we left the Reservation we were back from school in Farmington, and I had a faded khaki shirt from my scout uniform that needed dyeing. So one day when all the adults were behind the closed door of the daily business and prayer session, Danny helped me snatch the large pot of hot coffee that usually sat on the back of the kitchen stove. We rushed with it downstairs to our room, where I had the shirt ready in a big washbasin.

Yellowhair was busy washing the dinner dishes but noted our hasty departure, and just as I was pouring the steaming brew over my shirt a curious Yellowhair appeared at the open door, with wet hands and still carrying his dishcloth, to see what the boys were up to this time.

I tried to explain in Navajo what we were trying to do and, for that matter, why I needed to have a khaki shirt, but I did not convince him it was a good idea to waste good coffee on an old shirt. He never revealed our strange behavior to anyone, but I did have a little trouble explaining the irregular brown stains on my shirt to Mother.

BLACK BEAR ON THE MOUNTAIN

Yellowhair never joked or laughed much, but he had the keen sense of humor of most Navajos. This usually took the form of unexpected behavior.

One day the entire family—Dad, Mother, Aunt Clara, Yellowhair, Dan, Helen, and I—took a rare picnic and drove up a new road being built up in the Carrizo Mountains. After we finished our picnic lunch Dad suggested we should drive farther on the new road, which was under construction by the Navajo CCC, the tribal version of the Civilian Conservation Corps and one of many federal programs Franklin D. Roosevelt promoted to provide work during the Great Depression.

It was a wonderful road, by Reservation standards. Great walls of the cliff had been blasted down, rock and dirt shoveled, and trees felled, but we couldn't imagine where it led, so Dad said, "Let's explore a little and find out where it goes."

We all piled into the car, everyone except practical Yellowhair, who chose to stay and gather and cut wood while we were taking a joy ride up the mountain. And after about a mile the road just ended in a huge pile of rocks! The people from *waashindoon* (Washington) had built a splendid highway to nowhere. (The twenty-five Navajo CCC camps were successful, however, in many other projects on the Reservation and built hundreds of small dams to control the rampant erosion, erected windmills, and constructed dozens of storage tanks to provide water for the flocks of sheep.)

Disappointed, we turned the car around and started back down the mountain. Then, as we approached our picnic site, Mother suddenly yelled, "Glen, there's a bear!" All the kids sat up and peered out excitedly and sure enough, a big, black four-legged creature had lumbered out of the trees and was staggering across the road right in front of the car.

The kids started clamoring for us to stop, but Mother kept repeating, "No, Glen, no, keep going—keep going!" Aunt Clara was too stunned to say anything as the bear suddenly stood up on its hind legs and turned toward us: Yellowhair with his big black coat pulled up over his head.

Without a word Yellowhair proceeded to load into our already crowded car a small pile of wood he had cut and stacked along the road. He climbed in with the rest of us, and we rode home in silence. Yellowhair had spent a very satisfying day in his beloved mountains.

Years later I was driving back alone toward Teec Nos Pos after a short visit to the Four Corners monument and spotted a young Navajo walking along the road. He was ignoring the *bilagáana* tourist coming up behind him when, to his surprise, I stopped and offered him a ride as far as the trading post. He got in, and in the small talk of strangers casually meeting, we discussed small dams, erecting windmills, and providing water storage tanks to save the water that resulted, when I mentioned Yellowhair, and to my surprise he remarked, "He was my father."

At his age, he might have been a grandson, or he might have been referring to another man of the same name, or perhaps, in the Navajo way of speaking, he was referring to a clan relationship.

23   Life in the New Rock House

ad's first project after we returned from Clemenceau was to create more living space for his expanded family, and in his manuscript he wrote: "With the earnings from the work done during our absence from the Mission we built the east addition to the stone house and bought some furniture."

This was his modest description of a rather substantial building program that added some 24 x 13 feet, including two bedrooms and a walk-in closet that nearly doubled our living space in that little house.

CHICKEN DINNER

One day soon after we returned, my parents became unreasonable during the noon meal—we always referred to it as dinner—and kept insisting I would have to modify my behavior or be banished. The situation deteriorated, and finally Mother ordered me to leave the table. I objected that I had to have food and she told me to take it outside. I took my plate, stormed out the back door, and seated myself on a low retaining wall Dad had built around my sandbox.

A flock of chickens was working the area and soon came over to investigate the small boy eating his dinner outdoors. I tried to shoo them off, but the big red rooster kept coming back, and when I put down my plate to reach for a stone to discourage him, he saw his opportunity, charged in, snatched a portion of my biscuit, and ran off with it in his beak.

I ran back into the house shouting, "A chicken stole my biscuit!"—only to hear roars of laughter from both my unfeeling parents. They refused to take the situation seriously and told me to go finish my dinner. Feeling much abused, I slowly walked back outside just in time to see the whole flock finishing off my cookie.

WATCH YOUR STEP

One morning, just before noon, Mother was preparing dinner in the rock house, and Dad and I were down by the garage, involved in a particularly intricate job of repairing the engine of the car, when we heard her calling, "Glen," "Glen," "Glen?" Dad, both hands engaged trying to reinstall a connection in the engine, nodded to me and said, "See what your mother wants." I went to look but couldn't see anyone in the yard and returned and reported there wasn't anyone

Glen's finishing touches on the new Rock House.

out there, so he continued juggling the obstinate part until Mother shouted again in an almost panicked voice, "GLEN!"

Dad dropped his wrench, grabbed a rag, and, wiping the grease off his hands as he ran, left the garage with me pounding along right on his heels. I could see the kitchen door was open, but no one was in sight as we raced across the empty yard with Dad shouting, "Marie, what's wrong? … Where are you?" Suddenly, just as he reached the cellar steps, he glanced down, then called back to me: "Stop! Stop right there."

I stopped in my tracks but could see Mother below us on the bottom step with a pan of milk in her hand, warning us, "Don't come down, stay where you are!" Without looking back, Dad commanded, "Get the shovel, quick!" I turned and scampered back to the garage and returned to see both my parents just as they were, but on the second step below Dad I now saw a huge, coiled rattlesnake, buzzing and weaving its head back and forth—in search of something to strike.

Dad took the shovel from my hand, pushed me back with the other hand and then poked the shovel at the snake—who struck it like a flash. Dad jerked the shovel back, then forward in time to cut the reptile's head off before it could recoil. The invader was immediately removed from the scene and interred, but Mother took a little encouraging before she would climb down those cellar steps again, and, as long as we lived at Immanuel Mission, she was uneasy every time I ventured down into that cellar.

Mission solitude. Alwin with Mission in background.

RABBITS, RABBITS EVERYWHERE

For a while, one small room of the old trading post was used as a pen, populated by two white female rabbits and one Belgian hare I had named Frank Buck after the popular explorer of that time. The bunnies were Danny's and the hare was mine, and we took turns with the chores of keeping them.

One morning I came into the room and caught Danny trying to beat Frank with a stick. Frank had not behaved properly with Nibbles, one of his girl rabbits! However, nature took its course, and we soon had enough rabbits to fill a large outdoor pen, where they lived in deep burrows and became a major food source at the Mission for years.

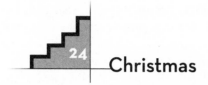

24 Christmas

Our Christmas presents always showed our parents' thoughtfulness about a child's needs. Most of the presents I received were not commercially manufactured, but practical articles of clothing, often handmade, or something that was not costly but had been lovingly crafted with considerable skill and much time by my family. One such item was a beautiful wooden sled that Dad built in the workshop one year. He wouldn't give me a clue about what his strange project was and was curiously unwilling to work on it when I was in the shop.

Mother also kept his secret but tried to get me interested in the cold weather sport by assigning me an essay on "My Sled." I strenuously objected on the reasonable grounds that I didn't have a sled and really didn't know anything about them, but the old adage "Ma's right even when she ain't right" still held, and I produced a very poor paper that proved my point.

On Christmas Eve I was amazed to see a beautiful sled with a big red bow under the tree—and even more impressed when, first thing on Christmas morning, Mother, who had been raised in the snows of cold Minnesota, immediately had me put on cap and mittens and took me out to the hill above the garden.

She showed me how to correctly hold the sled, then startled me by suddenly running to the edge of the hill, launching herself off the steep slope, and careening all the way down. I had never seen her participate in any outdoor sport before, and when she dragged the sled back up the hill I hesitantly took the snowy sled and, as an obedient son, threw myself over the hill and slid to the bottom, but with only indifferent success.

Years later, my wife, Marjorie, wrote two short stories based on a couple of the Christmas tales I told our children about my youthful misadventures at Immanuel Mission, which I will give in her words.

"CHRISTMAS AT IMMANUEL MISSION, 1929"
by Marjorie J. Girdner

Two men chopped and sawed dead cedars and piled them on the wagon. Alwin helped some but mostly played around the rocky hills chasing ground squirrels and looking for pretty rocks and potsherds. He made a game out of seeing how far he could go without stepping into the patches of snow. Glen called to him, "Alwin, it's time to find our Christmas tree."

Alwin hurried to his father. This was the first year he had been able to help get the tree because last year he couldn't walk after having polio. That made this year very special and a trip to the mountain a real treat. "I saw one over there that looks just the right size. Come see." He scurried over the little hill with his father and grandfather not far behind. "See, isn't that just what we want?"

Glen caught up with his son and wished the boy had picked out just a little smaller tree. He didn't want to disappoint Alwin on his first outing, so he figured he could make the tree fit into the small living room of the little stone house by sawing off the base to make it shorter. "That will be just fine," he told his son, who was grinning ear to ear because of his accomplishment.

His dad and grandfather soon had the tree down, and with some difficulty, loaded it on top of the wood in the wagon. The trip back was exciting, with Alwin anticipating putting up the tree and hanging the strings of popcorn that he had made himself. He wasn't sure what other ornaments his mother had stored away, but he knew it would be a beautiful Christmas tree.

"THE DAY AFTER CHRISTMAS, 1932"
by Marjorie J. Girdner

It was the day after Christmas. The celebration was over, his mother was next door, his brother busy, and he wanted to be busy too. "I'll take down the tree and surprise everyone," he said, mostly to himself because his brother Danny didn't care what Alwin was going to do, as long as he left Danny alone.

He carefully took off the strings of popcorn. "Where are the boxes Mother used? They must be hidden away, so I'll just hang them over the back of the chair." The glass balls presented a bigger problem.

Every place he put them, they rolled away. He finally put them in the soft easy chair and they nestled there like eggs in a nest.

The tiny clips which held the small candles he lined up on the table. The shiny garland coiled well on the floor. It was done. Now he had to drag it out to the woodpile.

He wished he had chosen a little smaller tree. He wasn't very strong after his illness and he wasn't a very big boy anyway. He almost knocked some dishes off a shelf. "I'll be in trouble if I break Mom's dishes," he thought. He tugged and pulled until he finally got the thing through the door. The wind was really strong and almost knocked him down as he struggled toward the woodpile.

Just then his mother came out of the big adobe house. "Alwin, what are you doing?" she said. "Why are you taking the Christmas tree to the woodpile? What did you do with the ornaments?" Alwin thought he had been very proficient and proudly announced, "Christmas is over so I took down the tree for you. I couldn't get all the icicles off but everything else is in the living room. I was careful with them and didn't break any of the glass balls."

Snow in the canyons.

Marie's anger showed in her face. "What do you mean, Christmas is over? The season lasts all through this week." Alwin hadn't seen his mother angry many times but knew she was mad now. He answered his irate mother: "Yesterday was Christmas when we got all our presents. There won't be any more presents under the tree so I thought I would help you by taking the tree down. I didn't have anything else to do and Danny was playing with his new puzzle." Tears welled up in his gray-blue eyes.

"You are right, there won't be any more presents under the tree, but we celebrate the season for more than one day. You had no right to take down the tree, especially without asking me. Go get the tree from the woodpile. We'll see what we can do."

Marie stormed into the house. There scattered on the floor, draped over chairs, and in the easy chair were the ornaments which she had so carefully put on the beautiful Christmas tree. There was no way she could recreate the lovely tree, and there wasn't really any reason to do so now that it was down. At least it was down and now she just had to put it all away.

As she stood there her anger subsided. "Alwin was only trying to be helpful. I guess I never explained to him about the Christmas tree as a symbol of the love we share at Christmas, not just a place where gifts were laid. He's a good boy and my temper gets hot too quickly."

She opened the door and could see the frail young boy making a valiant attempt to pull the tree back to the house against the strong wind. "It's all right, Alwin, we can't redecorate the tree. Take it back to the woodpile where your Dad can cut it up to use in the stove. When you come in we'll talk a little more about Christmas. I know you tried to help me."

When Glen came in for supper Marie couldn't help saying, "You'll never guess what your son did today." When he had done something good, Alwin was always "our" son, but when it was bad, he was "your" son.

Her anger was gone, but she thought Glen should know so he could do a little more explaining about Christmas and the season around it to both boys.

Alwin was sorry he had made his mother so angry. At least her anger wasn't because he had done something to Danny like it usually was. She did understand he was trying to be a helper, and now he understood more about Christmas. Next year he would enjoy the tree much more—and for a longer time.

25 Etta's Wedding

Etta lived near us for some time when I was quite young. A pretty girl, bright and cheerful, she had spent a few years away in school but was happy to be back to camp life, with just an occasional few days of living with the white people at the Mission. Etta was exceptionally good with me, teaching me Navajo words and carefully explaining Navajo customs to a small boy struggling with two cultures.

Several years after Etta's family moved away from our area, when I was about seven years old, she invited us to come up to their summer camp on the mountain and attend her wedding. The Navajo wedding ceremony was about the only Diné ceremony that the missionaries accepted, and I was delighted when Mother, Aunt Clara, and Beulah not only accepted the invitation but also decided I could accompany them, even though my bedtime was strictly nine o'clock in the summer and we knew the trip would take much of the night.

On the appointed evening, we started for the camp in the Model A and drove for several miles before we started up into the foothills of the Carrizo Mountain. The road soon became a rocky track winding through sandy arroyos and up and over hills until it ended abruptly on the bank of a deep arroyo lined with cedar.

The light had faded and there was a chill to the clear mountain air when we climbed out of the Model A, and we immediately caught the pungent smell of cedar smoke and knew the camp was not far off. We pulled on our jackets and started looking for a trail, but before we had walked more than a few paces away from the car a Navajo man came up out of the wash below with a flashlight. They had heard the sound of the car in the camp long before we arrived and sent a relative down to guide us across the sandy arroyo and up a steep wooded hill.

It was completely dark, but we heard barking long before we came up out of the arroyo, and then we heard voices and we saw the bright glow of a campfire. Our guide quietly ushered us past a large group of Navajos standing around an outside bonfire, to the doorway of one of several permanent hogans in the shadows just beyond the light of the big fire.

We did not knock, but someone silently lifted the blanket and drew us into the hogan. My first impressions were of the warm fire in the center of the lodge, the only light in the room, and the crowd of family and clan members sitting quietly on sheepskins around the brightly burning fire.

Etta was sitting on the far side of the fire in the back, facing east, and her father and the groom were beside her at the center of the crowded hogan. We turned right to the women's side to find a place to sit, and, as a small boy I expected to stay with Aunt Clara and Beulah on the woman's side of the hogan, and some Navajo ladies made room for us, but just as we were sitting down Etta beckoned. I was pushed along, a few old ladies made room for me to sit on a sheepskin just beside Etta, and she quietly greeted me in English.

The father opened the ceremony by pouring warm water from a can and washed the hands of the bride, then the groom, and finally himself. A lengthy talk followed before he drew out a basket of cooked cornmeal mush and placed it before the bride and the groom, and each then took a dip. After further ceremony the basket was passed around the circle and each guest took a small portion.

A messenger was then sent to Etta's mother, who was in a nearby hogan, to inform her of the completion of the wedding and that she now had a new son-in-law. Navajo custom is that a mother-in-law and her son-in-law must never see each other, as that could cause blindness.

A series of long speeches followed as the elders present took turns admonishing the young couple on how to live with each other in harmony and on the duties of each partner in a marriage. When we emerged into the cold clear night it was after midnight, and I only remember stumbling along behind our guide down a steep embankment into the wash and up a hill to the car, and then a long, sleepy journey home.

26 Kitchen Stories

The kitchen was the center of much of our life at Immanuel Mission, and many strange and unusual events took place in that room. Although our kitchen was not generally open to visiting Navajos, there were many occasions when they came in for various reasons. They were always given space to boil their pots of coffee on the busy big wood range.

One young woman of the Stronghorse outfit never failed to irritate Mother. When they were camped at the Mission, she would bring in her big pot just before our breakfast and set it on the stove in the middle of all the other pots and pans holding our meal, and then she would walk away and let it heat up and boil over, making a general mess of our breakfast.

BLESSED EVENT

Another young woman in an advanced state of pregnancy camped with her extended family for several days at the Mission and came in every morning to fill a pail of water from the bucket by the kitchen.

I was busy outside when a great commotion drew my attention to the kitchen and I rushed to see what was happening but was stopped and turned away at the screen door by a very agitated Mother. I managed, however, one glance back as I was banished but could only see a number of people milling around someone on the floor. All remained a mystery until years later when the facts of life were finally explained to me.

MISSING WATER JUG

Another experience involving the big kitchen range that dominated the kitchen occurred several years later. Mother packed a big picnic lunch and rounded up Danny, Helen, and me for a trip to *béésh 'ii' àhí,* as we then referred to Rock Point. We all got in the car and, when Aunt Clara joined us, we were ready to go … everyone except Dad, who was nowhere to be seen.

Finally, Dad rushed out of the house, jumped in the car, and was backing out when Mother cried, "Glen, stop! I forgot to put in our drinking water." Dad replied, "Marie, we have a canteen and won't need any more," and drove on toward the gate, even though Mother and Aunt Clara kept insisting we couldn't possibly have a picnic without our drinking water.

Outnumbered, as usual, Dad stopped, backed up, climbed out of the car, and sprinted back to the house with Mother calling after him, "The thermos jug is by the sink." At that time we were still carrying water from the well, and after Dad found the jug he discovered the pail was empty. He turned and spotted the large reservoir on the side of the stove and hurriedly dipped out a gallon of warm water, poured it into the jug, hurried back to the car, and we finally got under way.

Several hours later we stopped for lunch under a cedar tree and opened our lunch. The main course included boiled eggs, and Aunt Clara got thirsty and poured a large cup of water, took one sip, and shouted, "This is warm water!" Mother exclaimed in an exasperated voice, "Glen, why would you do such a thing?" and Dad sheepishly had to answer, "I just didn't think anyone would ever ask for water."

CALLIE

From time to time Mother would employ a Navajo girl from a nearby camp to help with the housework. I remember Callie being with us for some time just before Dan was born. She was slow to learn about how a house was maintained, which wasn't surprising for a girl who lived in a hogan, but she was very industrious.

The first day she arrived at the stone house, Mother took her on a tour of the place and explained in very basic English and some Navajo what she was expected to do. Callie didn't utter a word as she worked—until late afternoon when she was leaving. Then she turned and asked, "Miz Girdner, you want me come back tomorrow?" Apparently she had attended boarding school in Shiprock before returning to camp life and understood but seldom spoke a little English.

Mother often had Callie come back when she was overwhelmed with her multiple duties at the Mission during those early years, but they continued to have language difficulties. One afternoon she called to Mother from the kitchen, "Miz Girdner, I want to die." Mother answered, "I want to live!" and Callie called back "Oh Miz Girdner, I want to die in a wash pan," and Mother went along with the exchange and answered, "Well, Callie, I want to just die in bed." Callie then came into the room carrying a faded skirt and said, "Miz Girdner, I want to dye this red."

During the next winter, a baby sister was born in Callie's camp but soon developed serious stomach problems. The family brought the sick infant to the Mission and asked Callie to do something. Callie, still a teenager, had no idea what to do, so Mother took charge and bathed and tried to feed the tiny baby but she wouldn't eat and only screamed in a weak little voice. Mother worked with

Two young Navajo women visiting the Mission dressed
in their best clothes and all their jewelry.

her until late that night trying several kinds of medication and enemas to reduce her swollen little belly but with little success.

By morning the tiny patient had not improved, and Dad took her to the trading post at Sweetwater and arranged for the trader to take her to the Shiprock Agency Hospital on his regular run for supplies at the Progressive Mercantile in Fruitland. In a few days the infant was returned to the Mission with the diagnosis that the doctors said there was nothing more they could do for her. We immediately set out through the snow in the little Model A Ford.

About half a mile from the camp we ran out of track at the edge of a wash and had to go on by foot. Dad built a small campfire under the trees and, with Aunt Clara, hiked up the arroyo to inform Callie's people, leaving me to watch the now silent little girl wrapped in a blanket.

In a few minutes Callie's mother came running down the wash and not even looking at me, snatched up her baby and ran back up over the hill and Dad and Aunt Clara soon came silently down and we turned the car around and churned our way home through the slush and mud. There is no happy ending to this story as the baby died the next day.

27 | The Passing of Mary Holcomb

Grandmother Holcomb, whose dementia had worsened over the years, was finally confined to her room in the old rock house, as she tended to wander off when left alone. Her years of running a large family had made her assume responsibility, and Aunt Florence complained that she always wanted to direct everything.

Then Grandmother died in 1928, and Dad constructed a plain wooden coffin. A simple service was attended by the family and several friends, including Reverend Charles L. Campbell from the Presbyterian Mission in Shiprock, and C. C. Brooks, superintendent of the Methodist Episcopal Mission School in Farmington.

Grandfather Holcomb conducted the service, basing it on the Genesis account of Sarah's burial by her husband, Abraham, and she was the first to be buried in a new cemetery on the little hill just north of the Mission. It was important that a burial ground be separated from the Mission. Most Navajos would have hesitated to visit any place where a person was buried.

Soon after Grandmother Holcomb died, Grandfather took me for a walk and for once walked at a slow pace, engaging me in earnest conversation and explained that Grandmother had "gone to glory" and was now with the Lord. This was very good, and, in fact, he too would soon be up there on the hill beside Grandmother. My objections were silenced, and I returned to the Mission a little confused and with very mixed emotions.

California 1929

I n the summer of 1929 it was decided that Mother and Dad should make a tour of the West Coast Brethren Assemblies that were supporting the Mission and update them on progress at Immanuel Mission to the Navajos.

After several weeks of preparation they set out on the long trek to California in a Model A Ford with a two-year-old baby and a five-year-old son just recovering from a serious illness. In those pre-motel days it was necessary to camp under the stars, so a few cooking utensils and bedrolls were part of the baggage, and they planned to buy groceries as needed along the way.

Dad rigged an icebox on the running board, containers for dishes, a rudimentary medical kit, and storage for clothes and shaving gear in the tiny car. I remember him standing alongside the road lathering his face with a small brush and shaving with a straight razor by looking in the rearview mirror, all with one small cup of water. Actually this was much the same routine as at Immanuel Mission, except at home he usually shaved indoors with hot water and a larger mirror. Water became increasingly precious as we entered the sand dunes of the Mojave Desert west of Yuma, and every drop from the water bag hanging on the front of the car was carefully rationed.

I often wonder, when I look back on that trip, at the faith of a couple who would set out on a 1,000-mile journey through the sand dunes of one of the hottest deserts in the United States, in a car with a ten-gallon gas tank, no credit card, and, in the pre-cell-phone era, no way of communicating with anyone except the Lord. They had little money and no insurance but an unfaltering trust that the Lord would provide.

JUST LIKE BALBOA!

On a bright clear morning, our dusty little car reached the coast near San Diego, then a town of 148,000 people, and as we topped a sandy hill Dad suddenly said, "I smell salt water," and Mother exclaimed, "Glen, there's the ocean!" Danny and I, half asleep in the back seat, shot bolt upright and saw there down below us was more shimmering blue water than we had ever seen before, stretching away to the far horizon: *tónteel,* the "wide water." We had discovered the Pacific, but unlike the unfortunate Spanish explorer I was destined to cross that great body of water nine times in my lifetime.

We stayed in San Diego for more than a week at the dairy farm of Ralph Barker, brother of Florence Barker, who had been on the Navajo Reservation with us during the early days of Immanuel Mission. Ralph's wife was the former Louise Fauscutt, Mother's best friend during their school days at Oakland Technical High School.

Although Danny and I were familiar with range cattle, we had never seen dairy cows in such numbers and were absolutely astonished by the long lines of placid cows standing in rows being milked in the Barker barn. Ralph Barker was also involved in Heifer International, a humanitarian effort organized by the Brethren Church to provide female calves to the hungry people in the world in the belief that "giving a man a cup of milk will help for a day but giving him a cow may change his way of life."

Ralph Barker became very active in this organization and made several trips to Africa to help deliver heifers he had contributed to the program. By the year 2000, Heifer International reported that this program had reached over four million families world wide, and it continues in the twenty-first century.

On our first Sunday in San Diego, we attended the meeting of the Plymouth Brethren Assembly, and at the evening session Dad spoke of the work among the Navajos at Immanuel Mission. His message was well received, and we were given a warm welcome by the adults, but Danny and I were regarded with curiosity by the children. When we were asked if we spoke English at home I answered truthfully, "Sometimes."

DAY OF THE BOAT RACES

One day the Barkers took us to see the small boat races, a big event on a body of water near the town. We kids became excited at all the noise and activities, and the Barker son and I started running around imitating the speedboats, racing in and out of the crowd standing on the shore. I ran one way and he another around a group of men, and we met head-on as we rounded the corner.

I went down and received a cut just over my eye from a broken piece of pavement. When I saw all the blood, I started screaming. Mother and Aunt Louise arrived immediately, snatched me up, and ran to the car for some emergency patch work before we all bundled into the car and went speeding off toward the hospital.

Ralph Barker swerved in and out of traffic, ignoring all speed limits, and we soon caught the attention of a motorcycle policeman, who gave chase and pulled us over. Book and pencil in hand and a stern expression on his face, the cop walked up to find two men up front and two women, a small child, and a frightened boy screaming and bleeding all over the place in the back of the car.

The officer shouted, "Follow me!" He jumped back on his bike and we roared off with a police escort—siren blasting, kid screaming, two frightened women shouting directions, and two confused men trying to keep the car on the road.

At the hospital we were rushed into Emergency, and soon a doctor was sewing my brow while blood pooled up in my eye. Dad was standing by, holding my hand to give me courage when he suddenly fell over in a faint. The doctor didn't even look up from his work, just ordered, "Put him on the other bed." Dad recovered, and I stopped screaming when I looked over to Dad, lying about four feet away, grinning sheepishly.

MEXICO—OR NOT?

When it came time for us to continue our journey, we started up the coast out of San Diego, and soon after we left the city we reached a major crossroads where one sign indicated the road to Los Angeles and the other read "MEXICO 8 MILES." None of the family had ever been out of the United States, and Dad impulsively exclaimed, "Let's go to Mexico!" But Mother didn't think we should.

We pulled off the road and estimated how much we would need to continue our journey. Dad got out his billfold and counted some change, several bills, and a five-dollar gold piece he had been saving because they already were becoming rare, particularly to us, and then he repeated, "Let's go to Mexico." But Mother was adamant: "All the money we have was given for the Lord's work and we are the entrusted stewards. None should be spent for our own amusement."

Danny and I chimed in in favor of Mexico and the vote was three to one for Mexico—but Dad regretfully turned the car up the road marked "Los Angeles," and I was not to visit Mexico until my freshman year at the University of Arizona, when I went to Nogales by bus. Mother and Dad didn't go until I took them down, over a dozen years later.

Many years later I revisited San Diego and finally located where the old Barker dairy had been, in rural Mission Valley just below the old mission, now all covered by freeways in one of the most populated parts of the city.

CITY OF THE ANGELS

The Los Angeles area, at that time, was a booming metropolis of nearly 2,000,000, mostly new residents from Iowa. It was surrounded by farmland, miles of orange groves, empty beaches, and a number of small towns scattered along the Pacific Coast. We stopped at several small Brethren Assemblies along the way and stayed at homes of members of the congregations while Dad worked with each group.

I do not know how long we remained in Los Angeles but do remember it was long enough to have the stitches taken from my brow. I had no desire for any more activity in that area, but a gentle woman named Beth, a registered nurse, persuaded me to let her look at them, and before I knew what was happening they were all removed.

Several days after this milestone in my life it was decided that we would all go to Catalina Island. I was not in on this discussion, and perhaps we went as guests of our host family. Anyway, one morning we all drove to a covered dock in San Pedro, where the biggest ship I had ever seen was waiting for us to board. Above all else, I remember a throng of people on the deck, where we found starboard seats and settled in to enjoy a fresh morning breeze and the bright sunshine glinting off the blue ocean.

We left the harbor and moved out to sea, followed by a flock of seagulls, and soon Mother and our hosts were deep in conversation, Dad was walking around the deck taking snapshots with his new Kodak folding camera, and Danny, oblivious to all the great adventure, was snoozing peacefully on a bench, his face covered with a cap. I wanted to see everything at once and was so completely overwhelmed by the experience that Dad decided I could use some guidance and took me for a tour of the ship—which was as new to him as it was to me.

We went down several crowded decks and ended up at the shopping area, with displays of souvenirs, postcards, and all kinds of food that I didn't even recognize, as well as candies and ice cream, all for sale. We didn't buy anything but returned to the top deck, where Mother and her friend produced a basket of sandwiches and fruit they had brought aboard.

LOST AT SEA

The picnic on deck was wholesome and satisfying, but I was impatient and wanted to buy something from the stands down below. Dad was off taking pictures with his new camera again, and Mother wasn't interested in interrupting her conversation, and, to my utter astonishment, handed me the unheard-of amount of 10 cents to spend.

Excited, I rushed below, selected an ice cream cone, successfully completed my purchase, and, astonished to receive 5 cents in change, started walking through the ship, enjoying every wonderful new sensation. Suddenly I realized I didn't know where I was—not even which deck I was on. The more I wandered, the more confused I became, and panic began to replace the excitement of my new experience.

My ice cream now forgotten, I rushed from deck to deck but encountered only strangers. Meanwhile, Mother became concerned when her five-year-old didn't return and went in search of the little fellow who was so far off his Reservation. She eventually found me and shepherded me back to our seats on deck, and for the rest of the trip I did no further exploring but remained close to my family, just watching the blue water foaming from the prow of the ship as we ploughed through the blue sea.

Not long after, we arrived at the town of Avalon and spent a wonderful afternoon wandering the shops and running on the beach with Dad taking pictures of everything. We returned to the ship late in the afternoon. As we waited on the dock to board, I saw a line of portholes a little above the waterline, where a number of faces of crew members were watching all the tourists boarding the ship for the voyage home.

Back on the safe, firm mainland, two exhausted small boys were finally tucked in their snug beds for dreams of many strange and exotic places and events. However, the highlight of the trip was that I got to keep the 5 cents change for my ice cream cone.

I do not remember much of our long drive up the West Coast from Los Angeles, other than more empty beaches, small towns, and miles and miles of farmland, nor do I know if we stayed with friends or just camped on the beach some nights. One dramatic beach experience remains in my memory, however. We were wading along a sandy shore looking for shells when Mother suddenly warned me to turn my back, as a big wave was coming in, and above all, to keep my mouth shut!

Defying authority, I turned full face to the ocean and defiantly yelled at the wall of water, just as the big wave crested and swept me up on the beach, blinded and soaked, with a mouthful of cold water. Gagging and choking, I realized that Mother, as usual, was right, and at the same instant I made another great discovery—sea water is awfully salty, at least in the Pacific.

We finally arrived in the cool fog of the Bay Area, Mother's ultimate destination of the entire trip. This was the place where she had made her most lasting friendships and experienced the busy life of that great international seaport city that had sustained her during her lonely life on the dry, dusty Navajo Reservation.

We stayed in Oakland with Louise Barker's mother, who was glad to see Marie again, even though she did have a husband and two small kids in tow, and we spent a week or more exploring the wonders of the storied Bay Area. Mrs. Fauscutt was especially nice to the kid from the Reservation and would occasionally slip me little brightly colored cake decorations that I avidly ate by the handful, until the day I encountered in the mix a few sugar-coated anise seeds and lost forever my taste for cake decorations as well as for anise.

She also had in her closet an old skateboard fashioned of two roller skates and a board. Danny and I would coast down the steep walk in front of the Fauscutt house, and one day Dad took a picture, arranging Danny and me on the board with Danny in front. I objected that I was the oldest and should be the one in front but Mrs. Fauscutt mollified me by telling me that the pilot always sat in the back.

DAD'S TROUBLES WITH THE LAW
Driving in the Bay Area presented new challenges for Dad. An excellent, resourceful driver in the sandy canyon country, he was never comfortable with the heavy traffic, steep hills, and narrow streets of San Francisco.

One day he ran a stoplight and Mother yelled, "Glen, be careful, or you'll get a ticket yet." I asked what could happen, and she explained that breaking the law could lead to a fine and maybe even time in jail. I was appalled, and every time I spotted a policeman after that I would warn Dad not to attract attention as the police were already looking for that red light crime.

Another incident in Oakland added to my fear of the law in California. Dad had accepted an invitation to go up to visit San Quentin, and while he was on the tour of that federal prison he volunteered to experience solitary confinement for a dark minute or two, all alone. His story of this adventure struck me as a particularly awful risk, considering the fact he was already on the local wanted list.

My life back home at Immanuel Mission must have been very uneventful, as my lost-at-sea experience and the traffic incidents were about the only subjects frightful enough to make me get up in the middle of the night and stumble into my parents' room with questions like, "What if you had all gotten off while I was lost on that ship?" and "Will the police come to Arizona to ask about that red light?"

Those great California experiences in 1929 left a much more lasting impression on me than the hushed adult conversation about the big black newspaper headlines: "Wall Street Market Crashes!"

29 The Windmill and the Well

ater was the primary concern in all Reservation life, and it was the major factor in locating the Mission site. A small spring out behind the original stone trading post provided water for all drinking and household use. This eventually proved to be an unreliable source, as during the dry season the spring would dwindle, and one summer it just dried up.

Yellowhair, who had early assumed the chore of carrying all water to the house, went out scouting and soon located a water hole in an arroyo about a mile south of the Mission, and for most of that summer Yellowhair trudged up the sandy trail with two buckets of spring water. Occasionally I straggled along behind him with one small bucket, but it had usually sloshed almost empty by the time we reached the Mission. This source of water was always referred to as "the old man's spring" in honor of the man who discovered it.

DIGGING FOR WATER

In 1928, after we returned from Clemenceau, the missionaries decided the Mission needed a more reliable supply of water, and Dad and Grandfather Holcomb started prospecting. They finally chose a location for a well not far from the woodpile and started drilling a small hole with a posthole auger, a device originally used by cowboys to dig postholes for fences.

As they went down they had to extend the handle with lengths of quarter-inch pipe several times, but at 30 feet they struck water and found a source Dad described as "sufficient for the needs of that time."

Dad and Grandfather Holcomb began digging a large hole, about six feet in diameter, down, down, and down, through layers of wood chips, dirt, rock and sand. Their only tools were the auger, a pickaxe, and their shovels. The work was arduous, but the men doggedly kept digging. When they got down about six feet, Dad rigged a tripod of poles and a pulley to haul the excavated dirt up to the surface in a large bucket.

During construction it was necessary to devise a method for getting in and out of the pit, as well as lifting the dirt to the surface for disposal. Dad placed cross beams and rigged a pulley, attaching a rope with several loops and a bucket to lower the workers and also to send tools, pipe, and other materials down to finish the job. The labor was strenuous, slow, and dangerous, but Dad and the two Navajo men, George Hudajai and Roy Scott, kept digging and hauling up the dirt, bucketful by bucketful, and before the well was completed they had created a small hill.

The well became much darker as they went down, and neither George nor Roy had watches but they still kept track of time, and exactly at noon would call out, *'atné' é'ááh* (noon), and break for dinner. They also knew when it was *e'e'aahgo,* or sunset, but even I could figure that out without a watch.

THE RAIN OF PIPES

One day Dad was rushing to finish a load before noon, so he hastily loaded several lengths of pipes into the bucket and started lowering the cargo. The bucket snagged on a rock projecting from the wall, tipped, and sent the lengths of pipe rocketing down into the pit, crashing from wall to wall as they fell. He yelled a warning, and George, the man down below, flattened up against the wall and escaped injury. The incident became a story Navajos always found funny— but George failed ever to see any humor in the whole episode.

Both Roy and George assisted in other building projects around the Mission after the well was completed. For a time the Hudajai family camped nearby while George continued to help in construction, and I became acquainted with Denny, his son of about my age, and his younger sister.

COWBOYS AND INDIANS

Denny and I occasionally played together, sometimes the universal game of "Cowboys and Indians" that I had learned from the Foutz and Palmer kids at the trading post at Sweetwater. Incidentally, I was not the cowboy every time.

One morning we "captured" Denny's outlaw sister and knew our duty was to "string her up." Denny had an old soft rope about six feet long, and we looped it around our captive's neck and threw the end up over one of the vigas of the root cellar roof. We didn't have anything to tie her hands so we galloped away, leaving her teetering on the edge of the stairwell.

We didn't make our escape, however, as at this point in our melodrama the cavalry rode over the hill in the person of George, who had been working nearby, and the fair maiden was not only rescued, but a furious George turned on our posse and drove a yelping Denny from the Mission yard with a real lariat, and I do not remember Denny ever being allowed to play with the *bilagáana* kid again.

CHICKEN IN THE WELL

When the well project was finally completed, Dad built a board platform over the hole and designed a pole framework for a pulley so that water could be

Danny and Alwin with chickens.

drawn up with a bucket through a trapdoor in the platform that was supposed to be closed at all times.

Several years later we were entertaining company one cold evening when Yellowhair came in from outside and announced, "A chicken just fell in the well!" We all rushed out in the yard and sure enough, someone had left the trapdoor open, and we could hear a frightful squawking but could see nothing when we peered down into the dark hole, until practical Aunt Clara came out with a flashlight. Sure enough, a very confused hen was frantically floundering around and around at the bottom of the well and making a terrible racket.

After a lively discussion and several suggestions, a rescue operation was put into action, and Dad removed the bucket from its rope and rigged a boatswain's chair with a larger bucket. After another discussion it was decided that the seven-year-old boy was the one to send down, as he was the only one who could fit in the bucket, and, over the protests of Mother, I was bundled in winter clothing and barefoot, but equipped with a burlap sack and the flashlight, was secured in the bucket.

It was quite dark when all was finally prepared for the launch, and a small crowd had gathered, including family, a visiting pilgrim from Back East, and several Navajos, who watched as Dad, Yellowhair, and a Navajo volunteer carefully played out the line over the pulley and I slowly descended into the black hole to the helpful shouts of "Don't tip the bucket!" and "For goodness sake, don't drop the flashlight!" And about thirty feet down my feet hit cold water and I called "Back me up a little!" so I wouldn't join the chicken in the frigid water.

The unfortunate bird was perched on a small ledge at water level, and upon the appearance of an intruder with a light, started squawking and frantically floundering and splashing around again. I finally caught the chicken and managed to get the wet, flapping hen into my sack without losing my grip on the flashlight, then yelled: "Pull me up, pull me up!"

My frantic captive continued flapping around, and we were swinging wildly, bumping first one damp wall and then the other as we went up. Eventually the shivering, wet expedition reached the trapdoor and was pulled to the surface by a dozen helpful hands. The *bilagáana* visitor was astounded by the entire affair and wrote home all about his stay among the Indians and the primitive conditions and the exciting experiences of the missionaries stationed out there in the wilderness of the Wild West.

Later a small hand pump was installed, making the pulley and bucket arrangement obsolete. In real cold weather the metal handle of the pump froze, and Mother warned me that if I stuck my tongue on the handle it would stick to the metal. She was right, it did.

BIG BANG!

We had one other experience near the well that involved a chicken. It took place one year on Independence Day. The Navajo word for the Fourth of July is *naa'ahóóhai*, or "chicken," as traders often held a chicken pull, complete with a "feed," on that national holiday, to develop traffic at the trading post.

Instead of a live rooster, however, a small sack of silver coins was buried in the ground, and on a given signal, a number of Navajo men charged the site at full speed on their horses and milled around the buried prize, each man trying to jerk it out and race across the finish line with his prize.

One year on Independence Day at Immanuel Mission we were without funds to buy any fireworks at all, but Dad promised us we would celebrate the Fourth with a real "bang!"

He had found, tucked away among all the tools and equipment stored in the old original rock building, a single stick of dynamite left over from a road-building project. He cut a fuse, made a mud pack of explosives in an open space near the well, and covered the site with a large tin can. He then invited the eight members of the Mission family out for the celebration.

We gathered around and were waiting for the show to begin when Dad became worried about where all the flying debris from the blast would fall and decided that the safest place to observe the explosion was on the low roof of the old stone trading post building. It would not only be safe, but it would also make a fine grandstand.

So everyone, including Mother and Aunt Clara but not Yellowhair, climbed up the ladder and stood excitedly waiting for Dad to start the action by striking a match to the fuse. He had given himself a long fuse to allow time to sprint back and climb the ladder and join us on the roof. We all stood watching. The fuse sputtered toward the windmill—but nothing happened.

Just then the big rooster of our flock came wandering out from behind the woodpile, strutted over to the well platform, and started pecking around the dynamite pack. The whole family, except Yellowhair, was dancing around on the roof, shouting, screaming, and waving our arms to shoo the stupid bird away, when a lone Navajo horseman came riding down the trail.

Navajo style, dignified old *hastiin yázhi* trotted silently along the sandy trail by the Mission, looking straight ahead and paying no attention to the strange *bilagáana* missionaries dancing and chanting on the roof of the old trading post.

Hastiin yázhi politely had given no indication he had seen anything unusual and rode on his way, but I would like to have heard the story he told when he arrived at *tó łikan* trading post about the strange way the people over at the Mission had celebrated *naa'ahóóhai*. Finally Dad, after warning everyone to remain on the roof, climbed down and cautiously approached the site, only to find the fuse had gone out. He re-set the charge, and we finally got our promised "really big bang" for the Fourth of July.

Alwin in front of group of visitors at the Mission.

BÉÉSH 'II' ÁHÍ

Eventually, the Mission accumulated funds to make it possible to buy a fine new windmill, and Dad, with my "assistance," got it assembled and finally erected with the big wheel spinning in the breeze. Later he built a wood platform alongside and hoisted a large metal tank up on the platform with "Ford car power," pulleys, and rope, and Immanuel Mission finally had a dependable year-round water supply.

Not long after, I got my first introduction to the life of a blue-collar ditch digger. Dad and I dug what he referred to as a "freeze-proof pipeline" below the frost level to both houses. I then learned the basic principles of pipe fitting, as we struggled to cut thread and fit various lengths of pipe and elbows to install sinks and drains, with faucets over the two sinks inside the houses and a couple of outlets outside. When we finally completed the job, Immanuel Mission finally had running water in both kitchens, with one faucet over each sink, and that was all the plumbing at Immanuel Mission until long after I had left the Reservation.

We heated water in the large tank attached to the kitchen range in the adobe house and used it for cooking and washing. The used water was then hauled outdoors and poured on the shade trees or the flowers, just about the only irrigation they received.

On bath day we dipped water up by bucket and poured it into a metal washtub, followed by the inevitable sequel of emptying the tub after a bath in the same laborious manner. A traditional Saturday night event was the communal bath of the three "men" of the family, using the same tub of water for all in turn, thus getting reasonably clean and conserving both water and labor.

One week Mother didn't bathe two-year-old Danny until just before Sunday morning Breaking of Bread. She gave him a hurried scrubbing and dressed him in clean clothes, ready for the breaking of bread service, but just as she finished and had started combing his curly hair, he stepped back, lost his balance, and fell back into the tub.

I thought this was hilarious and was laughing uproariously at the dripping child when Mother, who had just about had enough for one morning, turned to me and said, "If you think this is so funny, you just empty this tub and haul in fresh water while I undress this baby and bathe him again." I never again laughed at another's misfortune.

We were constantly aware of the scarcity of and need to conserve water, as it was never plentiful at Immanuel Mission. This scarcity of water was reflected in our daily life during all my days there. I remember watching Dad outside the rock house on a warm summer morning, filling a small cup with hot water from the teakettle and taking it with a towel outside where he had a hand mirror hanging on a post. He dipped his shaving brush in the cup and lathered his face from a disk of soap, then proceeded to shave with a straight razor, using the single cupful of water for shaving and washing up afterwards. What shaving I did during my last few years at the Mission was by the same method.

COINCIDENCE IN PHILADELPHIA
Nearly twenty years after leaving the Reservation, I was in a hospital in Philadelphia and after several weeks, just before being released, I was walking around the ward. I stopped to talk to a young man in a nearby room and learned he was in for treatment of an old back injury.

I asked what had happened, and he said, "You won't believe this but I fell off a windmill!" Interested, I asked, "Where?" And he replied, "Oh, a place you never heard of out in Arizona called Immanuel Mission." I had not recovered from my astonishment when his doctor came by on his rounds and asked what all the excitement was about, but I don't think he believed my tale of building the windmill his patient fell from out in Arizona.

THE DESERT SHALL BLOOM LIKE A ROSE
The new windmill provided adequate water for household use, but when we started a garden below the Mission in the newly fenced area, it became necessary to look for a new source of water for irrigation. Grandfather Holcomb shouldered his trusty shovel and launched his own conservation project in the hills surrounding the Mission.

Over the years, water that fell around the mesa ran down into the nearby arroyo in small rivulets during rainstorms, and immediately flowed out of the area, so Grandfather built an earthen dam just inside the fenced area. Next he went out to locate every small channel and diverted them to the new reservoir. The water in the accumulated pond was then released through an irrigation box as needed to grow a small garden.

In time it became necessary to fence the entire ten acres of the Mission compound. First, hundreds of holes were laboriously dug with a hand auger. Cedar posts were then set, and the entire place was finally enclosed by a wire fence. Tamarisk was then planted just inside many sections along the fence, and soon the Mission could be seen from miles away as a cool, green oasis in the vast expanse of uninhabited desert between the canyons and the mesas.

Also known as salt cedar, tamarisk is not a native shrub of the New World but was introduced, probably from middle Asia, in the 1800s. It thrived under extreme desert conditions and was a valuable windbreak; but it was so prolific that it soon became generally recognized as an invasive growth.

Over the next few years Dad and Grandfather Holcomb developed a small garden that we carefully irrigated from the meager little pond of water that collected behind Grandfather's dam. We planted corn, tomatoes, peas, watermelons, and onions in neat little rows, and we also cultivated chufas, an ancient Egyptian earth chestnut also known as horchata. That tasty little nut became a favorite snack of mine.

Another feature of the new garden was that Danny and I soon became well acquainted with the hoe as an instrument to chop weeds.

30 — Grandfather's Last Hurrah

To me, Grandfather Holcomb seemed very tall and loving but a little formal and sometimes aloof with his grandchildren. He firmly believed each generation had its own place in the structure of the family, and little children were to be "seen and not heard." My earliest recollection of him is his seating me on his knee, trying to read to me for a few moments, and then dismissing me with the comment, "You're just too wiggly!"

Grandfather always walked fast, with great long strides, and never seemed to notice that the little fellow galloping along behind couldn't keep up. Sometimes he would stop, pick me up by one arm, sling me over his shoulder and walk on with me clinging to his back like a baby monkey. I remember his doing this with Dan also, but, in spite of Mother's predictions, one of our arms didn't become longer than the other, and as Grandfather got older he had to modify this procedure and would have the little fellow stand on the porch to mount up.

LOST IN THE WILD MIDWEST
In the summer of 1930, Grandfather decided to visit several assemblies in Albuquerque and the Midwest and then go on to see his daughters, Una Henion in Minnesota and Ruth Campbell in Michigan, before returning to Immanuel Mission.

Mother and Aunt Clara packed his black valise with the clothes he would need, carefully put together an itinerary of all the places he wanted to visit, charted them on the train timetables, and wrote up a detailed schedule, giving him one copy and keeping another so we would know where he was at all times. Dad drove him to Gallup, where he boarded the train and disappeared down the track.

We had no telephones on the Reservation, telegrams could only be sent in town, and we had only had occasional delivery of mail, so it often took weeks to get messages across the country. We did receive one letter from Albuquerque, reporting the Brethren there had enjoyed his visit to their Assembly. A few weeks later another short note came from Grandfather. He was in Kansas City and would soon leave for Minnesota as scheduled. But no further word arrived.

After several more weeks, Mother became worried and wrote Aunt Una in Minnesota, and in a few days she received a return letter saying Grandfather had visited her there but had left for Michigan. Days went by, still no word from

Marie, Glen, Yellowhair, Alwin, H. A., and Danny.

Grandfather. Mother wrote Aunt Ruth and, in time, a letter came back saying he hadn't arrived in Michigan as expected.

Grandfather had just disappeared, and all four of his daughters by then were frantically writing letters to all the relatives and Assemblies Grandfather was scheduled to visit, but there was not a trace of the missing missionary.

About two weeks later, he turned up in Michigan. He had decided in Kansas City that, since he had a minister's pass on the railroad, he would just go to St. Louis and visit the Assembly there. That proved so rewarding he went on to Chicago. He knew this put him a bit behind on his schedule, but he had all summer so didn't worry about a little change in plans—he just forgot to notify anyone.

Grandfather had a splendid, carefree summer visiting all over "Back East." Then one day he arrived back at the Mission in a pickup truck driven by a BIA official from the Teec Nos Pos area. He didn't volunteer much information about how he had gotten home from Gallup, and I don't think his daughters wanted to know. Grandfather was approaching eighty at the time, and Dad was amazed at his independent attitude and his zest for life. He was particularly impressed when the old man went back to the truck, jumping off the porch rather than bother with the three steps, and then trotted back with his overloaded valise and placed it on the porch.

Grandfather Holcomb continued his regular routine and chores, including correspondence and milking the cows, up until the day before he died in December 1931.

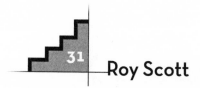

31 Roy Scott

Biwoo' łitso, "gold-tooth" in Navajo, was a charismatic young Navajo who shared the surname Scott with Walter, his older brother. Possibly this *bilagáana* name had been assigned to Walter when serving in the U.S. Army. Walter spoke very good English and now lived off Reservation but visited his family in the Four Corners area occasionally.

Roy lived near Immanuel Mission and spoke only Navajo but was a frequent visitor from the very early Mission days. He became a member of the crew who worked with Dad in experimenting with an adobe brick mixture for the big house in the spring of 1926.

THE CHRISTIAN WAY

Earlier he had become interested in the message the missionaries were bringing to his people and soon decided he would follow the Christian way of life. Aunt Florence referred to Roy Scott in her journal and mentioned his interest in the message the missionaries were bringing to the Navajo people: "He listened eagerly to God's Word and asked questions, even in front of other Navajos. We were delighted that Roy was so brave."

But Roy soon realized he was completely isolated from his own culture and all his relatives and friends, as religious dances and ceremonies were the Navajo social world. She continued: "However, the devil soon began his work, especially through George. It had dawned on the Navajos working for us that one of their number was actually believing God's Word. George poked fun at Roy in many subtle ways, and did all he could to draw Roy back into the old ways."

Florence Barker's journal carried on the story:

The older men also proceeded to fill Roy's heart with doubts. Then the devil arranged a dance five miles from the Mission and George persuaded Roy to go. It nearly broke me up when I found that Roy had gone to that heathen dance.

When Roy had first confessed Christ, the thought came to me, "This joy won't last; Roy will bring many heartaches and anxious moments," and so it has come to pass. My heart cries out in anguish to

Roy Scott at the mill by the original rock house.

God for Roy, one wee lamb gone astray and lost on a dangerous cliff with the coyotes hovering close by. The day after the dance we found that the boys had spent part of the night at a place of "ill fame." That made us all the more heartsick because we know Roy's former life and his great weakness.

Later that evening I talked with Roy as he watered the garden for me. He told me he didn't dance but only watched. He seemed to be a little repentant, but kept trying to turn the conversation to other subjects.

Now Aunt Clara became involved, and Florence Barker wrote:

Clara wanted to have an earnest talk with him but decided to bide her time and Roy worked until Saturday noon fixing fences and he became more like "our Roy" toward the end of the job. Clara questioned him and he talked freely to her.

The derision and laughter from George, and the doubts put into his ear by the other men had simply floored him. The loneliness of the path he had chosen seemed more than he could bear. However, he assured Clara that he would not throw away the things of God and would continue to pray, but to himself.

Florence Barker then remarked: "I guess it's better to be a silent believer than not one at all."

Roy next became interested in Black Hat's sister, Mabel, who had a reputation for being somewhat less than virtuous in her conduct. Aunt Florence had no use for her, always referring to her as that "vile woman" who would certainly lead Roy even further away from the Lord. In January 1927 Roy came over one day with Mabel, but Aunt Florence was not impressed by the young woman.

Roy, however, continued his quest and eventually married her. She immediately settled down and was a good and faithful wife for years, causing Roy to observe, "Marry bad girls—they become good wives." Roy was one of the first young Navajos to cut his hair, and I remember his going to Shiprock where he bought a new hat and came home to show off his "new look."

A LITTLE BIT OF WATER
Roy was my special friend for all the time I was at Immanuel Mission and took a special pleasure in instructing me in how to speak correctly. Once I asked for a drink, and when Roy poured only a little water in my cup, I commented it was "*alts'iisí*" to observe it was just a little bit. But Roy immediately indicated a short length of his rope and said "*alts'iisi*," then pointed at the amount of water in my cup and corrected me by saying, "*áłch'įįdí*."

Roy was Dad's interpreter when he took the census in the Sweetwater area in the spring of 1930, and he had much experience with our struggle to learn correct everyday Navajo conversation. Dad wrote that he had been of invaluable help in meeting with families rarely seen at the Mission and particularly good in finding their hogans back in the vast mesas and canyons.

DAATS'Í

Roy loved to ride with us on trips in the car, and one day he and I were riding in the back seat with Mother and Dad in front. As we drove over the old rocky road through *tsé tah,* "among the rocks," near the old uranium mine, Roy and I began speculating on possible names for a prominent rock pinnacle towering above us at the end of the Carrizo Mountains. We experimented with all kinds of names, following each suggestion with the Navajo word for maybe: *daats'i.* It could be a man, *daats'i,* or a big tree, *daats'i.* Finally Roy ended our discussion with the ultimate definition. "It was *daats'i, daats'i.*" Just maybe, maybe.

On another automobile trip Roy was riding in the car with Dad and me on our way to Shiprock, and just as we reached the intersection of the Reservation road with Dad's favorite road, the Gallup highway, Roy suddenly sat up in the back seat and shouted, "Look, look!"

Dad and I both glanced in the direction Roy was pointing but only saw a sign on the side of a little hill, spelling out an oil company name in hundreds of small, round stones painted bright red. We thought it unusual but not that exciting and drove on, but Roy kept looking back at the sign for a time, then settled back with an amused chuckle and said in Navajo, "I thought they were apples."

32 Above and Below Decks

THE GREAT HOUSE EXCHANGE

After Grandfather Holcomb died, everyone decided that the Girdner family should move into the big adobe house and Aunt Clara would occupy the smaller stone house across the compound. After much running back and forth hand-carrying clothing and personal belongings, we saw that our furniture and large household goods could be more quickly transferred by wagon than by carrying them over individually, one box at a time.

A morning was spent putting everything but the kitchen sink in the wagon under the watchful eyes of a group of curious Navajos, who had gathered to watch our progress with amusement that turned to hilarity when we realized that, for some unknown reason, horses were not available when it was time to roll.

Dad quickly recruited half a dozen of the young men standing by, laughing and commenting on the strange ways of the white men, and they gathered around the horseless wagon with Dad in back. I was standing just in front of the left wheel when, with a shout, the crew shoved off so rapidly that I was caught unawares. The steel-rimmed wheel ran over my bare foot, and I immediately retired from the entire project.

After the move the Girdner family settled into the larger house and Aunt Clara was established in the stone house, but most of her time was still spent in the largest room in the adobe building. This served as a chapel and community room for Navajos stopping off from their long ride on the trail to the Sweetwater Trading Post.

In addition to religious services, this room was used once or twice by government agents as a meeting place for informational and official BIA meetings as, in those days before chapter houses were established, no other building in the Four Corners area of the Reservation could accommodate large affairs. However, we had to exercise care so the Mission could never be identified as part of *waashindoon* and government activities.

At the southwest corner of the big adobe building, next to the community room, was a small bedroom that was used by whatever young lady was currently serving as a teacher for Danny and me. As its only entrance opened off the community room where the visiting Navajos gathered, the bedroom door was

Winter view of the Mission. The boys' bunkhouse door is visible on the lower level.

kept locked for privacy. Curious Navajos had a different view of property rights from those of the *bilagáana* missionaries.

One day when Inez Lockhart was with us, there were a dozen or more visitors sitting on all the chairs and the floor of the community room. One fellow was sitting on the floor in front of her door when she suddenly opened it to leave her room, and a very surprised Navajo rolled into her room and onto her feet.

The rest of the new adobe house—bedrooms, a kitchen upstairs, and a stairway down to a large basement that had a large storage space and several unfinished rooms with dirt floors—was the Girdner family living quarters.

THE KITCHEN

The east end of the new adobe building was a combination kitchen–dining room with two large windows facing the Carrizo Mountains. Just below these windows was a large table that usually seated eight but could be expanded to accommodate twelve for special occasions.

The east corner of the kitchen was Yellowhair's domain, with one chair by the window and a small table covered with oilcloth. He not only ate there but it was also his personal place in the room, and he always sat there when he was not busy with chores, resting, talking, "reading" the pictures in magazines, or often chanting softly to himself.

When cooking and baking, Mother would often place a dish of whatever she was preparing on Yellowhair's table, as he enjoyed his mid-morning snacks. One day she was making an angel food cake and had several egg yolks left over, which she set aside in a small dish on his table. She was busy and didn't notice when he came in from the woodpile and took his usual seat.

After a few minutes Yellowhair asked her what he had been eating and she glanced over, saw the little dish was empty, and said in surprise, "Eggs!" Yellowhair just remarked, "I thought they were peaches but they didn't taste very good."

A sink and work tables with large overhead cabinets lined two sides of the kitchen, and a huge iron wood-burning range dominated the entire room from the far wall. It featured an enormous oven that could bake a dozen loaves of bread at one time. This big oven had a steel door that opened down and could be a wonderfully warm seat on a cold winter's evening if one was very careful. Small warming ovens were located above the range, and the very important eight-gallon hot water reservoir on the side completed arrangements for all the cooking and baking. A large woodbox provided lengths of wood.

Beyond the range, beside the outside north door, stood a washstand with a pail of water, as there was no running water at Immanuel Mission during the early years. That corner of the room also contained a washbasin, several large towels, and the inevitable slop bucket for waste water. A broom stood in the corner just beyond.

Besides the kitchen, the center of family activities was another large room furnished with a huge woodstove, a piano with a great array of photographs on top, and a number of chairs. Several pictures hung on the walls, including one large painting called *Appeal to the Great Spirit,* showing a Plains Indian on a horse praying.

BELOW DECKS

The big adobe building was built on the edge of a small hill, so that the basement lay beneath all rooms except the southeast corner room. This was the only area downstairs that was finished with a wood floor, two regular windows, and a door that opened at ground level. This room was originally Grandfather Holcomb's office but later served as the boys' bedroom. Danny and I shared quarters with the tacit understanding that the side by the windows was his, and the other side was mine.

The windows on Danny's side were at ground level, and early one morning he was pulling on his pants when he heard a giggle and glancing over his shoulder discovered two little Navajo girls had crawled through the fence outside and were peering in the window enjoying the show.

We shared closets that ran along one wall, and each of us had our own iron cot in opposite corners of the room. By the first window I had a chair and small table that served as my desk. A modified fruit box bookcase on the wall behind the desk completed my "office."

My wall was covered with an eclectic collection of pictures dominated by a full newspaper sheet in color from one of Mother's London papers, which showed King George VI, in a splendid uniform, complete with a red coat and numerous medals. Beside the royal portrait of King George VI was a small picture, almost dwarfed by the British monarch as perhaps it should have been. It was the portrait of Haile Selassie, a diminutive ruler with an astounding title: Elect of God, King of Kings, King of Zion, Conquering Lion of Judah, His Majesty Haile Selassie the First Emperor of Ethiopia.

Benito Mussolini, Dictator of Italy, had just invaded that African country with his trained and well-armed Italian troops and airplanes, and the little emperor was putting up a heroic but futile resistance with his third-world army of tribesmen, armed with little more than rifles and spears.

Placed above all was a picture of "The Lone Eagle," standard at that time in the rooms of all red-blooded teenage boys in America. Charles Lindbergh, the young hero still in his twenties, was the first aviator to solo across the Atlantic in a small monoplane and was depicted here wearing his trademark leather helmet leather and gazing intently into the sky, oblivious to all earthly affairs— the essence of the All-American boy. I pasted this treasure up with wallpaper paste so permanently that it remained on that wall years after I had left the Mission. Aunt Clara eventually redid the adobe walls but first removed and carefully salvaged just the head and shoulders of the British King and mailed that fragment to me at Oak Creek.

I remember one episode that took place in our shared bedroom that has made me wary of eyewitness testimony. Late one night, Mother and Dad returned from a trip to Farmington and put a new pair of bedroom slippers under each bunk without waking either Danny or me. Early the next morning I jumped out of bed and, on stumbling over my new present, shouted, "Look what I got!" I pulled them on and started walking about.

Danny looked under his bed and replied, "I got a pair too—and a chocolate bar!" I rushed over to see his reward. Sure enough, there in his slipper was a big ten-cent Hershey bar! Stunned by this favoritism for my younger brother, I started back across the room…when I became aware of something hard in my left slipper, and snatching it off discovered I was wearing my chocolate bar.

There's a moral to this story: Dan recorded this same incident some fifty years later, with only one minor variation—he was the one who walked across the room with the chocolate bar in his slipper. Do not always trust an eyewitness account.

YELLOWHAIR'S DEN

Next to our room was Yellowhair's room, and his domain was never invaded by any other member of the family. However, we regularly heard his chants every night.

I did sneak a furtive peek at that den one day when he was away, but I had to exercise extreme caution as Yellowhair was a seasoned tracker and could detect even the slightest touching of anything in the room in spite of all my caution.

I was disappointed to find only an unadorned room with the plain dirt floor he preferred. There was only a single bed, a spare pair of shoes, a few clothes, and his big, black coat hung on a rack. One apple box stood on end beside his bed with his trusty flashlight resting on top, within easy reach from his bed— and an open box of very ancient Fig Newton bars, his favorite cookies.

Above, just at ground level, was one small, opaque window, Yellowhair's only source of sunlight in the entire room. However, he always kept his flashlight handy. This window featured in an episode involving an accident that occurred one day while I was outside, practicing with my big stone shot put. I carelessly dropped the heavy sphere and it rolled down to rest gently by his window.

It made only a small crack, so I quietly retrieved my shot put and went back to my designated playing field out in front of our room, assuming that my crime would not be detected as Yellowhair was not in his room at the time. However, within minutes I was on the carpet to explain why "Alwee" had "broken" his only window while he was out of his room. That little window was still not repaired when I left the Mission years later.

An open staircase led from the main corridor of the building upstairs down into the basement, a secure place available only to family members. This was a large room, and I designated it as "the hold," as that was the name of storage areas of ships in the sea stories I was reading at that time.

Halfway down these stairs, a screened "cooler" provided storage space for milk, butter, cottage cheese, and other perishable items, and our main food supplies were stored in the large room at the bottom of the stairs. After an expedition to Farmington we would have a considerable stock of foodstuffs down there, as we seldom made the trip to the orchards and grocery stores of Farmington more than once a month.

Metal canisters held stocks of rice, beans, and other grains, and a large covered crock held pickles. Potatoes, onions, and other vegetables were also stored in bins, and dozens of mason quart jars of peaches, pears, rhubarb, applesauce, cherries, and apricots as well as jars of tomatoes, beets, and other vegetables lined perhaps five rough shelves that Dad had built along one wall.

WHERE DID ALL THE PEACHES GO?

Mother also kept on hand a supply of wonderful jams, and I particularly liked her "Pinacot," a concoction of apricots, pineapple, and walnuts. Years later, the most appreciated packages I received during my time at Pearl Harbor, employed by the U.S. Navy, were two small jars of her jam, shipped all the way across the Pacific from Arizona. Mother kept a close eye on her handiwork and made

Alwin, Danny, and Helen with *bilagáana* visitor.

regular inventory checks of her treasured stock of canned fruit. She knew exactly what was on each shelf and knew she could only replace them when fruit was in season and available in Farmington.

She became suspicious one day when she noticed that jars were regularly disappearing. No one but family members had access to the basement, so she queried us all as to what was happening to her prized products, and after much sleuthing, discovered the leak was Yellowhair.

At that time the Black Goat outfit was camped less than a mile east of the Mission, and, as they were of his *bit ah ni,* or clan, Yellowhair made regular trips up to visit his clansmen. After a number of meals at the camp he realized he should be contributing to the festivities and began bringing jars of canned fruit on his visits, much to the delight of his Black Goat family. As all Navajos loved fruit, especially peaches, Yellowhair became a very welcome relative on all occasions.

After some discussion, it was agreed that Yellowhair could take a limited amount of canned fruit with him on his visits, but that he would always show Mother what he was taking and not just tuck them in his big black coat and leave. All seemed satisfied with the arrangement, Mother was again in control of her shelves, and Yellowhair continued to be popular with his clansmen.

The fourth room in the basement was not only the biggest room below decks, it was also completely underground. Six small windows lay at ground level, about eight feet above the dirt floor and just below the exposed beams overhead that held up boards that served as the ceiling for this room and flooring for the rooms above. The only equipment in this room was a swing set. We occasionally played in this area, and one of the few things Helen remembered of Immanuel Mission was pulling a cord fastened to the wall to accelerate her swinging.

Mother also had several wires strung in this room to serve as clotheslines when the weather outside was inclement. It didn't take the kids long to discover that if these heavy wires were pulled down and then suddenly released it would produce a most satisfying booming chord that reverberated throughout the entire house. The problem was that everyone in the house knew when we started a recital, and within minutes we would receive orders to cease and desist.

On several occasions Navajos asked to leave valuables at the Mission for safekeeping, and these were stored in this room. Once a man asked us to keep a carefully wrapped and tied bundle and left it at the Mission for several months. Some time after he retrieved his prized possession, we learned that the old fellow was a medicine man and the parcel was his medicine pouch.

On another occasion an old Navajo man was temporarily using a corner of the big room for a dressing room when Mother inadvertently opened the door and started to enter, then backed off and closed the door, but not before she saw the startled old naked man hastily covering—his eyes.

33   Establishing a Way of Life

ife at Immanuel Mission, although primitive to most people, seemed normal to me, as it had always been that way as long as I could remember. I was bewildered when visitors from Back East expressed astonishment at the "primitive" way in which we existed. Now, from a very different standpoint, I see that the Reservation was in many ways the last frontier.

DAILY LIFE AT THE MISSION

As Grandfather Holcomb grew older, Dad gradually assumed responsibility for maintaining all the grounds and physical plant at the Mission and dealing with the immediate need of housing for the increasing Mission staff. It was equally important to keep the automobile running and the roads maintained.

Mother was responsible for the day-to-day clothing needs of a growing family. She also planned and prepared all meals and did all the buying of groceries and supplies. This was no small task, as our remote location made it necessary to plan for a month or six weeks ahead. Except for what we grew, all fruit and vegetables and most of our food supplies came from Farmington, eighty miles away. Because we had no refrigeration, perishable foods were kept in a screened box along the stairway down to the basement, where it was usually dark and cool. Milk would last about three days and eggs, vegetables, and fruits had a somewhat longer shelf life.

Eventually we acquired an Electrolux refrigerator that ran on kerosene, and during the first days we had it at the Mission, groups of visiting Navajos came in to the kitchen to examine the new box and were astounded that it made ice cubes during the summer. One old man, on tasting ice water, refused to believe we could freeze water in a box and declared we must have been to the mountain for the ice. Making ice with fire was a little hard for him to understand, but after all, we were *bilagáana.*

Both cooking and heating at the Mission were solely fueled by cedar and piñon wood, cut and hauled from the foothills of the Carrizo Mountains, at first in a horse-drawn wagon, and later in a small trailer hitched to our Model A Ford. We unloaded it at "the woodpile" some distance from the buildings and chopped it into stove lengths with an axe outside. Grandfather Holcomb was

Girdner family at the Mission.

an expert with an axe and also often got out his wood saw, a relic of his days in the Northwoods, to cut a few lengths of log which he then split with an axe to make firewood.

Light was provided by small glass lamps fueled by kerosene that we always referred to as "coal oil." Occasionally we used candles at night, and outdoors it was a choice between lantern and flashlight.

We had no electricity as long as I was on the Reservation, but I was acquainted with electricity. During the 1920s the Girdner ranch was the only place in the Oak Creek valley with its own electricity. Uncle Stanley, who had developed considerable mechanical and electrical talent on several hydroelectric projects in the Verde Valley, put together a hydroelectric plant for the Girdner ranch, fashioned almost entirely from old automobile parts.

The entire system centered on the rear differential of an automobile, and the only part he didn't make himself was cast to his design by the Capitol Foundry in Phoenix. Thus, Shady Vale Ranch had a power plant and private "closed circuit" telephone years before the other ranches on Oak Creek.

At Immanuel Mission, however, the nearest electrical power was over fifty miles away. All Mission buildings lacked central heating, lighting, air conditioning, refrigeration, and telephones, and for years there was no running water or indoor plumbing.

NAVAJO VISITORS AT THE MISSION

Sometimes only a few Navajos would drop by in a single day, but at other times, especially during special events in the area such as sheep dipping, as many as forty people would come by the Mission in one day. Several times during bad weather they stayed overnight to shelter from storms—both snow and sand!

Visitors to the Mission were nearly always men. Occasionally a woman would accompany her husband, but otherwise women almost always came in groups and for a special purpose, usually to sew in the tiny room with the treadle sewing machine. It wasn't unusual for a number of ladies to arrive in a cheerful, talkative group bringing bright primary red or green velveteen to make into blouses, or yards of calico for voluminous skirts.

Navajo men usually came to the Mission alone. One would ride up and tie his horse to the hitching rail, identify the horses already standing at the rail to determine who was inside, then slowly make his way up the path to the door. Some of the more traditional would pause a moment before opening the door. Inside, a visitor would not greet everyone as a group but circle the room shaking hands with each person in turn before pouring himself a steaming cup of Arbuckle's coffee from the large pot on top of the stove, and then quietly selecting a seat.

Aunt Clara would welcome the visitor, and, after the regular inquires about family, where he was going, and why, she would sing a Gospel hymn in Navajo,

Some of the Misson's very earliest visitors: Charlie and his family.

accompanying herself on a small treadle box organ they called an "Iron Singer." And then she would give a short Gospel message, sometimes using large colored cloth posters with people dressed in Navajo costume, which she had prepared with crayon to illustrate the biblical stories.

At the end of the message there was always a respectful pause and then a discussion that ranged widely, from weather and local happenings to regional events, would start and gradually involve all those present.

This quiet conversation could go on for hours, as no one ever hurried, and all our visitors seemed to have unlimited time. Aunt Clara would take part in discussions for a time, but when they stretched into hours she would quietly leave the room for other duties until another visitor arrived, when she would come back and go through the whole process again. Many times a visiting Navajo would sit through several sessions, listening to the message over and over again—all so he could take part in the discussions that followed.

I often sat and listened to the message in Navajo and observed the reactions and personal habits of the Navajo men. I noticed that when men were sitting in a group they had a practice that always fascinated me. As most Navajo men have little facial hair, it was not necessary to shave, and they had only an occasional need to remove what little hair they had.

However, most adult men carried small metal tweezers they had fashioned out of a strip of metal cut from a can, and they used to take them out during a discussion and passively pluck stray facial hairs as they listened to the discussions. I was fascinated by this procedure and fashioned one of my own—but found little use for the small thing.

On one occasion a man came in and remained all day, sitting silently in his chair, working his tweezers and waiting for the next visitor to come in so he could take part in another conversation. He stayed overnight and until nearly noon the next day. I went in several times and sat watching him, but he just sat and never spoke or even acknowledged that I was in the room. This was not unusual behavior for a Navajo. When one had been busy and moving too fast, he would just sit for a while "and let his soul catch up." We white folks learned to follow that practice when we were caught behind a flooded arroyo after a sudden rainstorm. Without the tweezers, however.

Kinfolk, Pilgrims, and Government Men

Bilagáana visitors to Immanuel Mission in the early years were almost non-existent, as only a few vehicles of the time were able to negotiate the Reservation roads—or lack of roads. There were no paved roads on the entire Reservation, and Immanuel Mission was at the end of the track.

As a result, the arrival of any vehicle at any time was a major event, and when Dan and I were small, the second we detected the sound of a motor we would race each other into the house shouting excitedly, "Car! Car! There's a car coming—we can hear a car!" Mother would be embarrassed by such a display of naïve behavior by her sons and would try to quiet us with "Calm down, calm down. Now go out quietly and see who is visiting us."

There was only one road into the Mission from the outside world. We could see about half a mile up to where it came around the mesa, and we knew anyone coming down would have to stop at the Mission. We were familiar with the cars of the people we knew. The little blue roadster belonged to Miss Williams, the government nurse; a green pickup would be a BIA man; and other green vehicles could be a range conservationist or other government employee.

By the time the car bumped down to the gate we usually had identified the visitor, and Dan and I would be out to open the gate and welcome them to Immanuel Mission. However, if it was a strange car we would wait for Dad to do the honors. During all this time, the adults would be watching from a door or window, calm and discreet but curious, as Dad went out with the two excited little boys following close behind him.

Usually, unrecognized cars would turn out to be government employees trying to find their way to some other destination, but, confused by the dim track and lack of road signs, ending up at a dead end. Occasionally they had been assigned a specific project and were looking for a place to set up a base camp. Accordingly, we would give directions or make suggestions as to where they might find an accessible source of water, the most important factor in any campsite.

THE CAMPBELL FAMILY

The first kinfolk I remember visiting Immanuel Mission were Mother's sister Ruth Campbell, with Uncle Dick and my three cousins, who came in the

Dick and Ruth Campbell, Clara, Glen, Marie, David, and Bob,
with Ruthie and Alwin competing for space on H. A.'s lap.

early 20s while construction of the new buildings was still under way. An old photograph shows an uncomfortable Grandfather Holcomb seated outside the old rock house with four grandchildren, David and Bob standing at attention beside him and Ruthie and me competing for lap space. I do not remember much more of the Campbell visit, although there is an apocryphal story of a picnic in which Uncle Dick became disgusted with a cold cup of thermos coffee while eating the lunch in his car and attempted to throw it out a window that unfortunately was closed.

Eight years later I was to spend most of the summer with the Campbell family in Ypsilanti, Michigan, on my fabulous first trip Back East and up to Canada.

FAMILIE ARMERDING

The Armerdings were associated with the Holcombs during the early years on the Navajo Reservation and remained personal friends of our family for three generations. Carl Armerding, with his sister Minnie, established the Immanuel Mission at Winslow, Arizona, and she remained in this Navajo work when he left to attend the University of New Mexico and preach in Spanish at a little Mexican church. He also took a leading role in the Plymouth Brethren Assembly in Albuquerque.

Their parents, Ernst and Gebke Armerding, came to the United States from Germany long before the turn of the century and settled and raised a family of ten in New Jersey. A stocky man with a square beard and heavy accent, "Father" Armerding often visited his children in the Wild West. I met him on several occasions and was fascinated by his stories of life in pre–World War Germany, as they maintained strong ties to his home country until one visit to Germany with Carl, during the Nazi regime.

Father Armerding had great difficulties getting out of the country to return to his adopted home. This, and the fact he became extremely ill on that trip after overindulging in rich Old Country food, made him vehemently exclaim, "I learnt my lesson!" and he remained in New Jersey, never to stray again.

When Mother and Dad moved to Albuquerque in 1923, they lived for a short time in the same apartment building with Grandfather Holcomb's companion in the quest for the location of Immanuel Mission, Carl Armerding, and later Mother delighted in relating their experiences of the time.

Carl had one passion the good people at the Assembly probably never knew about. He had never lost his German love of brew, and, as such beverages were not available at that time of Prohibition, he often had his own home brew working in the basement. Sometimes he miscalculated his timing, and Mother and Dad would occasionally wake in the middle of the night to the sound of exploding bottles somewhere down below their little room.

Carl graduated from the University of New Mexico and continued his education, eventually receiving an Honorary Doctor of Divinity degree from what is now Dallas Theological Seminary. He had an active career as a missionary, itinerant preacher, and teacher in the United States, Canada, and New Zealand. He was invited by H. A. Ironside to join the faculty of Dallas Theological Seminary and later served at Moody Bible Institute and Wheaton College.

After decades of service on boards, church and mission station tours, and mission trips to Central America and Europe, he retired and died at the age of 98 in the Bay Area of California. Throughout the 1920s and 30s we continued to have contact with the Armerding family, but I have absolutely no recollection of ever meeting Carl Armerding.

Minnie Armerding, Carl's sister, was at Immanuel Bible Chapel not far from the southern Navajo Reservation for most of the rest of her life, and we met her often at the Southwest Bible Conference in Flagstaff and on other occasions. Once, on a trip home after a visit to the ranch in Oak Creek, we stayed overnight with Minnie at the Immanuel Mission in Winslow.

When I was about ten, Minnie Armerding drove out to our Mission with her fifteen-year-old nephew, Hudson. One day I took him down to see a unique small slot canyon several miles west of the Mission, where the *tó chin lin* (water going through narrow place) narrows into a short sandstone canyon perhaps fifty feet deep and, in places, less than ten feet wide. It was a sunny day, and we wandered through the canyon without incident, but after a cloudburst in the mountains, muddy runoff water would come down in a sudden flood, carrying brush and logs and maybe an unfortunate animal, and rage through the narrow slot. I have seen it foam up to within a few feet of the solid rock brink of the canyon.

On our walk back to the Mission, Hudson and I were collecting some small colored rocks when we passed a small hill and noticed that a recent sandstorm had blown away the sand and exposed what looked to be the top of a human skull. We stopped to examine the site and brushed away enough sand to find that it was the site of an ancient burial. We did not uncover any more of the skeleton, as I knew the Navajos would resent any actions that could possibly disturb an evil spirit, and we quietly walked on home.

Several days later, Minnie and Hudson left to return to Winslow, and Dad, Mother, and I accompanied them as far as Shiprock, the three of them following closely behind Hudson and me in Minnie's car. Hudson was new at driving but did a praiseworthy job of negotiating the sandy Reservation road, and he was exceptionally proud when he successfully applied Dad's instructions for driving a car through a drift of sand: "Put her in second, step on the gas, and don't stop or you will go down!"

Hudson followed the Armerding family tradition of higher education and went on to Wheaton College near Chicago, a college committed to intellectual integrity and historic Christian orthodoxy. He became president of the college in 1965 and remained in that office until 1982, the longest serving president in the history of that institution.

Several years later at the Southwest Indian Bible Conference in Flagstaff, I met another third-generation member of the Armerding family, a tall friendly fellow we called "Long John" Hurley. We took part in several events together and, after the conference closed, he and his mother came down to the ranch for a final evening in Arizona before they returned Back East.

THE TAYLOR FAMILY

In the early 20s the Taylors, a missionary family serving in Colombia, South America, came to the United States on furlough and visited Immanuel Mission for several weeks. How another family of four fit into the small Mission building I do not know, as I was less than two at the time, but pictures and stories of that time are part of our family lore.

A black and white Kodak snapshot shows their young son Leslie sitting with me on a blanket. In a recent encounter with some Navajo youngsters I had acquired lice, and the simple solution had been to shave my head, so I was completely bald and, worse, had no teeth. Leslie had the advantage over me with not only a full head of beautiful hair but a few teeth. In any altercation I would pull Leslie's hair and he would bite me.

The Taylors had a truck with Gospel messages prominently painted on the side panels, and one day while out driving, they started to cross an arroyo up in the *tsé tah* ("among the rocks") area that looked perfectly dry and safe. However, it had been raining up in the nearby Carrizo Mountains, and a sudden wall of floodwater suddenly came down and completely engulfed the family and their truck. Fortunately they managed to escape, but the truck was swamped, and it was several days before we were able to dig it out.

The traders ever after referred to the place as "Gospel Wash."

RAY MCALLISTER

At that time, it was popular for young men with the desire to "see the world" to work their way abroad on cargo ships, usually to Europe. Another early visitor to Immanuel Mission was Ray McAllister, who had recently returned from an adventure that took him to Japan as a hand on a grain ship, in which his sole assignment was to stay below decks with the large cargo of grain to detect any fire that might start. Not exactly an exciting voyage, but he had a number of great tales of his adventures in the Land of the Rising Sun once he arrived there. One experience that really intrigued me was his description of the Japanese "paper house" where he stayed as the guest of a Japanese family that gave him a mat and a wooden pillow for sleeping.

SHIRLEY FILLMORE

One summer, when I was about eight years old, I learned that Shirley Fillmore, a cousin on Mother's side of the family and a distant relative of President Millard Fillmore, was coming to visit. Although a stranger to us, Shirley was to be treated with respect at all times by Danny and me.

To our astonishment, the Cousin Shirley who arrived one evening was not a young woman but an old man of nearly eighty, who immediately caught my imagination when he first stepped out of the car, by casually remarking as we unloaded his luggage, "Careful with that bag, it's been up the Amazon twice." He then told us he just had it on loan from his son-in-law, who was involved in the Ford rubber production in Brazil, but I was greatly impressed and thenceforth treated him, and his bag, with the greatest respect.

Shirley Fillmore proved to be the most fun of all the visitors we had over our years at Immanuel Mission. Even though we considered him ancient, he insisted we call him just "Shirley," and he was always ready to take part in small-boy activities. He romped around with Danny and me in games we had never heard of before and entertained us with many tales of pre–Civil War life on a small family farm in northern Michigan.

I was particularly intrigued one day when we were driving through *tsé tah* and he remarked, "Those rocks just make my arms ache!" He went on to describe loading large boulders on a "stone boat" and dragging them out of the creek bed on their farm, and I wondered how a stone-loaded horse sled could be pulled up a hill as I had difficulty making my sled even go down a hill. Shirley's history stories were interesting to Danny and me, but his best stories, in our opinion, were the vivid details of how he survived a bus accident the year before and the tales of his great adventures afterwards in a hospital.

Shirley had a refreshing zest for living and also talked of all the great things he planned to do. Mother tended to dismiss his grandiose plans for the future, but some time after he departed, we were astonished by a letter relating his marrying a much younger woman and investing in a citrus grove near Phoenix. We haven't heard from Shirley since—but I am not sure we won't.

MR. HASKELL

A man with a first name which I never learned, although I'm sure he had one, arrived alone one afternoon, driving an old black car with a huge trunk strapped on the back. During his stay he unloaded that trunk and decided to leave it with us. Aunt Clara and Mother were not eager to accept the ugly old box, and there were several discussions as to what should be done with it. As soon as he departed, it was hauled up to the attic of the house as a place to store clothing. That old "Haskell trunk" remained in the family for over fifty years.

During his short stay at Immanuel Mission, Mr. Haskell was completely fascinated by the Indians and was determined to learn as much as he possibly could during the time he was there. He constantly tried to initiate conversations with the Navajos who dropped by the Mission, but they were reluctant to open up to the strange *bilagáana* asking so many questions and constantly writing in a small notebook.

One morning I happened by when he was standing at the well with his notebook and pencil, talking with Yellowhair, who had just drawn a bucket of water from the well. Yellowhair was patiently trying to help the old fellow learn the Navajo language by pointing and saying, "*deesk'aaz,*" cold. Mr. Haskell carefully made a note in his journal, then turned to me eagerly and asked, "Now, does that mean water or a well?" So much for scientific field research.

AROUND THE DEVIL'S BACKBONE
One morning Grandfather Holcomb, Dad, and Yellowhair left the Mission in the early morning to go up into the foothills to cut a wagonload of firewood. Much to my disgust, I had not been invited to take part in that wood-gathering expedition.

About midmorning after they left, two government men arrived in a pickup and asked to see Grandfather Holcomb. Mother and Aunt Clara were alone with two young kids when these visitors arrived and insisted they had to see Grandfather Holcomb. No one else at home knew how to reach the place where the wood party was working, but I did, and after much discussion Mother reluctantly offered my services as a guide. I was not eager to go off with these white strangers, and they looked at the barefooted six-year-old kid with consternation, but, as they had no alternative other than to wait at the Mission until sundown, they reluctantly accepted my services and we set off.

About two miles east of the Mission I directed them to turn off the "road" and follow a wagon track across an arroyo and up a hill, and soon we came to a black lava dike, locally known by the traders as the "Devil's Backbone" but always referred to by the folks at Immanuel Mission as the "Rock Fence," a rough translation of the Navajo name *tsé'iigháán.*

The outcropping of black rock blocked our way, but I knew the only gap in the formidable dike and pointed out the way through a maze of loose boulders. The two men looked at each other but drove on, and we found the opening, picked our way through, and continued grinding along very slowly. As we ploughed up yet another embankment the government men looked at me nervously, and asked, "Are you sure this is the right way, kid?" And then, "Will we be able to get back?"

I confidently answered that this was where the work party had gone that morning, as the wagon track was plain to see there on the ground before us, and we went several miles farther up into the foothills of the Carrizo Mountains and entered the trees. Just before the men decided the kid had gotten them hopelessly lost, we came upon a surprised Grandfather, Dad, and Yellowhair standing by a half-loaded wagon. They had heard the truck coming long before we appeared, but did not expect me to be riding with the visitors.

After a short discussion their business was completed, and the government men were ready to return down the hill, but in the meantime I had persuaded Dad I should stay with the work detail, so the government men were on their own. Evidently they were able to follow their own tracks back to civilization as we never saw them again. As for me, I had an unexpected but very good day with the men on the mountain!

LOST AND FOUND

Not long after my short career as a guide, another group of government agents came out from the Agency at Shiprock and stayed at the Mission for most of a day, discussing some proposed project in our area.

After this, they walked around the Mission grounds to inspect some of Grandfather's agricultural accomplishments with his system of small dams around the Mission, which created a channel for rainwater runoff into a reservoir from which he could irrigate his small vegetable garden. It also provided a degree of erosion control. I was in no way involved with this business and had, in fact, been discouraged from even tagging along to listen to their conversation.

The next day, I was checking the hillside where they had been walking and found a fat wallet in the sand. Excited with my discovery, I ran to the house and displayed my treasure. Mother was immediately concerned and questioned me closely as to where and how I had found such a valuable object. The rest of the family became involved with the discussion, and finally decided that the wallet should be opened to identify its owner.

It turned out to be one of yesterday's visitors, a large, important-looking man who, we had learned, was visiting the Agency from Washington, D.C. I was not allowed to further touch my find and no one looked further to see what else it contained.

About a week later it came time for Mother and Dad to go to Farmington for supplies, and they took me along. We passed through Shiprock just after sunset that evening and went directly to the Agency headquarters, which were closed, but someone directed us to the farm section of the Agency, down by the San Juan River.

We eventually located the men, playing horseshoes in the cool of the evening, and Mother, who had been holding the wallet for safekeeping, handed

Clara at the Black Rock Fence, known to traders as the Devil's Backbone.

it to me and told me not to open it but return it to its owner. I was to explain how I had found it, but under no circumstances was I to take any money from this man. I suspected there was a considerable sum of money in the billfold as I could see a stack of green edges but dutifully obeyed Mother's instructions exactly as given. Hesitantly I approached the group of men, who had stopped playing to watch us.

Immediately I identified the big man who had been at the Mission and walked up and handed him his lost fortune. He was thunderstruck that the pesky little kid that had followed them around when he was out on the Reservation should appear out of the dusk with his wallet.

He opened it to confirm it was his and see if it was intact, then thanked me profusely, pulled out a bill, and offered it to me. I really wanted that money, but, following orders, I thanked him and marched back to the car, leaving a puzzled man from Washington standing there wondering about a strange little missionary kid who refused to take money.

NEVER AGAIN

One summer several men assigned to a government project in an area near Immanuel Mission asked if they could rent the stone house for the several weeks they would be working in the area. The missionaries were not happy to allow such an arrangement but finally consented. We must have been very short on funds to agree to let any strange men live at the Mission. Still, they did, and for several weeks we had a couple of big green BIA trucks parked in our yard.

Our new tenants were quite an experience, and Danny and I watched them carefully to learn how white men behaved back in civilization. They seemed to smoke a lot and laugh and talk loudly and made considerably more noise than a group of Navajos. They also spoke a very colorful language with many interesting words we had never heard before and often didn't understand.

Mother, however, was not too pleased with having her young impressionable sons observing these men, and particularly offensive to her was the constant smoking and loud, uncensored conversation. Then came the incident that really turned her against them.

She invited the three or four men over to the big adobe house one evening for dinner, as opposed to our regular "supper." Mother appreciated the few fine things she had, and she carefully prepared a meal of several courses and set out the hand-painted china that Aunt Ruth Campbell had crafted for her years before.

The pale green plates and delicate cups with their tiny pink roses were her most prized possession, and she had once confessed that her attachment to them might be a transgression of the admonition in Scripture not to place faith in worldly possessions.

The visitors did not comment on the table and lace cloth, the china, polished silver, or gleaming glasses, even though they were highly unusual for this outpost in the desert, but immediately sat down and started serving themselves the first course without waiting for our customary opening grace. Mother asked for attention and a temporary hush fell as Dad quietly asked the Lord's blessing on the food and on everyone present.

The meal began again and our visitors demonstrated considerable appetite and fell to eating with vigor. Loud exchanges involving incidents of their day were made, but there was no expression of appreciation of either the table or the well-prepared dinner. Mother coolly remained the gracious hostess, and the meal was completed with a beautiful cake she had painstakingly prepared.

The man across from me, sitting next to Mother, put his serving away in a few bites, pushed his chair back, pulled out a pack of Camels, carelessly shook one out, and offered it to Mother—who politely refused.

She was speechless with horror, however, when he then proceeded to light up and throw the still burning match onto his plate. She recovered her ability to communicate immediately by snatching up the plate and wiping it with her napkin, only to discover a small burn had permanently smudged her treasured china plate.

Early one morning, soon after the plate incident, I spotted a couple of our visitors squatting and smoking outside the stone house and looking at a pile of potshards I had laboriously collected from an old Anasazi camp site I had discovered near the Mission. In addition to shards there was a metate and several grinding stones that I had also found and lugged home, and at first I was proud to see them examining my treasured bits of clay, painted with black and white and red designs ... But when I realized that, after looking at each piece, they were casually throwing it against the stone metate to see if it would shatter ... then I joined Mother in anticipating their early departure.

When that day finally arrived, we went in to clean the emptied house and found the heavy smoking had permeated all the curtains and fabrics. It took days to air the stench out of every room, and that was the last time any building at Immanuel Mission was ever rented to anyone!

MISS WILLIAMS

All government employees I ever saw on the Reservation were men, except for one proper little field nurse who was solely responsible for meeting the Navajo medical needs of our entire corner of the Reservation. She had all the niceties of civilization that were absent in our former tenants of the rock house.

Miss Williams—I never knew her by any other name—was a native Londoner but no stranger to the life of the frontier. She had lived for a number of years in India, and as she got to know us, she matter-of-factly related some astounding stories of life in that exotic, faraway place. She had worked as a nurse during the glory days of the British Raj. She had then come to the United States and somehow ended up in our far corner of the Navajo Reservation, with literally hundreds of Navajos to serve in a dusty, barren land with absolutely no paved roads at all.

She didn't often get as far afield from her headquarters in Shiprock as Immanuel Mission, so it was always an occasion when I spotted her little green car bumping down our road, and long before she reached the Mission fence, I was out with the opened gate to escort her in.

Often Miss Williams brought Mother old copies of newspapers her mother had sent from England, and I spent hours studying the pictures and reading articles about the strange, exotic activities of British royalty at the time of George V. If their activities had been as colorful as those of the present royal family, I am sure Mother would not have let me read her newspaper.

There was only one period when I didn't welcome Miss Williams, and that was while she was giving us a series of typhoid shots. Her schedule often brought her to the Mission on Thursday, and I hated that day and its needle and always felt great relief as soon as I had received it.

But only until the weekend. Then I would begin to think of the next Thursday's shot, with escalating terror, until she reappeared. I retained that dread of shots for thirty years until I was in the hospital for two weeks and received about a dozen daily shots, but Thursdays to this day still make me a little uneasy.

One afternoon Miss Williams ran into a large sand dune that had blown across the road, miles out in the desert, and she soon became so mired down

Superintendent A. H. Neal with Dan and Alwin
on a visit to the Mission.

that she couldn't go either forward or back. Not a car came along that day or the following night, and by the afternoon of the second day she ran out of water. Her situation was growing desperate when she suddenly saw behind her a convoy of three cars plowing through the sand toward her stranded car and thought she had started hallucinating.

It was not unusual for travelers to form a convoy when headed through sandy country, and the timely appearance of a dozen traders and government employees and a couple of Navajos relieved her anxiety. They all jumped out and set to digging her car out of the sand, and when she was free she was happy to join the convoy through the sand dunes.

She arrived at Immanuel Mission somewhat the worse for wear and unwillingly took a break at the Mission, but only because Mother insisted she eat and take a nap. She did rest for a short time, then dutifully pushed on, as she was already a day late in her schedule!

DERIC NUSBAUM

Two young men drove up to the Mission one day and stopped to talk with us. I was about nine at the time and had seen their car long before they arrived, so I was on the spot to listen in on the conversation when they introduced themselves, but I caught only one name, "Nusbaum." They said they were interested in Anasazi ruins, and had heard of *tsegi hoch cho* (twisted, rough, "good for nothing," per Aunt Florence) canyon just south of the Mission, and wanted directions on how to get there.

We had often been in the lower canyon and visited many of the Navajo camps in that area but were not very familiar with the many branches of the upper canyons. So Dad told them how to drive to within a couple of miles from the mouth of the canyon, where all semblance of a road ended, and then how to find a trail that would lead them into the many sandstone canyons and alcoves of the interior.

Dad also cautioned them not to attempt the trip so late in the afternoon and invited them to stay overnight at the Mission and start their expedition in the morning. They declined and chose to camp in a small arroyo not far east of the Mission. We gave them water and offered any other assistance they might need, and off they went.

A little later Mother called me and said she thought the visiting strangers should have firewood to cook their supper, so she instructed me to take my little wagon, go out to the woodpile, and get enough wood for a small campfire.

I was very hesitant to approach the white strangers, but I had my marching orders, so I loaded up my wagon and left on my errand. It was less than 100 yards to the campsite, but sand and brush made the going slow as I dragged my loaded wagon to the edge of the wash and down to their temporary camp.

I found both young men resting against one bank of the wash, eating a cold meal. They stopped eating and looked at the boy with a loaded wagon. "Where are you going with that trash, kid?" the one called Nusbaum asked sharply. "I just brought it down to see if you could use it," I replied meekly.

"Well, don't dump it here in our camp, take it on around that bend!" was the brisk reply, so off I trudged with my rejected cargo. I couldn't waste good kindling and firewood, so I climbed back up out of the wash and hauled my trash home and had a lot of explaining to do to Mother as to why I had failed in my mission. The next day the two young fellows were up by daybreak and headed on their way up the canyons, and I never saw either again, I was glad to say.

Research later revealed that the young man who didn't want my trash was Deric Nusbaum, adopted son of Jesse L. Nusbaum. The older Nusbaum was a leading archaeologist of the 1920s, who served for many years as superintendent of Mesa Verde National Park and also was the founder of the Laboratory of Anthropology at Santa Fe. Deric Nusbaum also established a reputation for himself by writing two very interesting books about his experiences as a boy growing up at Mesa Verde, *Deric in Mesa Verde* and *Deric with the Indians*.

EVERETT RUESS

One beautiful spring morning when I was ten, one of the strangest visitors we ever had at Immanuel Mission came riding by, mounted on a burro, with a collection of camping equipment lashed around him and hanging from the patient animal. I was busy in the yard with one of my endless projects, this time making sand castings of molten lead (blissfully unaware it was later to be declared poisonous) and had not noticed that he was in the Mission.

As soon as I saw the fellow I noticed he was not a Navajo but a white boy of nineteen or twenty, dressed like a Navajo in Levi's, well-worn shirt, and battered old hat, singing some unfamiliar song or chant at the top of his voice. I immediately forgot the sand casting and rushed into the kitchen where Mother was preparing dinner and excitedly asked who the white guy was.

Mother seemed slightly upset and answered in an irritated voice that he was some kind of a tramp who had not seen either soap or water recently. "Well, where was he going and what did he want?" I persisted, and she replied, "He wanted directions to Sweetwater but I think he was just hanging around to see if he could get some of this dinner." Surprised, I asked, "You didn't ask him to stay?" and received the short answer, "No. There was something about him I just didn't like." She didn't offer any further comment and when I got back outside the hungry stranger was disappearing down the trail to *tó łikan* (Sweetwater).

We had no idea who this lonesome stranger was, but about a year later we learned that Everett Ruess, a young man in search of beauty and oneness with nature, had roamed the Navajo Reservation for several years. He was in the Four Corners area not long before he disappeared in the canyons near Escalante, Utah, in the winter of 1935. Two burros and pieces of equipment were later discovered, but Ruess was never seen again. His fate remains a mystery to this day.

LONESOME STRANGERS AND ODDBALLS

Some of the people that appeared at Immanuel Mission in the early 1920s really defy description. One eager young man came out to Immanuel Mission when I was less than five years old and became enthralled with the Indians, their language, their sheep, their exotic customs, the land, the mesas, the canyons, and even the sand.

The evening before he was to leave, Mother and Aunt Clara packed a picnic supper, and we all walked out to the foot of the mesa just north of the Mission. While we were eating our sandwiches and drinking lemonade our visitor became enchanted with cliffs above us and excitedly asked if there was some way to climb up there.

There was no trail, but Dad pointed out a logical route that might take him up to the rim. The young man rushed off, but the family remained below, talking and enjoying the cool evening rather than making a climb up to the top of the mesa, but occasionally we heard our visitor as he picked his way through the brush and rocks somewhere up above us.

All was quiet for a while before we heard him rattling around directly above us, then heard him shouting, "I made it! I'm up here, can you hear me?" We shouted back that we could hear him but we were ready to go home and he'd better come back down before it got dark.

We started packing and were prepared to leave when suddenly a shower of small rocks started dropping perilously close to us, and then large boulders came crashing down. He was apparently unconcerned as to where they were landing. We beat a hasty retreat, and just before we got home he finally came panting up from behind us with the piteous query, "Why didn't you wait for me?"

Several years later a strangely dressed older man came wandering in one day, wearing what appeared to be old army khakis, lace-up boots, and a digger hat. He was packing an overloaded rucksack on his back and carried a stout four-foot walking stick. We couldn't understand his name, and he finally unfolded and showed us a worn piece of paper with a string of consonants scrawled on it, something we couldn't decipher: Letters like w, y, cz, sv ... with an occasional vowel spaced apparently at random.

He also spoke to us earnestly about a quest he was on, but we never did understand exactly what it really was. After joining us for a hearty dinner he strode off on the trail toward Sweetwater, much to Mother's relief. During the next few days, however, we began hearing stories about a strange *bilagáana* wandering among the Navajos and finally a wild story from the *ma'ii deeshgiizhnii* outfit camped above a small arroyo a few miles west of Sweetwater Trading Post.

One afternoon, a big man was seen coming down along the wash while it was raging with a flash flood from a rain in the mountains. He stopped just below the camp and sat a while watching the water churn by. He appeared to be praying and singing, then suddenly stood up and started shouting as he waded into the muddy water. He was immediately swept off his feet and went struggling off down the stream.

One of the Navajo men watching this little drama from above jumped on a horse and rode down to the flood, roped the poor drowning pilgrim with his lariat, and dragged him back to firm ground. The sodden stranger sat gasping and spitting water for a few minutes and then got up and stumbled off down the wash, never to be seen again.

A few years later, during the early 1930s, an unusual little group of mounted people—three men and one woman—came by Immanuel Mission one evening and stopped to ask directions. They had good horses, much better than the ponies the Navajos usually rode, fine tack, and saddles with what appeared to be Navajo saddle blankets. They were certainly well-dressed to be riding the dusty trails of the Reservation. After a short discussion they rode off toward *tsegi* canyon and we never learned who they were.

Years later, however, I found an account by Wanden M. Kane that makes no reference to Immanuel Mission but does describe riding in a group through the Four Corners area in the summer of 1930 with her husband, Oliver Lafarge. In her book *What Am I Doing Here?* she mentions that Earl Morris, Charles Bernheimer, and John Wetherill accompanied her on that ride. If Charles Bernheimer, who had referred to us in his book, was indeed a member of the small party that visited Immanuel Mission that afternoon, he must have been amazed at how the tiny Hookum Mission had developed from a two-room stone post to a three-building fenced compound in less than five years.

THE LONE EAGLE

A very few people who were not really kinfolk, pilgrims, or government men occasionally passed through our area during the early years of the Mission and always created tremendous excitement for me when they did. I remember one visitor very well, although we never actually met.

Once or twice a year at Immanuel Mission I would occasionally hear a sound, instantly recognize it as an airplane, shout an alarm, and start scanning the sky overhead for the first glimpse of a phenomenal visitor. A flash of sunlight on a tiny speck in the distance would resolve into a small monoplane slowly coming into view and then moving slowly across the deep blue sky above the Mission, and away. I couldn't really identify any detail, and my imagination speculated wildly, but I never knew who was up there, so near yet so impossibly far away.

Charles Lindbergh was then the best-known and most-admired man in the entire civilized world. He burst into fame in 1920, with bold newspaper headlines proclaiming his landing in Paris after making the first solo flight across the Atlantic from New York. Lindbergh and his plane *The Spirit of St. Louis* were instantly caught in a storm of publicity and official recognition that drove this quiet man, who preferred being alone with his machine, nearly to distraction.

Like every red-blooded American boy of the time, I had a large photo of the "Lone Eagle," wearing his leather helmet and gazing up into the sky, pasted on my wall and avidly read any news or article about him that I could find in the papers that filtered through to us, as well as stories in *Boy's Life* and other magazines.

In the summer of 1929, Lindbergh married Anne Morrow and shot back into the national spotlight and universal adulation. The newlyweds found temporary respite that summer on an impromptu visit to Earl Morris's remote "Antelope House" archaeological dig in Canyon del Muerto, and during their short stay they made several flights back and forth over the Reservation, taking the first series of aerial photographs of archaeological sites in that remote area. One of those specks I watched up there in our sky could have well been the Lone Eagle, and I didn't even know it until the next century!

Navajos usually were not much concerned about airplanes or other exploits of the whites. There was a story in circulation about the time a small group of Navajos was standing in a trading post when the trader heard a distinct drone overhead and rushed outside shouting, "Airplane, there's an airplane up there!"

Several Navajos followed him out of the post and stood casually looking up. "That's a *chidi naat'a'i,* flying car, up there," the trader said. Still no response. "Don't you understand, there's a man up there in the sky." Nothing for a moment, and then an old man remarked dismissively, "*bilagáana,* isn't it?"

Dad explained airplanes to me, and I had read about them in *Compton's Encyclopedia,* but I wasn't too sure I wanted to actually fly in one. My concern wasn't about crashing. I just thought the floorboards in a light plane might be a little flimsy and could give way, sending me on a short-cut back to earth while the plane flew merrily off into the blue.

35 | Trading Posts

During my time at Immanuel Mission, three families dominated trading on the Navajo Reservation: Hubbell in the south, Babbitt Brothers in the west, and Foutz in the Four Corners area.

JOHN LORENZO HUBBELL

A member of mounted Missouri Volunteers who came to New Mexico with Kearny, James Hubbell was discharged from the army, married Lina Rubi, a member of an old Spanish land grant family that dated back to the early 1700s, and settled in Pajarito, near Albuquerque.

Their son, John Lorenzo Hubbell, was born and raised in New Mexico and attended school in Santa Fe. Then, after a stint as a postal clerk in Albuquerque, he set out on a horse to travel through the "little-known country" far from the outposts of white civilization. He worked as interpreter and labor superintendent for the Bureau of Indian Affairs at the Fort Defiance agency, and also in several of the trading posts on the Navajo Reservation before launching into trading on his own.

In about 1878 he established a trading post west of Fort Defiance at a place the Navajos called *lók'aahnteel* or "wide reeds," which was also called Pueblo Colorado. (Confusion with Pueblo, Colorado, eventually caused the post office to change the official name of the place to Ganado.)

Gradually, over the years, Hubbell became known by the Spanish term of respect, Don Lorenzo. However, the Navajos referred to him as *naakaii sání*, "old Mexican." Renowned for his hospitality, Hubbell always had an open-house policy and by his own account entertained as many as 150 guests at a time. Over the years he hosted an incredible number of distinguished people at his trading post in Ganado.

Both President Teddy Roosevelt and New Mexico governor and author Lew Wallace were guests, as well as dozens of others. Writers included George Wharton James, Charles Lummis, Dane Coolidge, Hamlin Garland, and Leo Crane. Among the artists were Maynard Dixon, Laura Armer, Joseph Mora, Mary Colton, E. A. Burbank, and W. R. Leigh, as well as photographers Edward Curtis and Carl Moon.

Hubbell did not accept any payment from his guests but did encourage them to buy one of the splendid Navajo weavings in his rug room.

During his lifetime Hubbell had an interest in more than thirty other trading posts scattered across the southern Navajo Reservation from Ganado to Narbona Pass. He was also associated with C. N. Cotton in a thriving wholesale business in Gallup that supplied traders with trade goods and also provided a market for Navajo trade items. Today the Hubbell Trading Post National Historic Site is one of the few posts still operating as a store on the Navajo Reservation and is a very important tourist destination.

BABBITT BROTHERS

Five Babbitt brothers—David, George, William, Charles, and Edward—came to Arizona in 1886 and immediately got into the cattle business by buying a herd, it is said for $17,640. They established the CO-Bar brand, named after their hometown of Cincinnati, Ohio, and started an operation north of Flagstaff, right along the edge of the Navajo Reservation.

In 1889 they organized the Babbitt Trading Company as a general merchandising operation in Flagstaff, and they began supplying trade goods to the new trading posts springing up around the Little Colorado River. In 1891 the Babbitts acquired Lake Trading Post, the first of many posts they eventually operated all over the western part of the Reservation, including the post in Tuba City, very near the Mission at *kin łigaai.*

The numerous Hubbell and Babbitt trading operations were south and west of Immanuel Mission, and personally, I had almost no actual contact with these two fabulous empires. I did, however, have extensive contact with the Foutz family.

THE FOUTZES

Joseph Levi Foutz converted to Mormonism and crossed the plains to Utah at about the same time as Jacob Hamblin. After serving time as sheriff of Sevier County in Utah, he moved on to Tuba City, where he was a co-worker with Hamblin in missionary efforts with the Hopis and Navajos. When the BIA assumed control of Tuba City in 1903, Foutz moved with a number of other Mormons to settlements in Fruitland and Kirtland, in New Mexico, that had been established a few years earlier in the LDS Church's push to occupy the Four Corners.

Accompanying Foutz to New Mexico were his two wives, sixteen daughters, and thirteen sons. Six of these sons—June, Alma, Hugh, Jess, Leroy, and Luff—became prominent in trading. At the time I was on the Reservation, they and their sons owned or operated over twenty trading posts in the Northern Navaho Agency area, at a time when there were fewer than ninety trading posts on the entire Reservation.

Old Teec Nos Pos Trading Post.

PROGRESSIVE MERCANTILE
Soon after the turn of the century, the brothers-in-law June and Al Foutz and
Sheldon Dustin purchased a wholesale house in Fruitland, on a joint owner
basis, to provide a source of trading goods and supplies for the family posts in
the Four Corners area operated by the sons and sons-in-law of the Foutz family.

Supplies were purchased wholesale from Ilfeld's in Gallup and hauled
overland to Fruitland by teams of six horses pulling wagons and trailers. The
Progressive Mercantile later branched into a number of other activities, such as
sheep ranching and even Chevrolet and Maytag agencies.

TÓ ŁIKAN
Sweetwater was the trading post nearest to Immanuel Mission and the one we
knew best. Three miles straight north of Immanuel Mission by trail, and about
five miles by a primitive road around the end of a mesa, it was a bleak little place
with a couple of small buildings, a corral, and a water trough. It was completely
isolated by hills surrounding it on all sides, which cut off all view of the mesa
and mountains beyond. This trading post was also owned by the ubiquitous
Foutz family and operated alternately by two members of the family, Roy Foutz
and Asael Palmer, who was married to Lois Foutz.

Both had homes in the Fruitland area, and their families usually remained
in town during the school year but often came out to stay at the trading post
during the summer months. Asael Palmer was a staunch friend of the Holcombs,

who knew him as "Ace." During the critical early years of Immanuel Mission, although he was Mormon and Immanuel Mission was Plymouth Brethren, he was active in getting Navajo signatures on the original petition to permit Immanuel Mission to build on the Reservation. He was the first to appear with aid during the early disasters of fire and windstorm at the Mission.

On the Holcombs' first Christmas in 1922, Ace came over to the Mission with a surprise dinner of chicken, pickles, a big can of peaches, cake, and candies for the struggling Holcomb family. He also brought mail out to Immanuel Mission from the post office in Shiprock whenever he was in town on business, and he cooperated with the Mission in getting injured and desperately ill Navajos to the hospital in Shiprock.

The Palmer and Girdner families occasionally visited during the summer months, and I got well acquainted with three of his good-looking daughters, Bobby, June, and Marylou, as well as his two sons, Jim and Bill. The two families sometimes celebrated the Fourth of July together, usually with fireworks, when we were at the trading post.

I particularly remember the Palmers saving some of the best fireworks for the equally important Pioneer Day, a holiday in Utah that commemorated July 24, 1847, when Brigham Young, the prophet and president of the LDS Church, led the first band of pioneer Saints out of the mouth of Emigration Canyon, and, upon seeing the Great Salt Lake Valley below, declared, "This is the place!"

One summer Mr. Palmer was short-handed at Sweetwater and was also short on supplies for the trading post. Dad needed to go to town, too, so he volunteered to drive the trading post truck to Fruitland and pick up supplies at the Progressive Mercantile. I asked to go with him, and just as we were leaving Sweetwater, Bill Palmer decided to go along. So the three of us set off for Fruitland.

Soon after we concluded the business in Fruitland, made a stop in Shiprock, and were started home, Bill and I decided it was too crowded sitting three deep in the cab and chose to ride with the sacks, boxes, and barrels in the back of the truck.

Somewhat to Dad's discomfort, we began playing around back there, and when I flung up one hand my ring slipped off my finger and flew off into the brush. We signaled Dad to stop the truck by pounding on the roof, and all three of us jumped out for a futile search in the sand and bushes along the road. Today, somewhere out on Waterless Mesa there is a little lost silver ring set with a beautiful row of seed turquoise.

TEEC NOS POS

We gradually became acquainted with a number of the other traders operating trading posts in the Four Corners region at that time. The first stop on the road from Immanuel Mission to Shiprock was Teec Nos Pos, (*t'iis názbas*) or "Cottonwood Circle," established in 1905 by Hambleton Noel. It was sold to Burt

Dustin in 1913 and operated by the Foutz family for many years. The original trading post was an old rock building north of the present post, near the grove of cottonwood trees that gave the place its name. A small settlement consisting of a government school building and the house of the BIA representative, at that time the Gresham family, stood on the hill just above the trading post.

This trading post burned some time after we left the Reservation and was rebuilt near the present highway, paved Navajo Highway 160, and is the post office for that part of the Four Corners area, including Immanuel Mission. But in the early 1930s it took a couple of hours of strenuous driving from Immanuel Mission through *tsé tah* (the notorious maze of rocks), around the northern point of Pastoria Peak (the high point of the Carrizo Mountains), then across a treacherous area of permanent sand dunes, and down a steep dug way to reach the original Teec Nos Pos.

When I first visited Teec Nos Pos it was operated by Paul Brink, an experienced trader who had previously operated several trading posts on the Reservation. I remember one early visit when Brink showed us an old silver-mounted bridle that looked to be of Spanish origin. The Navajo man who brought the bridle in to trade told of finding it in the hills above the trading post, and it appeared ancient; however, by then many Navajos had become quite adept at copying silverwork.

BECLABITO

Just after the road to Shiprock, now Highway 64, crossed into New Mexico, stood Beclabito. This was a trading post originally built in 1911 by Billy Hunter and operated by Biffle Morris until Hugh Foutz, a brother of Roy Foutz at Sweetwater, bought the store in 1924 and operated it during our time on the Reservation.

At that time we understood the name to be a corruption of the Navajo *bi'klah bito,* "Left Hand's Water," as there was a little spring at the post, and we assumed it was named for an early left-handed trader. Today it is believed the name derives from *bitł'ááh bito'* or "water underneath." Regardless of origin, today it's pronounced "Beclabito" to rhyme with "grab your toe."

Hugh Foutz was a very quiet, soft-spoken man, but I was awed by the story that he had been a sniper in France during World War I and was reputed to be the best shot on the Reservation and could "shoot rabbits from a moving car." However, he never demonstrated any such activities in my presence. I do remember one subzero night when we were returning from town and he insisted we stay with his family overnight and continue our journey over the frozen road to Immanuel Mission in the morning.

In the foothills of the Carrizo Mountains not far from Beclabito, the road crossed a valley just under the foothills at a place the Navajos called "the place where the Mexicans cried." I never knew which Mexicans or why they wept.

But I imagine it was the site of a successful Navajo ambush of one of the many war parties that rode into Navajo country periodically to avenge Navajo raids along the Rio Grande, and perhaps pick up a few women and children for slaves while they were in the vicinity.

In this area there was also an unusual yellow cliff that featured a spectacular bold drawing of several galloping horses, probably a recent Navajo work.

DESHNA'S

After crossing into New Mexico, just on the other side of the bridge across the San Juan River, stood the first of the three trading posts in Shiprock at that time, which was owned and operated by Deshna Clah Cheschillie. This trading post catered almost exclusively to Navajo customers, but we occasionally dropped in to visit the man who had been so instrumental in getting the original Immanuel Mission charter signed.

A big grove of cottonwood trees stood across the road from this trading post, and sometimes on trips to Shiprock we stopped there for a picnic lunch. On one occasion it also served us as a campground by the river for Dad and me for a couple of nights when our car was having extensive repairs up at the Evans garage.

SHIPROCK TRADING POST

At the foot of the big hill on the south side of Shiprock was a trading post that had been established in 1897. It had been owned and operated since 1903 by an old-time trader called Will Evans, a cheerful round-faced man who was born in Wales. One quiet morning, Aunt Clara and I were in his trading post when he was reminiscing about his introduction to the life of a trader on the Reservation before the turn of the century. As a greenhorn in the winter of 1898, he was sent as trader to the remote Sanostee Trading Post on the eastern edge of the Carrizo Mountains.

This was his first trading post job, and that winter a deep snow so completely cut off that trading post that even the Navajos didn't come to trade. He was isolated for weeks, he told us, living on "beans, Irish stew, canned peaches, and Arbuckle's coffee, and I got so lonely I was reading everything I could find, including the fine print on the tomato cans, singing songs, telling myself stories, and writing atrocious poetry." I was intrigued by his use of the word "atrocious," and as soon as we got back to Immanuel Mission, I looked the word up in the dictionary and was rather disappointed to find it had a much different meaning than the word "salacious."

Years later this story appeared almost exactly word for word in his own book, *Along Navajo Trails: Recollections of a Trader 1898–1948.*

On another trip to town I was in Farmington on Memorial Day and watched as the annual parade of Farmington and Aztec high school bands, Boy Scouts, fraternal groups, cowboys, elected officials, and veterans in their too-tight uniforms all marched down Main Street, flying flags and waving to the cheering townspeople.

The last entry was an open car with "Grandpa Evans," a white-bearded old man, riding with two other men. They were three lonely old Civil War veterans who sat silently looking straight ahead and ignoring the cheering of the crowd. I do not know which Evans family he belonged to, Evans the garage man or Evans the trader.

BERNARD TRADING POST

Bruce Bernard, *niiyal* ("tilts his head") to the Navajos, was one of the best-known traders in the area. He came west from Kentucky in 1909 and bought and operated a trading post in Shiprock for some time before joining the army. He was stationed at Camp Pike near Little Rock, Arkansas, with Private Glen Girdner.

Dad once told me of going out one evening, before the war ended, with the fellow from New Mexico and sitting on a log in the unfamiliar wooded country and talking about back home in the Southwest. They were both discharged from the army in 1918, and Dad returned to Arizona. He had lost all contact with his army associates until, on his first trip to Shiprock after arriving at Immanuel Mission, he noticed a large building on the hill near the post office bearing the name "Bernard Trading Post," and he went over to see if it was really his old army buddy.

The moment he stuck his head in the door, Bruce shouted, "Hello, Red!" And after that, Dad frequently dropped by the trading post when he was in Shiprock to talk about "those times in the army" with Bruce. At that time Standard Oil was drilling one of its first wells at their new Rattlesnake Lease on the Navajo Reservation, some eight miles south of Shiprock. One evening Dad was in Bernard's trading post and watched as Bruce poured some liquid from a small bottle on the flagstone floor, then lighted a match and threw it onto the liquid, and it instantly burst into flame.

All the men standing in the bullpen crowded around the blaze to examine this strange liquid that was pumped from the ground just outside town, but Dad was struck by the fact that although the white men in the group started talking excitedly about this strange phenomenon of burning liquid, the Navajos turned away completely indifferent—or pretending to be.

Several years after the "oil incident," Mother took me with her to town, and when we stopped at the tiny one-woman post office at the top of the hill in Shiprock to claim the Mission mail sack, she gave me money and told me to go over to the Bernard Trading Post next door and buy some small items on her shopping list.

I entered the store with some trepidation and approached the counter, which was about even with my eyes. Mr. Bernard waited on me himself, and, after we completed the transaction, told me about knowing my dad long ago and very far away during the war. I was astonished that he knew me, but I didn't know what

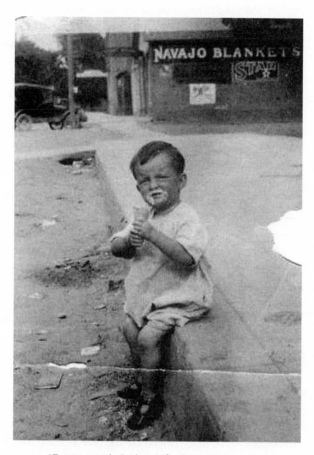

"Eat it outside:" Alwin's first ice cream cone
on a visit to Farmington.

to reply so, Navajo-style, didn't say anything. Bernard must have thought his old pal Red had a pretty slow kid.

RATTLESNAKE

I was interested in the oil-drilling operation near Shiprock but was also just a little uneasy about the place. Not so much about oil—we used that in our lamps at the Mission—but about the name of the place, "Rattlesnake." Snakes of all kinds were serious business in my young life, and the rattlesnake was the scariest of all.

One day on the way back home from Shiprock, Mother took the Rattlesnake turnoff at the "apples" sign, and we bumped along for some time until we reached the oil operation. The actual drilling site was something of a disappointment for me. My impression was of utter confusion, with a lot of noise, very large machinery, and rough-looking men rushing around turning valves and pulling up pipe from the ground. There also seemed to be a lot of mud involved.

RED MESA

Bob Martin abandoned his trading post at *dógózhii tah* in 1917 and was established at another store at Red Mesa when he first met Grandfather Holcomb. He remained at Red Mesa until 1933, when he sold the post to Willard Stolworthy and established a trading post south of the San Juan near Fruitland. During much of our time at Immanuel Mission, the Red Mesa post was operated by a nephew of Stolworthy, Roscoe Magee.

TSE LICHÍÍ' DEEZ' AHÍ AND NAAKII-TÓ

Rock Point, now called *tse' lichíí' deez' ahí,* was west of Immanuel Mission and the closest trading post in that direction. It could only be reached by driving over one of the most abominable roads on the Reservation, twenty miles of solid sandstone beneath the wheels of our struggling little car. Established in 1916, it was known then as *béésh 'ii' àhí,* "raised metal," for an early windmill erected there by a former trader.

One year Dad operated the Rock Point Trading Post for perhaps two weeks when Dan Christensen, the trader at that time, left the Reservation to take his wife closer to civilization when their baby was born. By that time Dad spoke creditable Navajo and was well received by the Navajos of the area, even though, as a missionary, he put the Bull Durham smoking tobacco down under the counter and moved the apples, another Navajo favorite, to the prominent spot usually reserved for the noxious weed. When Navajos asked for a smoke, Dad would truthfully reply it wasn't available at that time.

Dad also temporarily substituted once for Charles Ashcroft at Mexican Water, *naakii-tó,* another post run by H. B. Noel, just west of Red Mesa.

36 The Art of Trading

was most familiar with the trading posts at Sweetwater and Teec Nos Pos, and they were typical of most trading posts on the Reservation at that time. Most were just a small group of ugly, utilitarian buildings, usually unpainted and with very few improvements, as traders were licensed to trade on the Reservation but the land was leased and actually belonged to the tribe. All buildings would revert to the tribe if the post was closed.

A scarcity of water resulted in practically no trees or vegetation around the post, but there was usually a watering trough out front and a hitching post for Navajos to tie their horses. A gasoline pump for an occasional *bilagáana* visitor in a car stood to one side of the trading post, and the fuel was pumped by hand into a glass tank marked to show in gallons the amount being purchased. Regular gasoline was clear and a higher octane gasoline was purple.

Naalyéhé ya'sidáhí, roughly translated as "the fellow who sits watching his merchandise," was the Navajo description of a trader. He sat behind a counter that surrounded a large empty space called the "bull pen," with no furniture other than a large pot-bellied stove in the center of the room.

The flooring behind the counter where the trader sat was slightly higher than the bullpen, so the trader was a little above his customers. The counter itself, about elbow-high for an average man and far above the head of a small boy, was all of 40 inches wide to discourage an enterprising Navajo from reaching or jumping over for self-service when the trader was not looking.

Behind the counter were rows of shelves, often made of Arbuckle's Coffee crates, running all around the wall in a horseshoe that completely enclosed the bullpen, where the Navajo customers and onlookers stood or sat on the hard-packed dirt floor around the large stove in the center of the room.

On the counter up front by the trader was a glass case filled with hard candies, Wrigley's chewing gum, Prince Albert tobacco, and a slab of Bull Durham tobacco. Just outside the case, a small box of Prince Albert for cigarette makings was attached to the counter and accessible only through a narrow, spiked slot that allowed only a small sample pinch at a time.

Trade goods were arranged on the shelves to a height of about eight feet. First were the groceries, mostly boxed, bagged, or canned goods. Cans of

Navajo demonstrating a grinding machine.

tomatoes and peaches shared space with coffee, baking powder, lard, salt, and sacks of sugar and flour. A collection of enamelware pots, pans, and bowls came next, followed by a clothing section with colorful sateen shirts for men and wide-brim "Hoss Cartwright" hats and shoes, mostly in the smaller sizes.

Next were bolts of cloth in primary colors, including velveteen and bright calico yard goods for blouses, skirts, and shirts. Suspended from the ceiling were all kinds of goods: saddles, lanterns, buckets, rope, wool shears, Pendleton trade blankets, and dozens of other items.

The trader actually didn't have much time for just sitting and was usually busy working the space between the counter and the shelves, pulling items from the shelves or pegs and placing them on the counter as requested by the customer. As the trader had to walk around behind the counter to fetch items on the opposite side while the customer could turn and cross the bullpen in a few steps, some became suspicious that their Navajo customers were deliberately alternating their choices from one side to the other just to see the white man scamper.

It was impolite for a Navajo ever to point with his finger, and the wanted items were indicated by pursing the lips and lifting the chin, something like blowing a kiss. I thought this hands-free gesture very convenient until I tried it at home. Mother took immediate corrective action, and I realized she wasn't open to anything new in our social customs.

The outstanding product of all Navajo handicrafts is the world-renowned Navajo rug, at that time just becoming immensely sought-after in the United States and even abroad. At that time a 9 x 12–foot Navajo rug would bring perhaps $25 in trade and a smaller saddle blanket only about $10.

I remember one afternoon when we were visiting the Sweetwater Trading Post when a man suddenly opened the door and walked into the bullpen, where a number of Navajos were sitting around, and with a flourish unfurled the small bundle he was carrying under his arm to proudly display a beautiful little saddle blanket his young bride had just woven.

It was almost completely white, with very little of the traditional patterns that made the Navajo rug so much in demand, but it featured a small border surrounding one word in large block letters, a word she had carefully copied from a sack: SUGAR. The Navajos sitting around all murmured in admiration of the painstaking handicraft displayed in all its glory but Mr. Palmer glanced at us with a resigned shrug. It was extremely doubtful that he would ever find a buyer for that splendid little weaving.

Trading for wool was a profession in itself, and in larger trading posts one person would specialize in negotiating for wool. During sheep-shearing season the wool brought in for trade was bought by the pound, and prices offered by the trader varied widely depending on the market, something that most Navajos could not comprehend. A sack of wool was a sack of wool—why should the price change at the whim of the trader?

Wool was stuffed in bundles and sacks, and the trader packed it in huge 250-pound woolsacks that were hung on a wood frame just outside the trading post. As very young boys at *tó łikan,* Bill Palmer and I used the wool frame in front of the post as a monkey bar and often climbed up to swing from the board framework, usually when no adults were around to remonstrate.

Since wool and sheepskins were bought by the pound, as were many rugs, it was not unusual for a Navajo to try to increase the weight of the wool he was trading by wetting it just a little or by adding a few foreign materials—sand or maybe a rock or two.

One trader found a particularly heavy piece of metal tucked into the wool he was weighing. He did not say a word to the Navajo about it, but when the seller later purchased some grain in trade, the same foreign chunk of metal was resting in the bottom of his grain sack. Typically, the Navajo found this highly amusing, as most Navajos did when a trick was discovered.

Piñon nuts were another major economic resource for Navajos, and whole families could be involved in their gathering. Navajo women and children harvested them by spreading canvas or blankets under the piñon trees, then beating the branches with sticks to shake down the nuts. I loved these delicious little pea-sized nuggets and at an early age learned the Navajo trick of eating them by putting a handful in one side of my mouth, cracking the hard shell with my teeth and blowing the shells out of the other side. Mother thought the whole procedure was disgusting and it made an awful litter, so I was always encouraged to eat my piñons outside.

Much of the Reservation piñon crop was shipped to New York City, where many were sold by pushcart vendors to immigrants from the Mediterranean countries, who found the little nuggets very similar to nuts they enjoyed back home. Trade in New Mexico piñon nuts was estimated to be as much as 6,000,000 pounds a year at that time.

ART OF BARGAINING

Most trading posts did a large trade in sheep pelts and wool clip as well as livestock: lambs, sheep, and sometimes cattle. The trader, however, was responsible for getting livestock herded to market in the outside world. Trading had changed very little since the turn of the century, and though some Navajos occasionally had a little money, most transactions were still by barter. As the term implies, barter was conducted with little or no cash exchanged.

Transactions started when a Navajo man or woman arrived with something to trade: woven rugs, silver and turquoise jewelry, baskets, and other crafts were brought in to be exchanged for food, clothing, and hardware.

Navajo woman and girl visiting Rock House construction.

After the item for trade was duly examined and commented on by all present, it was placed on the counter, and the trading began. The trader would appraise the item, make an offer, and after a lengthy period of bargaining a price was agreed upon, and the trader would write the amount on the back of a paper sack and put it on the counter. The Navajo would then select the items he wanted to buy and the price of each was subtracted from the number on the sack.

Dollar bills might be used, but most Navajos were reluctant to accept paper of larger denominations, as they didn't read and were not sure of the numbers on the larger bills. Most found it very strange that one green piece of paper could be worth as much as five or ten other pieces of green paper. Actually, Navajos preferred silver, so big, round, silver dollars were usually neatly stacked on the counter with change in smaller coins.

Some early traders on the Navajo Reservation issued their own "tin money" of small stamped brass or aluminum coins in amounts from a nickel to a dollar, but these were seldom recognized as currency at any place other than the issuing trading post, and only a few of these coins were still in circulation by my time. Change was an important part of all negotiations, and dimes (*dootł'izh* or blue), fifteen cents (*gíinsi*), and quarters (*naaki yáál* or two bits) were piled alongside the bills.

Navajos usually selected the most important item first, and, after the trader took it from the shelf and placed it on the counter, paid for it from the pile of cash on the counter. Usually the first selection was flour, sugar, baking powder,

Roy Scott sporting his new short haircut
and his new hat.

or coffee, and others followed in order of importance. After each transaction the remaining money was counted several times, and I have even seen some old ladies actually tuck it away before selecting their next purchase and get it out again when that purchase was negotiated.

Every item was placed on the counter before the Navajo customer would start considering the next item to purchase. Then the whole process would be repeated. The final coins in the pile before a rug was "traded out" were used for goodies: canned peaches or tomatoes, apples, red soda pop, tobacco, and hard candies.

It could take a Navajo from ten minutes to half an hour to choose one item, carefully examine it, agree on a price, pay for it, and count the remaining balance before proceeding to the next item. It could take half a day for a single customer to complete his order, but the trader could sometimes deal with several customers at the same time. Most Navajos had plenty of time and would patiently wait their turn on stage, as trading was a spectator sport and all present would watch each transaction and make appropriate comments.

The language difference also added time to the process. Some Navajos spoke a little English, and most traders soon picked up what was then referred to as "traders' Navajo," but a lot of hand gestures were used and information was freely offered by helpful bystanders.

A woman negotiated for yard goods to sew into voluminous skirts, usually seven to nine yards for each skirt. Before buying a piece of calico she would take from ten minutes to half an hour to examine and choose the exact piece of cloth she needed. Then they discussed the price again before she decided the yardage and colors she wanted and the trader ripped the selected yardage from the bolt of cloth.

BRAND NAMES

Navajos were very discriminating in what they purchased. Quick to identify their favorite brands by the pictures on the container that identified the contents, Navajos would often refuse to trade for a strange picture.

Baking powder in the red can with the Plains Indian in a feather headdress was good, and the chewing tobacco with a star on the plug was preferred. The picture on the front of the can or package usually represented what was inside, and I often speculated on how a Navajo would react to the smiling picture of Aunt Jemima on a box of pancake flour.

Coffee was usually Arbuckle's Arioso, and a pound of the whole bean coffee sold for twenty cents; however, the coffee with the man in the yellow dress, the Hills Brothers brand, was usually acceptable. Folger's Coffee was my favorite, not that I drank coffee then, but because I admired the label, which showed a ship passing through the pre-bridge Golden Gate of San Francisco into the sunset, bound for some exotic port far across the Pacific Ocean in the mysterious Far East.

One reason for the popularity of Arbuckle coffee with the Navajos was that those beans came in a distinctive yellow package with a large signature on one side, which could be cut off and redeemed. I remember one old man coming in to the Sweetwater post with a stack of several dozen signatures. He flashed it around like a bankroll, much to the envy of all the Navajos sitting around.

Sugar, at ten cents a pound, was always popular and was bought at the same time as coffee, since all Navajos took their coffee strong and black, made by boiling large amounts of sugar and coffee together for a long time. However it tasted more like syrup than coffee to the discriminating *bilagáana.*

Flour was a staple item, and a local brand, Long Hollow, came in twenty-five-pound sacks and sold for about one dollar. It was identified by a picture of an Indian in a Comanche feather war bonnet, sitting on a horse below a towering Shiprock. A few years later the company changed hands and some marketing genius added a second Indian sitting on his horse some distance away with his hand to his mouth, shouting at the first Indian and the name was changed to "Long Holler." This was accepted by the Navajos but was viewed with some amusement by the *bilagáana.*

Another mill had an unfortunate picture on its flour sacks of a large wolf head, which was universally rejected by the Navajos who recognized it as *mą'ii,* the coyote, who was always treated with great caution, and they didn't need his likeness in their hogans.

PAWN

A credit system based on pawned jewelry was a basic part of trading, years before we came to the Reservation, and barter remained the mainstay of trade in the largely cashless society during all the time I lived there. A Navajo who was out of funds would offer as pawn a valuable object such as a piece of jewelry, a saddle, or other gear as security for goods purchased at the trading post. Then when he brought in wool or a rug, he would redeem the piece or make payment against the balance owed.

The trader always kept pawned items in a secure place, sometimes a locked pawn case in the corner of the trading area. Pawn served as an elementary bank account. It provided a source of credit and also a vault or safe place to keep jewelry and other treasured personal possessions, beyond the grasp of relatives or clan members. Navajos called the due date on anything *'e'e'aah,* sunset, and pawn not redeemed by that date was called "dead pawn."

Theoretically pawn could be sold by the trader after that date, but most traders treated the pawn in their store with the utmost respect and considered it as still the personal property of the owner, and it was not uncommon for a Navajo to come into the trading post and "borrow" a pawned item for some special event, then bring it back to be re-deposited in the pawn case.

Navajo rug on display.

One evening I was at Sweetwater with my folks discussing pawn with Mr. Palmer, and he opened the Sweetwater Post pawn case to show us the silver bracelets, rings, belt buckles, and strands of coral and turquoise necklaces. One beautiful old worked silver piece caught our attention, and Aunt Clara exclaimed that it must be a very valuable article. Mr. Palmer agreed but went on to comment, "That's actually a dead pawn but old *hastiin* is good as his word and I'm not selling it."

A trader had to be careful, however, in evaluating an item. When a piece presented for credit was overvalued, the Navajo might well decide to take the money and disappear, and eventually the trader would realize he had bought the piece. Occasionally pawn was not as secure as the trader thought, and it was not unknown for temporary employees to take advantage of their access to valuable items in the trading post pawn case.

One summer night, well after dark, Aunt Clara, Yellowhair, and I were alone at the Mission when we were startled by someone pounding on the door. Taking the coal-oil lamp in hand, Aunt Clara went to the door and encountered a young *bilagáana* dressed in new boots with spurs, embroidered shirt, and Levi's, with a large concho belt. He was also wearing a pawn case of silver in rings, bracelets, a bow guard, and several strings of coral and turquoise.

Aunt Clara stared in astonishment at the young fellow in all his regalia as he introduced himself as a summer visitor on the Reservation, staying temporarily at a local trading post. He said he had set out to see a native ceremony but lost the trail in the dark and needed directions to the Navajo camp where it was being held.

In his words: "Where are the Navies holding the big sing tonight?" After questioning him to identify the outfit from his version of the name of the family holding the sing, Aunt Clara translated it to Yellowhair for directions for finding their camp in a canyon, and the pilgrim rode off into the dark.

I often wondered if that young man ever found the ceremony, and if he did, whether any Navajo present that night recognized one of the pieces of jewelry the dude was flashing as his personal jewelry—supposedly safe and secure at pawn in the trading post? And, for that matter, did the trader know about part of his pawn going missing that night?

SOCIAL CENTER

A visit to the trading post was a social occasion for Navajos. Local news was shared and discussed in detail, and opinions were expressed. The latest happenings in *waashindoon* were always a popular subject for conversation.

Over the years the trading post also became the post office for rare letters sent home by students at boarding school, relatives working off-Reservation, and later by sons in military service. Most mail had to be translated into Navajo at the trading post or the Mission. Answering mail required even more assistance and tended to take much more time, as the Navajo way of talking could take pages to get to the point of the message.

Government notices were usually posted at the trading post, printed in the official obscure governmentese English, difficult even for the trader to understand and impossible to translate into Navajo. These important messages were universally ignored by the Navajos unless there was an illustration or picture in the notice that could lead to a discussion about such important details as the age of the horse and the equipment and the identity of the man.

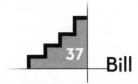

37 Bill

During those early years, Ace Palmer's son Bill and I were the only two *bilagáana* boys in our small corner of the Navajo Reservation. We were good friends, or as good friends as possible for two boys who rarely saw each other more than once a month. His name was not actually Bill but Willard, and for that matter he wasn't a *bilagáana* either, as Mormons were classified in a different category by the Navajos, who called them *gáamalii*.

HOLIDAY IN HONOLULU

In 1943, when I was at Pearl Harbor Naval Air Station in Hawaii, Aunt Clara wrote me that Bill's older brother Jim was also stationed in Hawaii, at the submarine base, which was just across the bay from Ford Island, where I worked. I located Jim by telephone—incidentally, my first serious encounter with a regular telephone, and we agreed to meet in Honolulu.

Two desert rats in the lush Hawaiian Islands, we toured the town together and ended the afternoon with lunch at the beach and a movie at Waikiki Theater. I wrote about this adventure to Aunt Clara, still at Immanuel Mission, and Jim must have been in touch with his family also as, when Aunt Clara contacted the Palmers on her next trip to town, Jim's sister Bobbie greeted her excitedly, saying, "Jim and Alwin got together in Hawaii and went to a movie," then covered her mouth and said, "I shouldn't have said that!" She knew Aunt Clara considered movies almost as bad as hanging around the pool hall.

At this time Bill was on the carrier USS *Enterprise,* and whenever the "Big E" came back to Pearl Harbor, Jim, Bill, and I had a "Reservation rendezvous" of perhaps the only three white guys from the Four Corners of the Navajo Reservation in the entire Pacific at that time. One afternoon, when the *Enterprise* was in port and anchored adjacent to the landing slip where I boarded the ferry to cross to Ford Island every day, Bill met me and took me aboard for a tour of his ship.

I was astounded at the size of that aircraft carrier, particularly the vast flight deck. Bill took me to his battle station on deck and showed me around that part of the ship, and then we went down to his quarters many decks below.

We were sitting on his bunk talking about our days on the faraway Navajo Reservation and then moved on to the present and a new movie scheduled for that night on the ship, when Bill suddenly said, "Why don't you stay on board tonight and watch it with me? My bunkmate has gone back Stateside on emergency leave and his bunk is available. You could stay over and catch the ferry to Ford Island in the morning. Nobody would know the difference."

I thought that sounded great, and we were enthusiastically discussing the plan when I began to have second thoughts. I knew Jonnie Whaley, my roommate back at the Navy cantonment, would be concerned if I didn't show up by blackout, and, as I had no way of contacting him, I decided not to sleep aboard after all and returned to the mainland and my own bunk for the night.

MISSING THE BOAT!

Before sunrise the next morning I got off the cattle car that hauled us back to the Navy yards, and after pushing my way aboard the Ford Island ferry, turned and looked up to see if possibly Bill was on deck of the *Enterprise,* which should have been silhouetted against the eastern sky—but saw nothing but a dark void. The USS *Enterprise* had sailed at midnight!

I never saw either the "Big E" or Bill Palmer again but returned Stateside near the end of World War II, married, and was very happy in sunny Arizona with our four kids instead of spending the next twenty years in a Navy brig for an unauthorized tour of the South Pacific. Bill Palmer returned to New Mexico after World War II and, soon after, married Lavone Ashcroft, the daughter of Carl Ashcroft, a longtime trader at Greasewood Springs and other posts in the southeast part of the Navajo Reservation.

CROWNPOINT

Bill and Lavone owned several trading posts on the Reservation and later bought the trading post at Crownpoint just east of Gallup, in the "Checkerboard" area of the Navajo Reservation. They ran it for nearly thirty years as the Palmer Mercantile.

Bill Palmer served as president of the United Indian Trader Association for a long time, and Lavone established the internationally famous Crownpoint Navajo Rug Auction in 1968, at a time when an oversupply of rugs made it difficult for weavers to find buyers. She developed an event where bidders could talk directly with weavers and bid on rugs at an auction held in an elementary school gymnasium. This became very successful in getting better prices for Navajo rugs. Bill sold the Crownpoint Trading Post in 1986 and retired to Kirtland, where he died in 1997. Our paths had never crossed again after we left the Pacific.

38 Windows on the World

Our contact with people, other than family, who spoke English was rare and came only at very irregular times. Sometimes we would make several trips to "town" in one month, but often we would be isolated for six weeks or more, usually when roads were blocked by snow or mud.

NEWSPAPERS

In our pre-radio days we heard little world or national news. Grandfather subscribed to his old hometown paper, the weekly *Kansas City Star,* and it arrived regularly at the post office in Shiprock but usually didn't show up at Immanuel Mission until several weeks later. Often two or three copies would arrive in one mail sack and were patiently sorted into chronological order before they were grabbed by the adults in order of seniority and avidly read to catch up on what was happening in the outside world, as if it was breaking news.

Mother was the youngest member of the adult family and often complained that the others commented on events and discussions that were well underway before she even read the articles. I also read some features and news in the *Kansas City Star* but usually turned first to the single cartoon panel of *The Intellectual Pup,* the adventures of a very wise dog. Dad and I also closely followed a serial story by one of the founders of the Swope Park Zoo in St. Louis, which held our interest for several months.

MAGAZINES

Magazines were another source of contact with the outside world in the early days of Immanuel Mission. We subscribed to a few religious magazines, such as the *Evangelic Lutheran* and the *Sunday School Times,* and also took the *Pathfinder,* a weekly news magazine of national and world events.

Grandfather was a lifetime member of the National Geographic Society, and I eagerly read the magazine each month, but when he died Aunt Clara notified the *National Geographic* that longtime member H. A. Holcomb was deceased and his subscription to the magazine should be cancelled. This was a severe disappointment to me, as I felt the people at the Washington office of *National*

Geographic would not have known of the event in faraway Arizona, and I could have continued to read it for at least a little while longer. As it was, I lost my best source of information on distant exotic lands.

Navajos would often ask for magazines, and we generally passed on our well-worn copies for them to take home and study the pictures. They were sometimes surprisingly interested and informed about current events and public figures, national and even worldwide. They referred to Hitler as "Smells his Moustache."

Dad was concerned, however, that some magazine pictures were not suitable to be distributed by a mission and asked me to censor everything we gave away so there would be no display of anything the missionaries considered disgraceful. Dad also felt ads for cigarettes and liquor shouldn't be promoted by the Mission—though at that time alcohol was very seldom a problem in our corner of the Navajo Reservation.

When I was about twelve, the folks gave me subscriptions to both *Boys' Life* and *The Open Road for Boys,* and these two magazines were very important to a boy living on a remote Reservation. I was particularly fascinated with the stories about aviation. In 1929 the German Hugo Eckener made a round-the-world flight in his Graf Zeppelin in twenty-one days. In 1931 Wiley Post, accompanied by Harold Gatty and determined to set the world record, circled the globe in eight days in his monoplane dubbed the "Winnie Mae." With his distinctive black eye-patch, dating from an early accident, Gatty was almost as well known as Charles Lindbergh.

Yellowhair liked to look through all picture books, newspapers, and magazines that came into his hands. He referred to all of them as *naaltsoos* (paper). He would sit at his little table by the kitchen window and pore over pictures that caught his eye, and then ask me to explain them to him, and over the years I spent many hours translating stories into Navajo terms he could understand.

In 1935 he spotted the account of the Wiley Post and Will Rogers plane crash at Point Barrow, and we had a lengthy discussion in which I not only had to describe in Navajo terms who they were and how they were killed in Alaska, but also explain details such as why one man had a patch over one eye. I thought of this session with Yellowhair when Marjorie and I visited Point Barrow about sixty years later.

Another illustration that instantly caught Yellowhair's eye was a dramatic picture of Ethan Allen and his volunteers storming the British Fort of Ticonderoga, and I was hard put to translate, "Surrender in the name of Almighty God and the Green Mountain Boys!" Years later I learned that Ethan Allen's demand was actually: "Come out, you damned old rat!" and was very happy I didn't have to translate that version into Navajo for Yellowhair.

MONTGOMERY WARD CATALOG

We did much of our Mission shopping from a big catalog of goodies that had many items that we never even imagined to be available. The U.S. Post Office became our shopping mall, long before anything like that was known in the outside world.

Navajos also were fascinated with the big *naaltsoos* they could leaf through at the Mission. It had pictures of all kinds of things they could buy and have sent to them. This required a great deal of explanation and writing, and I became the person at the Mission with time to describe items and order what they wanted to purchase.

Seldom did the Navajos have the slightest idea what was involved in catalog shopping, and the session usually entailed sitting down and leafing through many pages before they found what they needed. They usually wanted to examine every page and also wanted a description of many items. This could become a bit tricky as some items displayed were difficult to describe in Navajo. As a pre-teenage boy, I also had little knowledge of some items displayed in the women's clothing section of the catalog, and I eventually learned to remove a few pages we really didn't need when a new catalog arrived.

Men's clothing didn't require much explanation, although I remember one time when two young men were leafing through the catalog, and one remarked, "Oh, that coat must be bearskin." At this forbidden reference to a *shush,* or bear, the younger fellow soon found a curse of his own and replied, "And this must be *ch'įįdii* [evil spirits] skin!"

When it came time to prepare the order, I once drew an objection to my total from a Navajo with some education, who could read the prices in the catalog, and I had to explain *woshdę́ę́',* "from there to here" that had to be added to the stated price of the item pictured in the catalog.

During my last couple of years at Immanuel Mission, Montgomery Ward initiated a scholarship program that awarded a percentage of catalog sales, and I started a small account that was used for my further education when I enrolled at the University of Arizona a few years later.

RADIO

Our prized first radio was a five-tube battery-powered set acquired in 1926, and no child dared touch the mysterious dials on that splendid big black box, the center of attraction in the living room of our new stone house. Only Dad knew how to turn the dials to bring in KOB Albuquerque and occasionally the weak voice of KIUP Durango, Colorado. Some nights he could pick up signals from stations in distant cities—KOA 850 in Denver and KFI Los Angeles.

Then there was Dr. Brinkley, blasting out his message of goat gland therapy from the 50,000-watt Clear Channel XER, "the most powerful station in the world," with its huge 300-foot tower antenna in Del Rio, Texas. Actually Brinkley had lost his license to broadcast in the United States and was operating from Villa Acuña, Mexico, to avoid broadcasting regulations in the USA. This same "border blaster" radio station also broadcast some early Carter Family performances when they were first launching what was to become a very popular country music group.

One memorable night Dad picked up, through all the static, a signal from Calgary in Alberta and next morning entertained the family at breakfast with his account of listening to "Canada, actually another country," further kindling my lifelong interest in faraway places.

MIDNIGHT SERENADE

Herbert Redshaw, called *t'áá bi chidi* or "empty gas tank" by the Navajos, was a frequent visitor at Immanuel Mission. The Navajos named him this because a Navajo bought a car that ran out of gas. Redshaw explained that it was empty of gas, so they named him so.

A man in his fifties, Redshaw was a twenty-year veteran of the BIA and government farmer of the BIA Shiprock District. He lived near Aneth on the San Juan River. I only remember him as a man with a moustache, wearing a Western hat and vest, not the outfit one expected a man born in England to wear. When working in our area he sometimes stayed overnight with us while we were still living in the rock house.

Redshaw and Dad loved to listen to the radio, sometimes searching for signals from new stations well into the early morning hours. Mother tried to discourage this nocturnal activity because it often kept Dad glued to the set until well after midnight, but she complained very little—until one cold night they disturbed her rest with assorted howls and screeching, bits of talking, and cowboy music.

She leaped out of bed, pulled on her robe, snatched up her guitar, and started whanging away and singing at the top of her voice. Suddenly it became very still in the living room and Dad soon came creeping into bed. I was disappointed when I learned next morning that I had slept through and completely missed all the excitement, but that was the end of midnight radio searching.

Navajos also were not too keen about the strange box and its disembodied voices. Some suspected that all that static and squealing sounds could be *ch'įįdii*—evil spirits wandering around in the night.

After we exchanged houses and the Girdners were living in the big adobe building, Dad was able to make an aerial by setting a twenty-foot length of pipe east of the adobe house and stringing a wire to the radio in the main living room. This greatly improved the reception, but still only at night.

Radio became our main source of information and news of the outside world, and both Mother and Dad faithfully listened to the readers of the news that broadcast late every night. I gradually became interested in world news as

Alwin seeking shade on a hot summer Sunday afternoon.

I grew older, but during the early years most of my information still came from Mother, who would relay what she deemed important for young ears, especially information on the amazing developments in politics.

The disastrous flood in the Midwest kept us glued to our radio late into those terrifying nights of 1927, when we listened to the excited voices of "announcers" describe what was happening in the flooded states, as uncontrolled water surged over 27,000 square miles of the Mississippi Valley—an area larger than that of four small states.

In many places the furious water rose as much as two feet a day, breaking successive levees, flooding farms, roads, and towns, and forcing desperate survivors into over 150 hideous refugee camps in the mud of temporarily higher ground. Hundreds of children became lost to their families, and Mother was horrified when it was reported that many of these children's bodies were never identified. She immediately sewed our names into every item of our clothing, even though it seldom rained on our desert Reservation.

ONE MAN'S FAMILY

The entire family, except Yellowhair, faithfully gathered once a week for our special program, *One Man's Family,* a story based in San Francisco. Mother especially enjoyed it as she graduated from Oakland Technical High School in the class of 1919 with Bernice Berwin, the actress who played the part of Hazel, one of the leading characters of the story.

This was Mother's favorite program, and she sent for a booklet with pictures of the cast that brought back memories of her days in the Bay Area—so different from her present sandy, dry home in the desert. This serial eventually set the record as radio's longest-running show, with a total of 3,256 episodes over twenty-seven years.

While visiting the trading post at Sweetwater one day, Aunt Clara asked Roy Foutz, who was our trader at the time, if he listened to some of these programs, but he exclaimed, "No! I save my batteries for *Amos 'n' Andy*," the most popular program of all radio at that time.

These two blackface comedians must have been very important to this lonely trader. Later, when Dad and I made another visit to Sweetwater, Roy Foutz showed us an innovation he had devised. From the radio set in the living room a string ran up the wall, across the ceiling, and through a hole in the inner wall. He then took us around to the bedroom room and showed us the string coming through the wall and down to his nightstand so he could listen to *Amos 'n' Andy* at night, then turn the radio off from his bed. He had invented the remote control.

Two Navajo families visiting the Mission.

NAVAJO GRAPEVINE

We would occasionally learn of events through Navajo word-of-mouth accounts of local and even national news, which could be astoundingly accurate. The "Navajo Grapevine" network spread news, especially anything about the doings in *waashindoon,* with incredible speed across Navajo Country. In *To the Foot of the Rainbow,* Clyde Kluckhohn gives an account of a horseback journey across the Navajo Reservation in 1923, during which he heard the news of the unexpected death of President Warren G. Harding within forty-eight hours of his death, weeks before he was able to confirm it by newspaper.

39   Navajo Dress Code

I n the early days at Immanuel Mission, the dress of most Navajos was still very traditional. Most old-timer men continued to wear traditional white unbleached pants, often made of flour sacks, slit to the knee and topped by a white blouse.

But younger men preferred Levi's, usually tight, with almost inaccessible pockets; and vests were popular as they had multiple pockets for carrying many items. Shirts were usually cotton or sateen and could be quite colorful. Both older men and women wore leather moccasins, but by the 1930s, many of the younger men preferred *bilagáana*-style work shoes or boots. A wide leather belt with a splendid worked-silver and turquoise buckle and a hat completed their costume.

The women wore plush bright red, green, or blue velveteen blouses, very elegant—but with open underarms and worn outside the skirt. Rows of little, peaked silver buttons or dimes decorated the sleeves and front of the blouse and also served as a petty cash fund to be cut off and used as cash when needed at the trading post.

I remember many dimes, and sometimes quarters, with a small loop soldered to the back. Many other coins in circulation had a small residue of solder remaining on them where the loop had been removed and the coin recycled into the economy. (These coins didn't work all that well in vending machines.)

Women also wore multiple long sateen or calico skirts, which they had adapted from the dress of officers' wives at Fort Sumner during the time of *hwééldi*. An average skirt required about nine yards of cloth, and the Navajo women insisted it not be cut with scissors but torn by the trader. As Navajo skirts had no pockets, most women carried some sort of bag or sack for small objects and personal items, and also some things that were not so small.

In cold weather both men and women wrapped themselves in colorful blankets, not woven by the Navajos as most white people assumed, but Pendleton blankets bought at the trading post. Men used Pendleton blankets not only as a wrap but also as a cover when sleeping, and women favored fringed Pendleton shawls.

Some women wore leg wrappings of soft white deerskin, and most women and many older men wore red soft leather moccasins with a white sole and a silver coin or button fastener on the side. Navajo women did not use any kind of

Roy Scott and his older brother Walter in his military uniform.

makeup, but in summertime did wear bright red clay on their faces as protection against the sun.

Some traditional Navajo men wore headbands, but most young men preferred high-crowned "Hoss Cartwright" hats, often black and decorated with a hatband of leather, with silver ornaments and sometimes a band of beadwork. A few men wore silver *ketohs,* or wrist bow guards, and silver belt buckles. Both men and women wore strings of turquoise or tubular red coral beads, sometimes silver with a *naja* (pendant), but I do not remember seeing any Navajos wearing feathers at that time.

Men and women alike also wore everything they could afford in necklaces, bracelets, and rings, as jewelry was an indication of the importance of the person, almost as much as owning large herds of livestock, especially horses. Most men wore turquoise pendants in their ears and many had belts and hatbands made of intricate beadwork, a craft in which many men were very skilled. I learned this art form and produced some creditable beadwork pieces, but, as I did not wear a hat, soon acquired a surplus of beadwork with no market for my wares.

Working silver and turquoise jewelry was an art the Navajos learned from the Pueblos and became a specialty of Navajo men and soon brought wide recognition and a source of income. Many other exchanges did not require money. In one rather unusual transaction, Dad traded a three-piece suit to a Navajo man for a very wide, beautifully crafted bead belt. He soon found the little glass beads were too fragile to survive everyday use but continued to wear that splendid piece on special occasions for years.

As for the suit, I have often speculated about that exchange—how did that Navajo keep his pants from falling down without his belt, and, for that matter, how did a dress suit adapt to camp life?

MISSIONARY BARRELS

Occasionally an Assembly of Plymouth Brethren would have a drive and collect items, usually clothing, to send out for the Indians. Most were practical and useful and welcomed by us, but some people apparently had no concept of camp life, and we often had to improvise. A necktie could be used as a headband, but suits, dress shoes, sequined evening wear, and fancy hats were not very useful to people living in a hogan.

On one occasion, years after we left the Mission, I was telling a Sunday school class in New Jersey about the precarious Navajo economy out in New Mexico, and the class immediately put on a drive and soon sent me a donation for Navajo children—100 new toothbrushes. Yet I knew it was almost certain that kids carrying buckets of water a mile or more for family use would not be too concerned about cleaning their teeth, and, for that matter, I also knew that yucca soap makes terrible toothpaste. And don't get it in your eyes!

THE "BOSTON AUNTIES"

One Assembly in Boston had a group of ladies that took particular interest in missionary children and included something for them in every shipment to Immanuel Mission. We referred to this group as the "Boston Aunties" and eagerly gathered around to watch the unpacking of every new box from the Boston Assembly.

Sometimes the presents were games or, more important, books, but usually they were clothing. Evidently there was a small professor at Boston College with my neck size, as quite often several elegant shirts were included in the missionary box, so during my teens I wore beautifully tailored, pinstriped broadcloth shirts to Sunday morning meeting—quite a contrast to my daily garb of a plain shirt, made by Aunt Clara, and bib overalls.

Once I also received an expensive pair of wool knickerbockers that pleased Mother, as "short pants" were considered correct for young boys at that time and graduating to "long pants" was as important an event as getting a driver's license is today. Knickers made me look like Little Lord Fauntleroy, a popular fictional character in the 1930s, and I despised those knickers and wore them as seldom as possible and then very grudgingly. Somehow they soon were ripped on a barbed wire fence in a very unfortunate accident.

On another occasion, a pair of lace-up leather women's boots caught my fancy, and I clumped around in them for several months. Those big boots laced up over my pants and must have looked completely ridiculous, but I soon forgot them as they were very uncomfortable and hard to lace up every day.

40 | The Word in Navajo

My first memory of an encounter with any spoken word, either English or Navajo, is of sitting in my high chair in the primitive kitchen area of the old stone house and eating my breakfast early one morning. Grandmother Holcomb was correcting me and told me I was eating "shredded wheat," not "broom."

Just then I heard a distant crowing and said, "Chicken!" only to be wrong again. Aunt Clara said, "Rooster." Both were still laughing when the outside door opened and Mother stepped over the stone sill and down into the room, carrying a pan of milk.

She was immediately regaled with the tale of my difficulties with the English language, and everyone thought it very funny, but I failed to see the point of all the hilarity. Anyway, they were all misinformed; the word for the bird actually was *naa'ahóóhai*. Mother later said that learning both English and Navajo at the same time was not a problem for me, and she always insisted that of my first ten words, five were English and five were Navajo.

This is not surprising because at that time not one in ten Navajos spoke any English, and almost none were fluent in that strange language. For almost the first four years of my life I was probably the only white child within fifty miles of the Mission, and Indians were the only people I saw for months on end, other than family. The occasional white visitor was a curiosity and deserved to be pitied, as he spoke no Navajo at all.

I started young enough to develop a good feeling for speaking the Navajo language and mastered the difficult glottal stops in speaking, and I acquired a good vocabulary, particularly of nouns, but structure and usage were completely different than English. For example, the correct answer to the question, "You don't want this?" for a Navajo would be, "Yes, I don't."

I also had difficulty with the endless ways a verb could be changed, and one simple word could have many forms: "mother" in Navajo was *shimá* for "my mother," *nimá* for "your mother," and *bimá* for "his mother." I knew hundreds of nouns and had perfected the accent but was never fluent in constructing correct sentences that expressed more than a simple message. However, that didn't stop me from talking with Navajos, and they were polite enough to act as if they really understood me.

At Immanuel Mission we spoke English among ourselves, but our conversation was liberally sprinkled with Navajo words and phrases, particularly when we were speaking of Reservation people and places. Aunt Clara was more than a decade older than my mother, and Mother always referred to her as *shi 'ádi,* "my older sister." Yellowhair was addressed as *shinááhai,* "older brother." We had to speak Navajo in all our conversations with Yellowhair as he did not understand English, or perhaps just chose not to.

MANNER OF SPEAKING

From the Navajo point of view the *bilagáana* was always in too much of a hurry and had no appreciation for silence. He would make a statement or ask a question and, if he didn't get an immediate reply, would plunge on, repeating the same question over again, and not recognizing the need to think before attempting a reasonable reply.

A white man would also ask personal questions that any child would know were private information, such as "What's your name?" Even the white man's manner was abrupt, loud, and even rude, with an insulting way of looking you directly in the eye when talking. He also pointed with his finger and laughed a lot.

The *bilagáana* wanted to rush directly to business without the polite Navajo preliminaries and often became impatient, even angry, when a Navajo chose not to answer. Sometimes it must have been tempting for a Navajo to be rude and just disagree with a nosy white man.

Navajos almost never directly made a statement of fact and usually would begin a statement with a qualification, "Perhaps it was…" or "They say that…" An example of this was a statement made by Emily Johnson, a Navajo woman who worked with Dad at Southwestern Bible School. Dad had loaned her Earle Forrest's book, *With a Camera in Old Navaholand,* and after reading it she wrote, "In all my life I never heard of Navajos eating dog or puppy meat," but then, Navajo style, she added the disclaimer: "They must have in those days. I have heard the Sioux tribe still eat puppies."

EARLY TRANSLATIONS

The first Americans to have contact with the Navajos had no idea how to reduce their guttural language to writing, and they recorded speeches and agreements as it sounded to them—often resulting in serious misunderstanding by both the military men and tribal leaders as to what was actually said in "treaties" made at that time.

Dr. Washington Matthews was a surgeon who had served in the regular army. Beginning as early as 1865, he was stationed at a number of western military outposts and became interested in the Sioux, Hidatsa, and Arickarees living along the Missouri. He gathered extensive ethnographic material that resulted in several works on grammar and philology that were published in 1877 by the U.S. Geological and Geographic Survey.

Matthews was assigned to Fort Wingate, New Mexico, in September of 1880 and started studies of the Navajo language and religious activities. He collected information on a number of Navajo chants, ceremonies, and ceremonial healing methods. After Matthews, a number of army officers and civilian scholars worked over the years to reduce the difficult language to writing.

Missionaries, however, were responsible for the organized translation of the Bible into Navajo, and the Franciscan Fathers at St. Michael were particularly dedicated to that task. Father Berard Haile, OFM, played an outstanding part in this translating during his sixty years of service with the Navajos from 1900 to 1961. In addition to working to convert Navajos to Christianity, Father Berard also developed a phonetic Navajo alphabet and completed three other works on linguistics before his death in 1961 at the age of 87. He contributed more to the creation of a written Navajo language and to the documentation of traditional culture than anyone else of that time.

LATER TRANSLATIONS OF SCRIPTURE

Alexander Black and John Butler, two Presbyterian missionaries of that early period, also translated portions of Scripture into Navajo. L. P. Brink worked with the Zuni language at the Christian Reformed Mission at Rehoboth before he also began rendering the Bible into Navajo.

Through years of diligent study and practice, Aunt Clara became one of the most effective *bilagáana* translators of everyday, conversational Navajo, even though at the same time her co-worker Aunt Florence Barker found the language, with all its glottal stops, a "mess of sounds." Aunt Clara had a lifelong dedication to translating the Bible into written Navajo and, beginning with the Gospel of St. John, worked through much of the New Testament and eventually translated a very respectable body of Scripture.

Many Navajos, first at *kin łigaaí* and later at Immanuel Mission, took an interest in her work and spent hours patiently explaining the workings of their difficult language to her. She particularly remembered one man at Moenkopi and wrote: "He wanted one of us to go and live at his hogan so that he might help us with the Navajo. I asked if we both could live with them sometime and he said, 'No, that would not be good. You cannot learn Navajo that way. If one of you lives alone with Navajos, and there is no one to whom you can talk English, then you can learn quickly.' "

Navajo conversation at that time was always carried on at a slow, deliberate pace, and this made it easier for me, as a youngster trying to master two languages. All this has changed, however, and once years later on the long drive from Flagstaff to Gallup I picked up a radio broadcast on KTNN in what I recognized as Navajo, but it came in such a flood of words that it sounded like a

Marie and a visitor support Alwin, a cradled Navajo baby,
and a visiting *bilagáana* toddler with a broom.

television pitch for used automobiles. I couldn't distinguish a word—nor would a Navajo of seventy-five years ago.

Local dialects were not all the same in all parts of the Reservation, and a number of words were pronounced differently. For instance, *chidi* was the common name for an automobile on most of the Navajo Reservation, but we pronounced it "*chuggi*" in the Four Corners area.

White men on the Reservation developed a "traders' Navajo" that was spoken not only by traders but also by military men, anthropologists, and government employees. But there was to be no universal standard for written Navajo for many years.

GERONIMO MARTIN

Bob Martin, our friend since the founding of Immanuel Mission, had three sons, Robert, Fred, and Geronimo, the youngest, who was born at Red Mesa Trading Post. He was just a small boy when I first saw him at Immanuel Mission. Geronimo joined his two older brothers at the Methodist Mission boarding school in Farmington but had only been there a few months when a fire destroyed the dining room and the boys were sent home for the rest of the year. Geronimo then attended the Christian Reform Mission at Rehoboth, and, after finishing the eighth grade there, rejoined his brothers at Albuquerque Indian School.

After he graduated, he became an interpreter for the Christian Reformed missionary at Toeadlena. But his eyesight soon became so bad that he was transferred to work with Reverend Vanderstoep at Shiprock. Geronimo was completely blind by the time he was twenty-five years old, so his sister Susan ordered a correspondence course in Braille, which he learned to read. When the American Bible Society furnished him a Braille Bible, he returned to bringing the Word to the Navajo camps, serving with the Christian Reformed Church in Farmington.

During the early 1940s, two white missionaries, Faye Edgerton and Faith Hill, met at the Navajo Methodist School in Farmington. Soon after, both joined the North American Branch of Wycliffe Bible Translators in Farmington, and they began attending the Christian Reformed Church, where they met Geronimo Martin. Together they began a lifetime project of translating the Bible into Navajo.

Over ten years later, this team completed the Navajo translation of the New Testament, and it was dedicated at the Christian Reformed church in 1956. The American Bible Society had printed a Navajo translation of the Book of Genesis and the Gospel of Mark as early as 1911, but portions from other books of the Bible, Gospel songs, and the rest of the Bible were not completed until years later.

Geronimo Martin and his wife, Lois, encountered many problems in translating the books of Leviticus, Ezekiel, and Job. The ancient words and concepts were often hard to explain. For example, Geronimo had never seen a pomegranate, so Lois bought one, and, after they ate it, he worked out a descriptive sentence in Navajo.

After they finished the whole book of Job, Lois was traveling to Tucson when a suitcase came loose and slid off the top of the car. The full translation of Job in that suitcase was never found. Someone right behind them must have picked it up, and Lois wondered later what they thought of those "chicken-scratches." Job was patiently re-translated, and Geronimo commented wryly, "Well, we can understand some of Job's tribulations better now." Lois thought the second version was "probably a much clearer translation."

NAVAJO HYMNS AND SONGS

L. P. Brink, a prolific translator, had over thirty hymns to his credit, including the universally loved children's song, "Jesus Loves Me," or "*Jesus ayoaso'nih*" in Navajo. Eventually he compiled a Navajo hymnbook that included many songs. When Immanuel Mission was founded, the only Navajo songbook was a recently printed translation of some sixty songs, but a number of missionaries of several denominations were working separately to find Navajo words for our familiar old hymns.

Aunt Clara translated a few hymns into Navajo: "Nothing but the Blood of Jesus," "Room for Jesus," "Such Wonderful Love," and "Solid Rock." But Fred G. Mitchell in Ganado had the record for translating the hymn with the longest title: "*Yisdáshiiniltnigii' 'ayóo 'aninosh'ní*" ("My Jesus I Love Thee").

Equally important was the untiring work by a number of Navajo Christians. Alice Gorman translated an astounding thirty-five hymns and Albert Tsosie translated twenty hymns into their native language.

WORKING TOGETHER

The scattering of missions across the Navajo Reservation, primitive travel conditions, and lack of funds and time made it difficult for the missionaries to share their translation efforts, and most worked in isolation. The work of translating was not done for personal recognition only, however, and every effort was made to share their studies whenever possible.

Aunt Clara and Dad both traveled occasionally to other missions to compare translations in progress and coordinate their work with that of other missionaries.

In 1928 Dad took me with him on one long trip down to the southeast corner of the Navajo Reservation to meet with Fred Mitchell. A veteran missionary, Mitchell, who had considerable experience at Tolchaco and was conversant in Navajo, was appointed in 1920 as the first superintendent of the new Presbyterian Mission at Ganado. After miles of driving we eventually encountered a sign:

GANADO MISSION

LARGEST INDIAN MISSION IN AMERICA

40 MILES OVER THE WORST ROAD IN ARIZONA

Here we found Fred Mitchell, who was then retiring to concentrate on his work in Navajo translation. Mitchell was assisted at that time by John Curley, the young Navajo who had worked for a short time at Immanuel Mission during its early days.

At Ganado Mission we also met Dr. Clarence Salsbury, a veteran himself of Presbyterian missionary efforts in China. At that time he was reluctantly taking over as acting superintendent of Ganado Mission in addition to his duties as medical director in charge of developing the facilities at Ganado that became the renowned Sage Memorial Hospital.

Sage Memorial Hospital not only provided an excellent health care facility, it also trained health specialists at its Ganado Training School for Nurses, the first organization to be accredited by the State of Arizona for Indians. Eventually it trained members of some twenty Native American tribes and several foreign countries. Terence Egan provides more historical background in *Old Ganado Mission*.

On this visit to Ganado, after introductions, I was taken to a classroom of Navajo children and spent the day playing with them while Dad worked with Fred Mitchell, and I remember little else of that visit except for a very unpleasant episode on our return trip to Immanuel Mission. We had stopped for the night in Gallup and were in a small café for a late supper when I suddenly had an attack of nausea, and I vividly recall Dad standing behind a small boy as he was violently ill on Front Street.

Some years later L. P. Brink came to Immanuel Mission for a session with Aunt Clara and Dad, and he brought with him a boy probably a little older than I was, possibly a grandson. Although I barely recall the prominent Reverend Brink that day, I do remember a lively discussion of postage stamps with the boy who came with him, which ended in my selling him some of my rare West Africa stamps. I do not think my parents or the good Reverend Brink ever learned of that commercial transaction.

THE MAN WITH NO SINS

When Dad arrived at Immanuel Mission in 1922, he spoke not a word of Navajo, but immediately set out to conquer the complicated language and spent days studying printed Navajo material and writing down hundreds of notes on various usages. He would talk with visiting Navajos for hours to work out all the uses of a single verb, jotting down voluminous notes in pencil for further study. He continued to be a dedicated student of Navajo for the rest of his life.

One night when Dad had been on the Reservation only a few months, he was helping Aunt Clara conduct a service with several visiting Navajos but only understood a few of the words spoken. Aunt Clara was translating bits of the conversation into English when one Navajo remarked that this man *damoo łichíí,* "red Sunday," had no sins.

This intrigued Aunt Clara, and she was even more puzzled when she relayed his statement to Dad and he replied shortly, "Well, I always knew that but didn't expect anyone to say so."

At breakfast the next morning she asked Dad if he really thought he was holy and had no sins, and an astonished Dad replied, "Of course not, why do you ask?" Aunt Clara repeated their exchange of the night before, and Dad laughed uproariously, then explained: "I thought he said I had no sense!"

A latecomer but a diligent and tireless student of the Navajo language, Dad never published his work, but he did compile hundreds of handwritten notes and comments on endless conversations and studies of Navajo word usage and Navajo expressions. In 1954, long after Dad had retired to the Girdner ranch on Oak Creek, he and Mother went to the Navajo Children's Home in Clemenceau for a short time as houseparents, and then a longtime friend, Gordon Fraser, persuaded him to join the faculty of the Southwest School of Missions in Flagstaff.

The Southwest School of Missions was not large, with only some twenty faculty and staff, including Geronimo Martin and his wife Lois teaching in the Navajo Language School. Dad served as a dean of the Navajo Department at the Southwest School of Missions from 1959 to 1972. He taught seventeen credit hours of Navajo classes in reading, writing, spelling, and conversation in a school that served adult Navajo students learning to read Navajo and a few white missionaries studying the Navajo language.

Dad reviewed many of the books about the Navajos now in my library, which were written by early visitors to the Navajo Reservation, such as Elizabeth Hegemann's *Navaho Trading Days* and Earle R. Forrest's *With a Camera In Old Navaholand.* He penciled detailed notes on the margins on some and also recorded a number of comments and personal experiences, but Navajo-style, he never directly contradicted any author.

Years later I inherited all of Dad's papers and found boxes of information including a "Chart of Accompaniment Verb Forms," with his detailed comments on "Stems with Consonantal Initials," and a discussion describing two classes of paradigms in the yi-imperfect: "The disjunct having no adverbial prefixes, and the conjunct, having adverbial prefixes require the yi imperfect in contrast to the conjunct zero imperfect. However, the yi- prefix does appear in all forms of such verbs...."

That was dense enough to completely discourage me from ever attempting to learn to read Navajo.

41   Prayer and Thanksgiving

n addition to the difficulties in learning to speak the language in words and terms the Navajos could understand, the missionary had to contend with the task of presenting a message that challenged the entire structure of myths and ceremonies that Navajos had followed for centuries. New concepts, with all the talk about death, completely baffled them.

Aunt Clara became aware of the enormity of her mission very early in her work on the Navajo Reservation. One woman with whom she was talking made a sobering statement: "I do not know what to believe. I have known our religion for a long time and yours for only a little while. Now I will think about what you tell me, for about four years, then perhaps I will know which is right. You should talk to one person every day for a long time and then he would understand well."

With very few exceptions, all early missionaries felt a personal obligation to carry out the charge to bring the Word of God to the entire world, and this was the sole reason the Holcombs chose to establish Immanuel Mission on the Navajo Reservation in the early 1920s. Everything they did was to further that effort, as they believed implicitly they had been called to this work. They had a deep, unshaken faith in the power of constant individual and group intercessory prayer for guidance in everything they did, and they had only one desire, and that was always to comply with the will of God, as they understood it.

Most missionaries on the Navajo Reservation had an all-consuming commitment to a way of life that offered few of the earthly rewards most Americans considered basic. They did not expect power, fame, or even personal recognition in this world and had no regard for financial gain, life or health insurance, or pension or retirement plans.

DAILY SERVICES AT IMMANUEL MISSION

Every morning the entire family, including Yellowhair, gathered in the living room immediately after breakfast for Morning Prayer. After singing one hymn, either Grandfather or Dad would read one chapter from the New Testament, followed by prayers from one or more of the adults present.

Every night after supper we again gathered for Evening Prayer and a session of singing, with Mother accompanying us on our antique piano. Everyone present got to choose one favorite hymn, usually resulting in eight or more hymns every evening.

Singing was followed by reading aloud a chapter from the Old Testament, in rotation around the room. Everyone who could read took one verse at a time in rotation, and by the age of seven or eight we had learned to wade through thickets of "begats" and could sound out almost all the names of people and places. By the time I left the Reservation I had read the entire Bible about three times and the New Testament many more times.

Evening meeting then ended in prayers. Everyone knelt at their chairs. Then, beginning with Grandfather Holcomb, everyone prayed aloud in rotation by age. Yellowhair was always last and prayed in very soft, often almost incomprehensible Navajo, and usually offered the longest prayer of the evening.

THE LORD'S DAY

At Immanuel Mission the worship service on Sundays differed from that of mainstream Protestant churches with a Communion service called the "Breaking of Bread." This was a morning meeting attended by the entire Mission. Guests and children attended but did not partake in the actual Communion, yet were expected to remain quiet and very respectful for the entire service, which always lasted for an hour or more.

The service opened with several hymns sung a cappella, then prayers were offered and portions of the Bible were read in unison. No formal sermon by a minister followed, but rather a long session of silent prayer during which anyone present could stand and read a particular passage and speak to it with their own comments, exhortation, and praise. No children and only members of a recognized Brethren Assembly participated in the actual breaking of bread and taking of the cup of wine (grape juice in small individual glasses).

The Bible stated that we were to obey our father and mother and therefore parental instructions carried the same obligation, and penalties for disregarding them, as a disobeying of the original Word. This authority extended to all the adult members of the family, and it was years before I realized that neglecting to wash my hands before a meal, even if I was alone, didn't actually violate Scripture.

From our earliest days we were grounded in the principles of fundamental Christianity and were expected to conform to a strict code of behavior that allowed no exceptions. Our elders interpreted Scripture literally, and Danny, Helen, and I were very well trained in what was expected of us. Observance of a complete code of house regulations shaped our daily life at Immanuel Mission.

As a teenage boy Jeffrey Staley lived with his missionary parents at Immanuel Mission two decades after I left. Many years later he wrote in his autobiography,

Reading with a Passion: "In our Plymouth Brethren home, scriptural meaning was always simple and crystal clear. Interpretive conflicts did not arise from honest intellectual questions but from willful acts of rebellion."

SIN IN THE SAND

One afternoon, when I was about seven years old, Dad had reason to drive out on the mesa about ten miles from the Mission on an errand. As he and Yellowhair were getting in the car to leave, I implored Mother to let me go along.

I was recovering from a cold and had been under the weather for several days, and she unwillingly consented to my going—but only on one condition: I was not to leave the car without putting on my shoes!

I grabbed my shoes and the book I was reading and ran out to the car, where Dad and Yellowhair were waiting. At our destination, Dad and Yellowhair walked out on the mesa to visit a Navajo camp, but I decided that, rather than put on my shoes, I would remain in the back seat of the car with my fascinating book, and for over an hour I quietly sat reading.

As the sun started to go down and blue shadows began to lengthen across the desert, the beautiful quiet evening beckoned, and just before sunset I got out of the car and started tracing roads in the soft sand just behind the car. When it began to grow dark I returned to the back seat of the car, and soon Dad and Yellowhair returned and we drove home.

When I picked up my shoes to go in the house I suddenly remembered my original instructions and realized I had broken the law, and, after some internal struggle I confessed my transgression.

Mother severely admonished me about obedience and then applied a few strokes of the switch. I have to add, however, that although Mother often resorted to the switch or, for major offenses, the razor strap, she never was severe and any major damage was only to the pride and dignity of the transgressor.

When any child stepped over the line, Mother's reaction was always swift, and she would sharply call out our full name: "Alwin Girdner, you come here!" At other times it would be a decisive snap of fingers, a frown, and even a thump on the head with a forefinger—particularly effective when she was wearing a thimble.

A QUESTION OF FAITH

From my early days I wondered about the competition among various Christian missions on the Navajo Reservation. All seemed to have the same God and basically they worshiped in the same way, and as I grew older I began to wonder about the other peoples of the world. Jewish people also worshipped one God as we did. So did the Muslims, although the latter of course were descended from Abraham's son Ishmael, who was "a wild man; his hand against every man, and every man's hand against him."

Glen reclining at the rock gorge on a Sunday afternoon with Alwin held in his legs and Marie sitting at his feet. Mary Holcomb, Clara Holcomb, and Floyd Tilson are in the background, and Stanley Girdner, Glen's brother, is at far right.

In Foxe's *Book of Martyrs* I had read the many stories recounting how people were killed by the hundreds for worshipping God but in a wrong way. Written in the sixteenth century, this tome was originally titled *Acts and Monuments of These Latter and Perilous Days, Touching Matters of the Church.*

I had also had read many other accounts of the Crusades, the Spanish Inquisition, the Hundred Years' War, the burning of witches in Salem, the driving of the Mormons out of Missouri, and the continuing Irish troubles.

Why all this conflict in the name of the same God?

Even our own tiny denomination was divided into Open Brethren and Exclusive Brethren. How had so many lost the way? This confusion caused me a great deal of concern and, after a long period of questioning and confusion, I finally went to Dad with my problem concerning the differences and conflicts between missionaries on the Navajo Reservation—weren't they all really of the same faith? Catholics and Mormons, of course, were somewhat different, but the Baptists, Presbyterians, Christian Reformed, and Methodists all called themselves Protestants—but seemed to be in competition with each other.

Dad's explanation of faith as two men standing beside two pillars that joined together beyond their sight might seem a little simplistic, but it gave me some hope for the future of mankind. I accepted this and later expanded the theory to include many pillars that joined to form a great dome over us all. Man, like an ant in a hogan, had no concept of what was up there above him, and I realized that the name Immanuel Mission meant "God With Us," not "God With Us Only."

On the Trail with Dad

s I have said, Dad devoted countless hours to learning the difficult Navajo language and constantly made voluminous notes that he studied and painstakingly revised over and over again after talking with Navajo visitors. To this day I have boxes and boxes of his handwritten notebooks, lists and pages of revisions of Navajo words and phrases, and his comments on usage. As soon as he could put simple sentences together well enough to make himself understood, Dad started visiting camps.

At first he walked the sandy trails of the mesas and canyons around the immediate Immanuel Mission area. Then, as primitive tracks were developed into roads, he drove the little green Model A Ford to the far-flung camps of the Navajos scattered around the Four Corners.

He always carried his own annotated copy of *God Bizaad,* the Word of God in Navajo, and a few comments in that language he had laboriously put together. He did not carry a hymnbook, however, as Dad never attempted singing any of the songs recently translated into the Navajo language.

On several occasions when I was quite young Dad took me along on one of his summer hiking visitations to Navajo camps around the Mission. One of my favorite trips was up the *tó chin lin,* a small stream that ran several miles above the Mission to the *tłízí łizhin* outfit, a hike of several miles.

About halfway up we would stop at a favorite dell and rest in the cool shade of several large cottonwood trees. We had a refreshing drink, and as a light breeze ruffled the leaves over our heads, Dad would read aloud a passage from a book he had carried along. This is one of most treasured memories of all my Reservation days.

HALF A DOZEN OLD NAKED MEN

One morning Dad and I were visiting camps in this area and left our pleasant dell to follow a trail on a shortcut across the hill above the stream. As we approached the water we heard a whooping and splashing down below and came to the rim just in time to see half a dozen completely naked men tumbling out of a *táchééh,* "sweat hut," and rushing down the bank to leap into a small pool.

They were so busy splashing around that they did not see us standing above them on the other side of the stream. I wanted to stay and watch but

Alwin's first Navajo sweat hut experience, with Glen,
in *tsegi* canyon, c. 1924.

Dad insisted we move quietly on before they knew we were observing their cleansing ceremony.

Farther upstream we saw an old man standing in a small corn field just above the stream. As we approached he called out, "I didn't do it! I didn't do it!"—a Navajo way of joking with friends. He was Old Wagon or *tsinaabọọs sani,* grandfather of the Black Goat family and one of only two people still in the area who had walked the Long Walk, the trek home from the confinement of the Diné at Fort Sumner in 1867.

When Dad and I went hiking in the desert we usually carried one small, padded army canteen that couldn't have held much more than a quart of tepid water, and we always walked as long as possible between drinks, as Dad had cautioned me that taking occasional sips of water would only make our thirst worse.

Somewhere I had read that desert travelers sometimes relieve their thirst by putting small pebbles in their mouths, and we tried doing this but only succeeded in walking along the trail with something hard and dry rattling in our mouths.

CENSUS OF 1930

In April of 1930 Dad was selected as one of the "enumerators" for the census of the people of the Reservation. For about six weeks, sometimes with the help of Roy Scott as interpreter, Dad attempted to count every man, woman, and child in our corner of the Navajo Reservation. He later remembered this as a valuable experience and wrote that it "improved rapport with our neighbors and added some who were utter strangers."

I was only six at the time but remember his leaving every day with his big record book, sometimes on horseback, more often walking, in search of every living soul in the canyons, mesas, and hills around Immanuel Mission.

Occasionally Dad took the car on his census rounds, and one day, when he was working alone, I accompanied him, visiting camps on the far side of Walker Creek, probably not more than five or six miles from the Mission. But the road we had to take went around the mesa, past *tó łikan,* and then followed a wagon track to the top of another mesa.

We parked the car and hiked down into a small canyon to look for an elusive outfit Dad had been trying to locate for days. He had asked at other outfits about this camp, and the Navajos had always laughed and given vague directions for finding the "Woman's Family." We arrived late in the afternoon and sure enough, it was inhabited only by women, a *ma sani* ("old mother" or "grandmother"), several daughters, and a couple of small girls. Not a man in sight.

Dad was a little uneasy entering a hogan occupied only by women, but the fact he was with a little boy added some propriety, and we entered and sat down at the indicated place on the ground, surprisingly, on the north side of the hogan, while all the women arrayed themselves across from us on the south side, usually reserved for men.

After we were seated, Dad opened his big black "Schedule" and started explaining what *waashindoon* wanted this time, and, after many questions and much discussion, he was asked to proceed. The first question was not promising, as it asked the given name, initial, and surname of every person in the camp, and of course no Navajo willingly shares this private information with an outsider.

The next question, "Age?" also took a great deal of time and no little invention on Dad's part. If available at all, one's age was usually vague, since Navajos had no calendars and also count a baby as "one" when born and "two" on its first birthday. In addition to this, they counted the years as winters, so usually the figure for "age" entered for the record was, at best, only a guess.

The questions then became more difficult and ultimately even a little ridiculous for Navajos: "Is home owned or rented?" "What is the value of the home?" "Is there a radio set in the home?" The Navajo ladies answered most of his queries, usually with some amusement, but they refused to give any information at all on a few of the questions.

All this happened in a cooperative, friendly manner, however, and we did not leave the camp until after sunset. Our way home, so near but such a long way round, meant we arrived back at the Mission well after dark.

The Census of 1930 recorded 39,064 Navajos living on the entire Navajo Reservation, but by the end of the twentieth century the Navajo Nation numbered over 250,000.

ROCKS, CAVES, AND SAND

In Dad's camp visitations he gradually worked farther afield by car, and on one long trip Danny and I took with him, we crossed over into the red mesa country of southern Utah.

Between camp visits, we stopped one day at noon for lunch near a red cliff, and while eating, we spotted a small cave in the rocks above us. When we had finished our sandwiches and cookies we took time for Dad's favorite sport of "exploring the country." Over the years Dad had taken Danny and me on a number of "expeditions" into the canyons around the Mission and as far north as Utah. We had examined many ruins up in the rocks, some with walls plastered with mud with century-old fingerprints where women had patted the mud into place.

On this trip we scrambled up the side of the mesa to the cave, and just beyond the entrance we saw that the floor of the cave sloped down much farther than we anticipated. It was almost dark down in the main room. We spent half an hour or more stumbling around in the musty gloom and found some traces of fresh smoke on a wall, indicating recent habitation by someone, and then, farther down, shards of pottery and tiny dry corncobs, traces of a much more ancient Anasazi occupancy.

Dad had his trusty little folding camera, but in those pre-flash days, it was too dark to photograph anything in the cave, so he had me climb back up and stand near the opening, silhouetted against the bright outside light, and took what became one of my favorite pictures.

On another trip Dad and I visited that same area and, after several calls on camps, arrived late in the afternoon at an outfit on the edge of a huge sand dune. I was tired and didn't want to put on my shoes, so Dad told me to just wait in the car while he went to the hogan.

After a few minutes an old woman with a cane came hobbling by, and seeing me sitting alone, hobbled over to the car and demanded loudly in a shrill, querulous voice, *ha' át'iishǫ baa naniná*? What was I doing just sitting there?

I understood the question but couldn't think how to explain why I was there alone, so just sat silent. She raised her voice and angrily repeated her question, but I remained silent. This really irritated the ancient lady, and she walked away, waving her walking stick and shouting words I didn't want to understand about rude *bilagáana* kids.

A little later, I got out of the car and ventured over to the edge of the sand dune, then slid down part-way and just lay there enjoying the cool sand and warm sunshine. A Navajo boy saw me and came and lay down about ten feet away, without a word.

After a few minutes of silence he looked over at me, then started a slight flipping of sand with one hand. I followed suit, and we were introduced. We then started playing in the sand, rolling down the dune. The Navajo boy and I did not exchange a word during all our time together.

NAVAJO WAY OF DEATH

The Navajos believed that any contact with a dead body could be deadly, as the *ch'įįdii,* or evil spirit of the dead one, would remain long after other life had left the body. If an individual died inside the hogan, it had to be sealed, and anyone who participated in the burial was isolated for at least four days. On one occasion a man died in a camp near Immanuel Mission, and we provided some hot food to members of his family as they were sitting outside, alone in very cold and windy weather, for the prescribed number of days.

This deadly fear of evil spirits prompted many Navajo families to ask the trader or someone from the Mission to help with a burial when there was a death in the family, as the *bilagáana* didn't seem to be affected by the evil spirit.

I was first involved in such requests when I was about eleven, and a death occurred in a Navajo family who lived some distance north of *tó 'ádin* (waterless) mesa just north of the Mission. They sent a relative to the Mission to

First riding lesson. Alwin was pulling leather just to stay
on that horse.

get help with the burial, and Dad immediately put a pick and shovels in the car. Unwillingly, he allowed me to accompany him, and we set off in the Model A, with the Navajo messenger as guide.

After improvising the final few miles over a trail through sand and brush, we finally located the isolated camp not far from the Utah state line and drove up to a substantial winter hogan with about a dozen family members standing outside, a few yards away, around a smoldering campfire.

After a few quiet words of greeting, Dad and I walked to the hogan and raised the blanket and saw the body of a man in his thirties who had died of tuberculosis, lying on the packed clay ground in the back of the hogan, wrapped in a Pendleton blanket, with his saddle, lariat, and other personal possessions piled around him. Most of the family belongings had been taken outside the hogan, probably before he died.

Dad returned to the group outside standing around the fire and said he needed a volunteer to help us.

After quite a discussion, the mother of the dead man stood up, and angrily berating the men of the group, took off her turquoise necklace, a strand of coral, a bracelet, and several silver rings and handed them to the young woman standing by her. She didn't want to have to discard them because they had become exposed to *ch'įįdii*.

Then, to my utter astonishment, she pulled off her green velveteen blouse, hung it on the hitching post, and, still muttering, pushed past us and strode topless into the hogan.

I was speechless, and even Dad appeared a little bemused, but we gamely took up our pick and shovels, followed her inside the hogan and set to work digging a shallow grave, all the while carefully keeping our eyes on our shovels. She immediately started to pull down parts of the logs overhead, causing dust and bits of bark to pour over her hair and everything else.

The most difficult part of this funeral was lifting the heavy, wrapped body into the grave with the determined little woman grimly helping us. All of his things had to be destroyed, so she smashed several cups and dishes, and then we went outside and told the men still standing around the fire to help us seal the hogan.

After some hesitation, several men came over and pulled down the outside logs, and the hogan was then abandoned, never to be approached again by any traditional Navajo.

They simply said, "We don't walk there anymore."

43   The Only Girl

Helen Jean Girdner, the only member of the family to be born in a hospital in Farmington rather than at home, arrived on March 17, 1931 (St. Patrick's Day), at midnight, and, as the attending doctor was named Moran and the head nurse was Gallagher, Mother was always suspicious that the clock might have been set ahead for just a minute or two that night. They were delighted that the little girl had red hair but quite disappointed when she wasn't given a proper Irish name, such as Colleen or Erin, but Helen she remained.

Mother had her hands full in managing the daily life of a largely male extended family, including a husband, two boys, and an elderly Navajo man, so there was precious little time for small-girl activities. Aunt Clara was very fond of Helen, and whenever she had spare time would sew nice clothes for Helen, but Aunt Clara was always busy and preoccupied with her life's work as a missionary.

Little Navajo girls, unlike Navajo boys, seldom visited the Mission, so Helen had no contemporary playmates and tried to tag along with two older brothers in their activities. But they resented her intrusion into their strenuous boy's business and occasionally even hid from her.

Mother noticed this behavior and one day called me in for a little conversation in which she pointed out our thoughtless behavior and asked me why we were hiding when we knew Helen was looking for us. I gave an evasive answer, and then Mother said something I will never forget: "You know what I hear? A lonely little girl calling for someone to just notice her."

When Helen was seven, in 1938, the family moved to the Navajo Methodist Mission in Farmington. But she was still the only white girl of all the children in Miss Huffman's room, who had names like Eva Begay, Lucy Benally, and Frances Curley.

Helen, to some extent, was a pilgrim for most of her life. In 1957 she married Martin Waldron, a tall, dashing young man just out of the British army, and they soon left for the scepter'd isle where she exchanged the spacious skies, mesas, and desert of Arizona for the plush fields, rolling downs, and chalk cliffs of the English Channel.

They made their home in East Sussex and, like Rudyard Kipling, who had moved to England from India some fifty years before, Helen remained for over half a century in Hailsham, not far from Bateman's, Kipling's home in the nearby village of Burwash. She never returned to live in the high desert country.

Alwin displaying his new sister Helen.

44 A Splash in the Tank

WATER BOXES

Except for school recruitment, there was little government activity in the Four Corners part of the Reservation during the 1920s. However, early in his administration of the Northern Navajo Agency, Superintendent Kneale became aware of the scarcity of water for the flocks of Navajo sheep. He immediately initiated a program to develop the many small springs on the Reservation to provide a clean and constant water supply for the Navajos and their flocks of sheep.

The water flowed underground through galvanized pipes from the source of spring water to a 25 x 3-foot concrete water box, to make about eighteen inches of water available year-round. A pipe fed in the water at one end, and a spillway let it run over the far end of the tank, where it seeped back into the earth. Sometimes a little grass and even patches of moss would grow around the overflow area.

The nearest tank to us was about a mile south of the Mission on the wide, sandy bank of *tó chin lin,* a small, usually dry wash that ran down from the foothills of the mountains. This tank was right on the main trail that led from the *tsegi hoch cho* canyon to the Mission and eventually on to Sweetwater Trading Post.

Danny and I discovered this tank on one of our hikes to *tsé sa'an* mesa, and it became a convenient rest area for a drink of "cool" water and perhaps a sit on the edge of the tank.

One hot afternoon we stopped for a drink before the last mile home. The water looked so inviting that we couldn't resist stripping off our clothes and swimming in the shallow water box, unconcerned about the strong sheep odor but keeping a wary eye on the trail for any lone Navajo horseman who might come riding over the hill to discover two naked little white boys splashing about in the Navajo stock tank.

SHEEP DIP

In the early 1930s the Bureau of Indian Affairs decided that all sheep on the Navajo Reservation were to be dipped annually to control ticks and other parasites. Some 250 sheep dip tanks were constructed across the Navajo Reservation, each consisting of long concrete trenches lined with a metal tank about two feet wide and four feet deep.

Bob Martin at the government sheep dip
just south of the Mission.

Sheep dip.

Sheep-dip vats were filled with an insecticide, Black Leaf or toxaphene, a bright yellow, vile-smelling solution made with a mixture of a great number of chemicals, but claimed by many to be a mixture of sulfur and tobacco. Some 20,000 gallons would be pumped into the vat every day and emptied and refilled every night. (Toxaphene was permanently banned as a sheep dip in 1986.)

Down in the valley about a mile west of Immanuel Mission, the BIA installed a permanent sheep dip facility and branding corral, and during the summer of each year it became the scene of great activity. All the families in the area brought their flocks to be dipped, and campfires lighted the hills and valley at night as dozens of outfits waited with their sheep for their turn to put their animals through the noisy, smelly, dirty process.

When the time came to dip, the youngsters of the outfit drove their flock into a holding pen where they had a long wait as, one at a time, each animal was thrown into the smelly yellow liquid and struggled through the length of the trench. The final insult was having their heads shoved under the chemicals with a pole, although the horns of some billygoats were too wide for the tank.

The bewildered wet animals finally reached the end of the tank and climbed a set of steep steps for another wait to drip off on the "dry off pad" before finally being driven to the post-dip corral. Then the first unfortunate animal of the next flock could be dumped into the foul solution.

A pungent, decidedly unpleasant odor filled our small valley for days and could be detected at the Mission over a mile away to the east, which was overflowing as men, some of the women, and a very few kids came to visit during the wait for their turn at the dip.

VISITORS AT SHEEP DIP TIME

So many Navajos visited Immanuel Mission that Aunt Clara was in the common room from sunup to sunset every day during dipping season. One rainy September night during the early 1920s, forty Navajos sought refuge on the earth floors of the kitchen and sitting room, and once two women spread their blankets on the bedroom floor.

A discarded metal tank rested on its side in the back yard of the Mission for years and served as a metal trampoline for visiting as well as Mission kids, who jumped and bounced up and down on our own private "ramdie, bamdie flamdilater" for many a noisy hour on long summer evenings.

45 The Breath of Life

Ruach, the ancient Hebrew word for wind, was also used in the Christian tradition to define the Spirit unseen that had neither limits nor any recognized destination—God. *Níyol,* wind, was also a tremendous force in everyday life on the Navajo Reservation. A sudden windstorm could suddenly blow in at any time without warning, and we soon learned to stay inside during a major windstorm as it howled around the corners for days, obscuring the sun and sending clouds of sand blowing and tumbleweeds rolling. Anything unsecured could blow miles away, and we ventured outside only for chores and other important duties during a big wind. It didn't help that the outhouse was some distance away from the house.

After every major sandstorm we would find a fan of fine red sand sifted on the floor just inside every door and piled in ridges along every windowsill, and we were in for a major housecleaning. Dad's notes mention "sweeping up twenty pounds of sand after just one fierce two-day blow." One wild night, as sand rattled the windows, Dad put his hand on the wall and then motioned for me to come over and join him. As soon as I touched the wall I could feel the whole building trembling from the force of wind. It surprised me but I knew it would not collapse. Dad had built it.

Reading James K. McNeley's *Holy Wind in Navajo Philosophy,* I learned that wind was also an important element in Navajo belief. They thought of breath as a holy wind, the spiritual part of being. Through wind the holy ones could give them guidance for their thoughts and behavior, provide support, and warn of the consequences for some act committed long ago.

When I was quite young Yellowhair pointed out to me that my thumbprints had a whirlwind pattern just like that of a sand dune and then explained to me at length the significance of wind as the breath of life, a concept I didn't fully comprehend until years later.

The Reverend Shirley Montoya is a Navajo who once served as associate pastor of Christ Church United Methodist of Tucson. She pointed out in a Christmas message (reported in the *Arizona Daily Star* on January 12, 2004) that she saw no reason her culture and her religion needed to be mutually exclusive. She pointed out the parallels between them:

THE BREATH OF LIFE

The Navajo believed that breath is a holy wind, the spiritual part of a being. That's something like the Holy Spirit. The Navajo ceremonies teach about wholeness and wellness: the body, spirit, and mind must be in tune. In Romans the Apostle Paul talks about his struggle between his mind and his will. We wrestle with that.

She went on to say that her people on the Navajo Reservation were wrestling in other ways: "Diabetes is rampant. The old ways are being lost. Few know how to make cornmeal mush or dry meat or sweeten cake with wheat germ." But she illustrated how her Tucson congregation could learn from the Navajo: "People cut down Christmas trees without much thought to their life and then throw them away. Back home the Navajo way is to offer corn pollen to ask for forgiveness, then use every part of the tree. Needles are burned at ceremonies. The wood facilitates cooking."

Many years before, in *Navajo Windway and Chiricahua Windway*, Father Berard Haile discussed the part wind plays in Navajo belief, noting that a Wind Soul enters at birth, influences all thought and behavior during life, and departs only at death, "something like the Holy Spirit."

Navajos also believed that if a mother-in-law and her son-in-law looked at each other, one or both could eventually go blind, and as a result many families lived together for years without these two ever seeing each other. If bystanders sighted a son-in-law approaching, they would call out "*naadaani*," "son-in-law," and he would stop and not approach the group until she either retreated into the hogan or covered her head with a blanket.

Whirlwinds or dust devils were also bad luck, and when one was discovered coming toward a Navajo camp someone would always call "*naadaani, naadaani*," so that the whirlwind would veer off and avoid their hogan. The ever-present curse of trachoma among the Navajos may have had something to do with causing this particular taboo about seeing your son-in-law, but I understand some people in Mongolia have been known to practice this same custom.

Usually Navajo men came to the Mission by horseback if they were alone or as part of a group of men, but they often came in a springless wagon if they were accompanied by their family. When the mother-in-law came along too, the man sat on the bench seat facing forward, his wife and baby sat beside him, and the mother-in-law sat behind him on the flat bed of the wagon box with the older children. The mother-in-law always faced backward, wearing a blanket that she could draw over her head if the son-in-law happened to look back. An entire family could spend a whole day traveling together in a wagon without either the man or his mother-in-law ever seeing each other. On arriving at their destination they took turns leaving the wagon.

Reservation Postal Service

EARLY DAY DELIVERIES

For years we picked up our mail only once or twice a month, since we went to town only when we needed supplies or had other business to transact. This was a long interval for a faith-based little Mission whose only source of funds came in checks from various assemblies across the United States. However, the trader at Sweetwater made occasional trips to town to restock his supplies from the Progressive Mercantile in Fruitland, and when he passed through Shiprock on the return trip he always picked up the mail sack for Immanuel Mission.

This sporadic mail service produced a feast and famine at Immanuel Mission, especially during the early days, and after a long period of no mail we could expect an avalanche when it did come. On one occasion Aunt Florence received fourteen letters at one time, and one New Year, forty letters and cards arrived in a single sack.

CHRISTMAS GREETINGS

In 1930, November was unseasonably cold, and everyone worked industriously to get all their cards, letters, and packages ready, We completely filled a canvas mail sack, locked it, and sent it over the mesa to the Sweetwater Trading Post by way of a passing Navajo in late November. We had already had an early snow that year, and we were determined to have everything in the mail before the Christmas rush.

After the big push we all settled down to wait for our return Christmas mail. A big snow fell on the Reservation that winter, blocking all roads and delaying all travel, so we waited, and waited. No mail came, so we waited some more.

Finally, the day before Christmas, a cold and complaining Navajo on a tired old horse came struggling through the snow with a bulging wet bag of mail.

We thanked the courier, rewarded him with hot coffee and a loaf of bread, and set him, lightened, back on the trail. Then we eagerly gathered at the kitchen table while Grandfather unlocked the bag and turned it upside down. Out tumbled packages, letters, and cards—the same packages, letters, and cards we had so eagerly "mailed" six weeks before!

POSTAGE STAMPS

Both Grandfather and Aunt Clara passed on to me the stamps from the letters of their voluminous worldwide correspondence, and at a very early age I had amassed a respectable collection: exotic stamps, postmarked in Argentina, Bolivia, Cape of Good Hope, Ceylon, Charkha, Chile, China, Colombia, Congo, Ecuador, Egypt, Fiji, Guatemala, Guinea, Honduras, India, Kenya, Lebanon, Maroc, Nejd, Nigeria, Palestine, Peru, Portuguese India, Salvador, Senegal, Soudan Français, South Transvaal, Straits Settlements, Uganda, Union of South Africa, Upper Volta, and West Africa.

Grandfather and Aunt Clara apparently didn't know anyone in Zambia. The most unusual item in my stamp collection, however, is an envelope from a mission in the mountains of Colombia that had no stamp at all but an ink notation in English: "mail carried from this place does not require postage."

Early on, my folks had presented me with a loose-leaf stamp album, and over the next few years I carefully mounted my assortment with the prescribed little hinges on printed spaces in the album until the little album became completely filled. Then, just before we left the Reservation in 1938, they gave me a splendid red Scott album, and I started transferring stamps and, although I later stopped collecting them, this album still contains a great collection of ancient exotic stamps.

PEN PALS

My stamp collection was augmented by an active overseas correspondence of my own that I discovered by reading *Boys' Life,* published by the Boy Scouts of America. At that time "pen pals" were being promoted by the Boy Scouts and other organizations to create understanding and good will among young people worldwide, and they published lists of names and addresses of young people in many foreign lands who wanted to contact someone in the United States.

I early learned to type a little on Aunt Clara's big upright typewriter and at about the age of eleven began corresponding with a boy my age in Denmark, Henning Pedersen, who lived in a town with the improbable name of Kjellerup. Henning wrote in English and proved to have a gift for descriptive prose about his home country on the North Sea, but I had the advantage of living among the "red Indians," so for years we regularly exchanged letters, photos, literature, and stamps.

Henning had another pen pal, a boy who lived in Gutenberg, Sweden, who also understood English, and we developed our own three-way correspondence club. This exchange was to continue until the onset of World War II. Henning's last letter described German parachutes coming down near his village, and I lost all contact with him. I also wrote to Keith Scarr, another boy in Hobart, Tasmania, for a number of years with similar exchanges, but we also lost contact during the war. I developed several other pen pals, too, including a girl in London who sent me her picture, but Henning always remained my special friend.

A postscript came over sixty years later, when I started to write about my days on the Reservation and began wondering what happened to my boyhood pen pal in Denmark so long ago.

Thanks to modern e-mail, I was able to find the library in the town of Kjellerup and had the luck to contact a most extraordinary, helpful person, Hanne Vestergaard, who almost immediately replied, saying every Pedersen listed in Kjellerup had been phoned, but Pedersen was a common name and no one remembered a Henning. I e-mailed my grateful thanks for the unusual cooperation and dismissed Henning as lost.

Nearly a month later I was surprised by another message from the faithful Hanne Vestergaard. *Midtiyllands Avis,* the local newspaper, had printed a story about my quest, and a relative of Henning read the piece. Henning happened to be in Kjellerup to attend a wedding, learned of the article, and contacted the newspaper. They interviewed Henning for a story, and Hanne Vestergaard got in touch with me again for a picture of the long-lost American who found the local boy he had known before the war, for a follow-up story in the paper.

Unfortunately, I have never been able to locate either of the two fellows in Hobart and Gutenberg—or that blond girl in London.

47 Fun and Games

The isolation of Immanuel Mission made not only medical and church activities impossible, but many basic services were also unavailable. Sidewalks lined with gasoline stations, garages, and grocery, hardware, and drug stores were a day's journey away, as were theaters, art galleries, concerts, lectures, and organized sporting events.

Entertainment, as such, was not considered important at Immanuel Mission, and although we kids were often told to "go outside and play," organized fun was regarded as somewhat dubious and probably "worldly." Dancing was strictly forbidden, but that wasn't much of a problem as there were no partners available anyway. Movies were also frowned on, but that, too, was no problem out on the Reservation.

Pool halls were known to be hangouts for people with no purpose in their lives, and gambling, of course, was strictly forbidden at all times. I never saw a deck of the sinful cardboards or poker chips at the Mission. Dice were also looked upon with disfavor, although later they were allowed a few board games such as Monopoly.

There was a croquet set at the Mission, and Mother and Dad would guide us through the strangely arranged wickets by knocking the wooden ball with a long-handled wooden hammer. Without grass, the hard dirt court was always dusty, and we usually succeeded in getting ourselves sweaty and dirty on hot afternoons.

Although playing cards were considered sinful and never allowed, nevertheless we did play some card games with other cards, and Pit was extremely popular with the whole family. On many a winter night any Navajo in the vicinity would have wondered at the uproarious laughing and shouting sessions at the Mission, which drowned out the howling of the cold wind around the corners of the house.

PROVERBS

Aunt Clara was usually reading or occupied with other tasks and did not participate in most of these activities, so it came as a surprise to us when she introduced a new game she called "Proverbs," adapted from a popular game at that time, Authors. She selected twenty subjects from the Book of Proverbs,

Showing off bows and arrows,
almost obsolete by then.

taking four proverbs from each subject, and typed them all on eighty pasteboard cards. We followed the rules of the original game and learned the ancient wisdom of the Old Testament rather than the works of modern writers.

Proverbs remained popular with us for years, and several young, educated Navajos learned to play the game with us. To this day I can season my conversation with profound bits of wisdom: "Be not wise in thine own eyes," "As cold waters to a thirsty soul, so is good news from a far country," "A soft answer turneth away wrath," and "Rejoice not when thy enemy falleth."

BOARD GAMES

Dad, an excellent checkers player, taught me the fundamentals of the game, and over the years I became fairly proficient and introduced checkers to several young Navajos. We played with a rather loose interpretation of the rules, as they considered many regulations, such as not moving backward or diagonally across the board, to be silly and unnecessary and just wanted to get on with decimating the other guy's warriors and getting caps on their own chiefs.

As early as I can remember, we had a complete set of black dominoes, but I wasn't as interested in playing a game that involved matching up spots as much as I was fascinated by making great circles of the wooden slabs, then pushing one over and watching them fall in a rippling tide.

Board games became an important part of recreation at the Mission, and I became so absorbed in the financial deals of Monopoly one afternoon that Yellowhair complained. When I wanted to finish my game before going after the cows with him, and he walked off alone grumbling about my "gambling," I suddenly realized I was creating a very bad impression for him and the Navajos.

The Navajos considered gambling as an activity that put one out of harmony, much the same as sickness did, but many Navajos were inveterate gamblers, and it was not unusual for a man to gamble away just about everything he had. So it was important that we did not do anything at the Mission that would suggest that we approved of any kind of wagering. Navajo gambling was perhaps the biggest vice during the 1930s, because liquor was not yet readily available, at least in our corner of the Reservation, and we were aware of only a few drunks in that area.

DILTH-DILTH

Navajo boys had a stick dice game they called *dilth-dilth,* and one summer when I was alone at the Mission with just Aunt Clara and Yellowhair, three boys I knew gathered in the back of the Mission and started playing. I hung around watching the action, and they introduced me to the fundamentals of the game.

It was essentially a dice game without dice, played by dashing two small, painted boards against a large stone. The color combination that fell out determined how many spaces a stick marker could be advanced around a circle of small stones.

I learned the basics of the game and started playing with them and enjoyed the experience until I realized we were playing for money or personal articles such as pocket knives or other valuables, and then I dropped out. Evidently Aunt Clara was unaware that it was gambling, but still I didn't tell her of my involvement.

The boys became so engrossed in their game that they stayed over and continued the play the next day. Then Aunt Clara discovered the purpose of the simple game and became concerned that Navajos would think we condoned gambling, so she told me that if they didn't leave by noon she would have to disperse them.

I didn't want to be involved, so I started walking up to my favorite "pottery flat" to see if I could find any new shards exposed by the wind that I could add to my collection. As I passed a clump of bushes growing by the arroyo, a black-tailed rattlesnake began rattling, and I returned to the Mission, grabbed a shovel, returned to the scene, flushed the big reptile out, induced it to strike at the shovel, and when it did, cut off the head and buried it.

Carrying what was left of the snake on my shovel, I headed back to the Mission to show my prize to Aunt Clara. As I approached the gamblers they began to heckle me about having to work while they could play, and then one fellow asked what I was carrying in the shovel. On impulse, I tossed the snake on their blanket, put down my shovel, and walked on into the house, leaving them scrambling in a panic to escape the sudden evil that appeared on their blanket.

When I told Aunt Clara what had just happened, she became excited and ran to the back door—but there wasn't a boy in sight. They had decamped and only a rumpled blanket and scattered little counter stones remained. She was concerned that the Navajos would consider the Mission under a curse and not come near the place. I had committed a serious error in public relations. But as it turned out, nobody ever mentioned the incident.

The boys may have decided it was best to keep everything to themselves. In any event Navajos continued coming to the Mission and, in time, the boys disappeared, but we never again had a problem with gambling around Immanuel Mission.

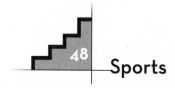

48 Sports

ROLL IN THE SNOW

Navajos always emphasized physical activity, and the men encouraged their boys to be active in their everyday life. In wintertime this included rushing out of the hogan and rolling naked in the snow. Dan and I learned of this vigorous Navajo practice and decided we could do likewise. We chose late at night for modesty, stripped in the kitchen, rushed out into the cold dark night, and flung ourselves into a bank of snow.

It literally took our breath away, and I found it almost impossible to force myself to roll over. With perseverance, however, I finally was able to complete two and a half rolls—I didn't know how many times the Navajo boys could roll over in the snow, but surely this was a new world's record for white missionary boys.

RUNNING RABBITS

A popular sport with young Navajo men was the rabbit hunt. A dozen or more fellows on horseback would ride in a group through the brush until they flushed out an unfortunate bunny. Immediately all would give chase, yelling in a high falsetto at the top of their voices and lashing their horses to run their best as the rabbit dodged in and out of the brush.

Riding in a pack, they were unable to avoid all the trees, boulders, and small arroyos, thus adding a handicap to the contest as they screamed along in pursuit. Eventually the rabbit would either find sanctuary in a hole or ledge, or would be run down by the brave hunters.

One day a young educated Navajo was standing with me out on our front porch watching as a large group of his tribesmen on the ridge south of the Mission excitedly charged through the bushes in pursuit of one hapless rabbit, and he turned to me with a deprecating grin and said, "They will get less than one square inch of rabbit each."

NAA'AHÓÓHAI

As I have mentioned, the chicken pull was a favorite Navajo sport traditionally sponsored by traders as a Fourth of July event, so Navajos always referred to Independence Day as *naa'ahóóhai* or rooster. I only witnessed this event once at Sweetwater Trading Post, when I was about five. Roy Foutz, the trader there at

Alwin showing off his gymnastics skills.

that time, buried a small bag of money rather than a rooster on a flat place near the trading post and covered it up to the neck of the bag in sand.

A number of young Navajo men were milling around on their horses waiting for the signal, and when Roy dropped his handkerchief they all came screaming down toward the "chicken" and tried to grab it by the neck, pull it out, and carry it on a mad dash for the finish line. To add to the excitement, Roy Foutz stood by the "chicken" with a small quirt and, as the Navajos came charging down, he flailed about, switching the horses to make them shy away from the prize. Out of the chaotic mob of yelling men, plunging horses, and clouds of dust, one young fellow managed to lean down, snatch the prize, and fight his way out of the confusion to gallop toward the goal with all the others crowding around, shouting, and trying to snatch the prize from him.

Chicken pull was good for bringing customers to the trading post, but it was all excitement and confusion for a five-year-old kid from the Mission.

Navajo boys also loved to wrestle, and some were always eager for a match with the red-haired *bilagáana* kid when they visited the Mission. Mother didn't appreciate my desire to scuffle around on the ground getting my clothes filthy. However, Dad encouraged me with rudimentary lessons in the manly sport he had learned in the army, and I grew proficient enough to take on boys even bigger than my own flyweight.

I remember one bizarre match when a boy about my size climbed to the top of a gate and challenged me to remove him to settle a disagreement. This was too much to ignore so I climbed up from the other side of the fence, and we engaged in a rather precarious wrestling match astride the shaky gate. In the process his bright green rayon shirt was completely destroyed, and he rode his burro home wearing a blanket, accompanied by his two older brothers, who were laughing at his predicament. But when a dirty, disheveled boy marched in boasting of his triumph, both Mother and Dad took a dim view of his offending the very people we were trying to show the Christian way of life.

BILAGÁANA GAMES

The isolation of the Mission made it difficult to organize any kind of team sports, since usually only Dad, Danny, and I were available to make up a team. Helen was too young to compete with her older brothers, and Yellowhair, the only other available player, took a dim view of all pointless activity that entailed running about for no apparent purpose.

Sports were featured in both my prized boys' magazines, *Boys' Life* and *Open Door for Boys,* and I developed an academic interest in contests. I even learned something about tennis, soccer, and lacrosse, and eventually acquired not only a softball, but also a football and a basketball, and I tried to learn the fundamentals of each game.

Softball was simple. Just throw a ball straight up in the air and then catch it when it came down, but pitching alone soon became tiresome, as I had to walk out and recover each pitch when it came down. In football I encountered the same problem of no receiver, so I was limited to kicking. At that time the drop kick was in vogue, and I assiduously worked on that, with only indifferent success.

Basketball offered more opportunities. Mother had become interested in the game as a student in the Bay Area, and one Christmas I received a beautiful regulation basketball. Dad had never played basketball but duly mounted a backboard and net on the far side of our windmill and carefully marked out the free throw line, where I spent many hours lofting the ball but never developed much proficiency in the art. There wasn't much point in running about dribbling the ball as it didn't rebound well from the ground, and of course it usually was a solitary game of "take the ball and run around."

DISAPPEARING BASKETBALL TRICK

Occasionally I tried to teach the fundamentals of basketball to Indian boys but with only indifferent results. Then one day, when I was alone at the Mission, a boy I didn't know came by, we threw the ball around for a short time, and he seemed to take an interest in the game.

After a time Walter Fairfield and some other Navajo men arrived, and I took a time-out to return to the house to welcome them. When I returned to our game, however, the boy had disappeared and so had my basketball. Apparently the boy had taken more interest in my equipment than in my game.

I walked back in the house, where the men were still sitting and talking, and reported the missing ball. Walter commented that on his arrival he had seen the boy leaving and had noticed that the boy was all hunched forward on his burro as if he was hiding something under his shirt.

Some weeks later Aunt Clara was visiting a summer camp on the mountain and spotted a basketball lying in the bushes near the camp. She started asking questions, but the outfit expressed surprise that it was there, and no one would acknowledge knowing anything about it or how it had gotten to their camp, so she just picked up the unclaimed ball and put in her car.

That evening after supper she casually remarked, "Oh, you might be interested in something I have out in the car." She would say no more, so I rushed out and opened the trunk—and there was my long-lost basketball, but somewhat the worse for wear. Apparently it had been kicked into cactus, as it had numerous spines sticking from the cover. The bladder had been pulled out, and a sour smell indicated it had been used to carry goat's milk. Further, it would no longer hold air for more than a few minutes. I tried to repair my ball with indifferent success, soon lost interest in basketball, and turned to other sports.

ONE-MAN OLYMPICS

The 1936 Olympic Summer Games were held in Berlin, and the black American runner Jesse Owens upset all Adolph Hitler's plans for a master race triumph by winning four gold medals: the 100-meter dash, 200-meter dash, 400-meter relay, and broad jump. This fired the ambition of a twelve-year-old would-be athlete on a remote Indian reservation in Arizona to stage his own Olympic games, so I prepared a private stadium in an empty area just east of my room at Immanuel Mission.

As track dominated the stunning news stories from Germany, running events dominated the makeshift arena. So lanes were laid out, willow cuttings were stuck in the ground for use as hurdles, and a plentiful supply of sand was used for the jumping pit. Pole vault standards proved to be beyond my engineering capabilities, so I abandoned that sport. A smooth, round rock the size of a soccer ball made an excellent shot, and although the possibility of its being dropped on a bare foot was ever-present, I ignored that hazard.

All weights, distances, and times were arbitrary. Because I had no idea of the official standards for time or distances for any of the events, I used a yardstick and a big pocket watch to set my own regulations. The nice thing about this was that I could adjust the rules at will as the events progressed.

The next problem was the not-insignificant matter of finding competitors to perform in this magnificent facility. I recruited Dan, but soon found that an eight-year-old was not exactly enthusiastic about all that running and jumping, as he had no chance of ever winning any event, and anyway, he couldn't even lift that big rock shot put.

Indian boys my age seldom came by the Mission, and those who did come by were usually busy rattling their cans of rocks to keep their herds of sheep together and had no time for just jumping and running around. This left me not only the athlete and official judge but usually the only spectator, although an occasional passing Indian would stand by the fence and watch the activity with a bemused expression, and occasionally Dad could be persuaded to come see a very spectacular event.

My Olympics did not escape notice by passing Navajos, and sometimes I overheard comments about the strange activities of that *bilagáana* kid. These remarks were not intended to be offensive, for blunt comments were not uncommon in Navajo conversation.

As my stadium had no shade during the day, most games were played in the cool of the evening and usually continued until I could no longer distinguish the markers in the gathering dusk. In every contest it was only possible to have one performance at a time and therefore there was a lot of repetition, as I had to run and jump for several countries, one at a time. All jumps were easy to decide, but determining exact results for running events was confusing. The pocket watch indicated about the same time for each run, although the later runs tended to be a little slower than earlier ones.

There was always a winner and that was me, and there was always a loser, and that was me also. This led to some ambivalence on my part, since victory was always accompanied by defeat. It carried over into my adult life, and I never have been able to really enjoy a big win, because there is also the element of how miserable the other fellow must be feeling to lose. This tends to temper the triumph, and as a result I always lacked the "killer instinct" that motivates the successful athlete. Of course, lack of ability may also have some bearing on results, but being vindictive and jeering the losing opponent always seemed very distasteful.

Dad reinforced this "no loser" attitude, and, although he enjoyed the competition of playing games like checkers, he would never finish a game. When the game reached the point where he was certain to win, he always came up with an excuse for the match to be terminated early, sometimes by just "accidentally" knocking over the board and scattering the remaining pieces.

49 Roundups and Ruins

A BOY, THREE COWS, AND AN INDIAN

One afternoon, when Yellowhair was away, it fell to me to round up the cows. But unlike Yellowhair, I had not kept constant watch on their wanderings during the day and only knew they were somewhere west of Immanuel Mission. I was not as adept as Yellowhair in tracking, and, even worse, I was not very familiar with that particular canyon, but in late afternoon I set off in the general direction where I thought the cows had wandered and trudged along nearly an hour without a clue as to where to look for the animals.

Several miles from home I climbed a little hill and found tracks going in both directions. I was sitting down to study my situation when I spotted a Navajo man galloping up the slope below me. I was impressed by the fine, spirited pony he was riding, and as he drew near I recognized him as a hot-shot young fellow who had visited the Mission several times and impressed us as something of a dandy, with fancy clothes and an abundance of jewelry.

He pulled his horse up in a dramatic cloud of dust and asked me the Navajo greeting question, "*Háágóó sha?*" ("Where?") Not wanting to admit I didn't know where I was going, I gave a short answer: "*Béégashii.*" Cows.

He laughed, pointed with his lips in the opposite direction from the way I was going, and said my lost herd was on the other side of the hill, then set spurs to his mount, and tore off. As I stood looking after him with mixed feelings of relief and chagrin that I had not found the cows myself, he suddenly wheeled his horse, trotted back, and, again pointing with his lips, told me, "There's water just under the hill!" and with a flourish, thundered off again.

As we never packed a bottle of water on a trip of only a few miles, I was really thirsty, so I started down the hill. It almost immediately dropped off into a little hidden canyon with sheer sandstone cliffs, and down below, tucked under a ledge of stone, was a tiny spring, dripping clear water.

It was after sundown, but I took time after a long draught of the cool water to sit down by the pool. I was watching a number of swallows flying around in the evening sky when I noticed they were dipping in and out of a small cave high on the steep canyon wall above me.

Cows grazing, *tsé sa'an* in the background.

I climbed up the cliff a little farther and saw a small Anasazi ruin tucked just under the rim and hidden from the pool below. Swallows were darting in and out, busily building nests on the wall just below the overhanging cliff. Carefully working my way on up the cliff, I explored the small fortification and found pottery shards, very small dried corncobs, burned places on the walls, and other signs of habitation by ancient man.

Suddenly the thought came to me that as this ruin was so far away from any road it was possible no white man had ever been up here before. Navajos have a morbid dread of entering any place associated with dead people, and I might well be the first person to stand in these ruins in over 1,000 years. I wanted to stay longer and explore this little canyon ruin but had cows to find and miles to go before I slept, so I dutifully climbed up and out. I soon found the cows contentedly waiting exactly where the young Navajo rider had pointed and started my little convoy slowly plodding homeward.

It was completely dark when we finally came in sight of the Mission, and I sighted a small light. Mother had become concerned about her prodigal son and his small herd and walked the 100 yards to the edge of the Mission to hang a lantern on the corner fence post to guide him home through the night.

HIDDEN RUINS

Just beyond *tsé sa'an,* the red butte two miles south of Immanuel Mission, was a seemingly endless network of canyons and little side canyons with hundreds of little rock and mud Anasazi ruins. Some were just above the canyon floor, and others were in small sheltered coves that were completely hidden from the canyon floor by the overhanging water-stained cliffs, blended with the sandstone walls. These lofty ruins were usually accessible only by small hand-holes pecked into the almost-sheer cliff, and many appeared untouched by the centuries.

One day while exploring in the *tsegi* I found, in addition to the usual corncobs and pottery shards, a tiny herd of little molded clay figures and started stuffing them in my pocket. When Aunt Clara arrived at the cave I excitedly handed her one of the little clay cows.

She examined the little figure and identified it as recent, probably the work of a Navajo boy herding sheep on the canyon floor, and told me to put the cows back where I had found them, as they belonged to him. I did as I was told but have never forgotten that small herd of clay figures.

Although nearly all ruins were up in the canyons, there was evidence of temporary camps closer to home. I had a favorite area, my own "pottery flat" in a clay area just beyond a small arroyo east of the Mission, and there I found hundreds of shards, mostly black-on-white but some red ones and even a few yellow fragments. Perhaps it was a place where the ancient ones gathered to fashion pots, bowls, and other pieces for everyday use.

After a rare rainstorm—or more frequently, a violent sandstorm—a new layer of shards would appear, and, in that period before there were many rules and regulations, I gathered hundreds of shards and a few arrow points, grinding stones, metates, and even a piece of a stone axe. A prized find was the broken stem of a small pipe, with traces of smoke still evident.

At Immanuel Mission we also had a few bowls acquired through trade with an occasional Navajo visitor who brought them in to sell. They were careful to not disclose where the pots had been found, and we lacked the expertise to discern if they were of Anasazi origin or were crafted by more recent Indians. We also had a sense of respect for the ancient people and their sites and were careful always to leave a ruin intact by never damaging walls, defacing petroglyphs, digging, or otherwise disturbing ancient sites. Nor did we ever discover any intact piece of pottery in any ruin.

The artifacts I left in my "Mission museum" may still be there, tucked away in some old wall and long forgotten, much as they had been for the centuries before me.

"POT HUNTERS"

The Four Corners area at that time was so inaccessible that most old sites had not yet been trashed by "pot hunters," although a number of people had started to excavate pots and artifacts. Pottery, arrowheads, and other relics were considered fair game by most white people, and some traders proudly displayed

Beulah Neff at Anasazi cliff dwelling.

their beautifully mounted arrowheads, bowls, pottery, and other artifacts alongside their extensive collections of Navajo rugs.

Perhaps the best-known amateur collector of the time was Richard Wetherill, who is the subject of a biography by Frank McNitt, *Richard Wetherill–Anasazi*. Wetherill discovered the great cliff house ruins of Mesa Verde in 1888, and by 1890 had mapped the cliffs and canyons of the area and explored nearly 200 cliff dwellings. Wetherill and his brothers started excavations in the ruins and uncovered numerous mummies, corncobs, pieces of pottery, bone implements, stone axes, bows and arrows, strings of beads, blankets, and items of clothing such as sandals, buckskin caps, and cedar bark breechclouts, as well as hundreds of other artifacts, which were exhibited at Chicago World's Fair in 1893.

As they had no formal education in archaeology, they have been referred to as "professional pot hunters." However, Wetherill painstakingly recorded everything recovered and marked every relic for identification. Early on, he contacted the Smithsonian Institution and offered the collection for the "cost of excavating," but the Smithsonian politely informed him that "due to the lack of funds, they could only accept donations."

The Wetherill collections were eventually acquired by several institutions, including the Colorado State Museum, the University of Pennsylvania, and the National Museum in Helsinki, Finland. Several scientific expeditions of university and museum archaeologists started to research Anasazi sites at that time, but most concentrated in the western and southern sectors of the Navajo Reservation.

Richard Wetherill located dozens of other Anasazi sites, and by 1890 he had explored and mapped much of the Navajo Reservation. He later operated a trading post in the Pueblo Bonito area of Chaco Canyon, described by Frances Gillmor and Louisa Wade Wetherill in *Traders to the Navajos*. I had the distinct privilege of attending a class under Professor Frances Gillmor while attending the University of Arizona a few years after the book was published.

EARL H. MORRIS

A native of New Mexico, Earl Morris started his archaeological research early. His father was active in collecting artifacts, and Earl Morris later told this story, which is quoted in his biography by Florence and Robert Lister, *Earl Morris and Southwestern Archaeology*:

> One morning in March of 1893, Father handed me a worn-out pick, the handle of which he had shortened to my length, and said: "Go dig in that hole where I worked yesterday, and you will be out of my way." On my first stroke there rolled down a roundish, gray object that looked like a cobblestone, but when I turned it over, it proved to be the bowl of a black-on-white dipper ... Thus at three and a half years of age there happened the clinching event that was to make of me an ardent pot hunter, who later on was to acquire the more creditable, and I hope earned, classification as an archaeologist.

In 1923 Aztec National Monument was established by President Harding, and Earl Morris was appointed the first custodian. He also led several of Charles Bernheimer's expeditions to explore the Navajo Mountain area and "disturb the past to inform the present." Morris was particularly interested in comparing the relationship between the late Basketmaker period and what was then called the Early Pueblo. In 1923 he was also very interested in the unknown canyon lands south of Immanuel Mission, where he wanted to explore the headwaters of the Red Wash and look for the Lost City of the Lukachukai Mountains.

Earl Morris's wife, Ann Axtell Morris, discussed this legend in *Digging in the Southwest*. "Somewhere in that torn and broken labyrinth," she wrote, "one alcove hides the lost city of the Lukachukai." She went on to relate the story of the Franciscan fathers Anselm and Fintan, who

> were trying to return to St. Michaels by wagon through the trackless Lukachukai with a Navajo guide and stopped at noon in the heights. Below them the great gashed canyons of Del Muerto and De Chelly

are just perceptible and along the horizon was Black Mountain, the last stand of the old-style Navajo, some of whom have never seen a white man.

The two priests were busy preparing lunch when they realized their Navajo guide had disappeared. He eventually returned with an enormous Pueblo III water jar under his arm. He wouldn't say where he had found the jar, only pointed into the canyon with his lips and said there were "houses down there" in a high alcove.

The priests had no time to explore but pressed on—determined to return and find the lost city, but they never did, and it remains lost to this day.

ROCK ART

Mysterious petroglyphs were chipped on rock walls around the base of cliffs in many canyons near Immanuel Mission, and sometimes we found elaborate whirls and strange little figures that conveyed some unknown message we couldn't decipher. On a smooth yellow cliff below Pastoria Peak in the Carrizo Mountains, one large fascinating sketch depicted a group of running wild horses, manes and tails streaming in the wind, probably a recent work by one or more Navajos. Navajos loved to draw horses. Fortunately spray paint had not yet been invented in those innocent days.

Canyons were the heart of Navajo Country for me, and to this day, when I think of my Reservation days, the first picture that flashes through my mind is of the sheer, red sandstone walls and ruins up in the alcoves of *tsegi hoch cho* canyon. And I get maybe just a twinge of regret that I didn't live on the Reservation long enough to explore all those mysterious canyons and perhaps find that Lost City of the Lukachukai.

50 Names

n our prevailing white culture we are proud of our names and carefully recite them upon meeting a new person. We are pleased to have our name remembered and used in a conversation. We put our names on our houses, shops, and business cards and are proud to see them in print, especially if they are spelled correctly.

Having a name put on a building, park, school, library, bridge, or even a water fountain is the ultimate honor for the *bilagáana,* but not for the Navajo in the 1930s. Then a name had a personal, spiritual significance, and its power could be diminished by making it public. In *Along Navajo Trails,* Will Evans wrote of some customers hesitating to reveal their names even for pawn records, and on one occasion a man answered Evans's query about his name with, "I don't know, ask someone else."

When meeting someone, the white man would always introduce himself by giving his own name and follow by asking the other person's name: something like, "Hi, my name's Tom Jefferson. What's your name?" To the Navajo this was as rude as if the *bilagáana* said, "Hi, my name is Tom and I make $80,000 a year. What do you make?" An intrusion into personal affairs like that doesn't even deserve an answer.

Only a few Navajos ever knew another's private name, and nearly everyone was referred to by what we would today call a nickname, reference words based on a relationship or personal characteristic. Thus the son of *tł'ah nééz,* "big left-handed," was referred to as *tłah nez biye'* or "son of big left-handed."

Biye' has become anglicized to "Begay" and is a very common family name among Navajos, as is *binálí,* "his grandfather," which now is often spelled Benally. To avoid saying a person's name, Navajos usually employed a descriptive nickname, often referring to some physical feature: "big nose," "left-handed," "gold tooth," or "man who limps." Others were named for their costume ("brown hat," "no shirt") or their economic status ("many goats"). Navajos also gave descriptive nicknames to *bilagáana* traders, government men, and missionaries. Aunt Clara was known as "singing woman," Dad was always referred to as "red Sunday," and, naturally, I was "little Sunday."

NAVAJO CLAN NAMES

When Navajos met for the first time they did not mention their personal names, but would introduce themselves by first giving their mother's clan name and then their father's clan, thus identifying who they were. If they shared any of the four clans they immediately recognized each other as family and had responsibility for each other.

This was most important when a young man met a girl, as there were very strict rules for social behavior. Marrying within the clan was cause for ostracizing a couple, because related men and women could never have informal social contact.

There were four original matrilineal clans of the Navajo, but different events and new groups joining the tribe over the years resulted in over sixty clans by the early 1930s. They included clans with names such as *tł'ízí łání,* Many Goats; *mą'ii deeshgiizhnii,* Coyote Pass People, for descendents of Jemez refugees from the Pueblo Revolt of 1680; and *naakaii,* Mexican People, for those descended from Mexicans who joined the tribe, often as captive women and children taken in Navajo raids over the years on settlements along the Rio Grande.

THE CLAN *BIT AH NI*

Yellowhair, of course, was a *bit ah ni* or one of the Folded Arms People. As Yellowhair lived in our home nearly all the time I was on the Navajo Reservation, and as Mother always referred to him as her elder brother, *shinááhai,* it seems to me that if Yellowhair was my uncle, I should also qualify as a member of the *bit ah ni.*

NAVAJO NAMES IN ENGLISH

Some Navajo names were translated literally to English. One of our nearby families was called in Navajo *tłízí' łizhin* and so was logically "Black Goat" in English, but another neighbor, *'aseezį́i siláoo*—literally "gossip policeman"—became "Mistaken," and that took some explaining. As a young man he had acquired an army jacket and could therefore be mistaken for a soldier or a policeman.

At Immanuel Mission we also adopted the Navajo custom of assigning nicknames to visitors for our own use in identifying them in the future. Some were based on physical features or habits or manner of dress, and others on some incident that had occurred involving them.

POCKETS AND CONSTELLATIONS

When Mother first came to Immanuel Mission, one Navajo man went into great detail explaining the meanings of the word "pockets" to her. There were all kinds of pockets: pockets in coats, pockets to carry something in, and they had a variety of uses. Thereafter he was always referred to at our house as "Pockets."

Wee Navajo girl all dressed up.

Another young man took Dad and Mother out on a hill on a starry summer night and pointed out all the stars and constellations that were important to Navajos: *náhookǫs biʼką',* the North Star; *náhookǫs biʼáád,* Cassiopeia; *átsé étsʼ ozi,* Orion. He also explained the creation myth: when the stars and constellations were being placed and named by Fire God, Coyote snatched the leather pouch that contained them and blew all the remaining stars into the sky to create *yikáisdáhá,* the Milky Way.

Ever after this man was referred to as "Constellations," later shortened to just Con, and he and his wife, Grace, played a very important role in my young life.

NEW ANGLO NAMES

In the early 1930s Navajos started leaving the Reservation in search of employment in the outside world and found they needed a *bilagáana* name in white society. They would often come to the Mission or a trading post to discuss an appropriate new name, preferably one they could pronounce.

We gave consideration to the personality of the person and to his Navajo common name and even the clan name. Other sources for a new name were places where the person lived or what he did. As missionaries, we came up with quite a few biblical names both for first names and surnames, such as John, Peter, Paul, Joseph, Daniel, Mark, or Benjamin.

Names we suggested were usually readily accepted, but we failed completely with one young man. We suggested the name Zeke, but he refused it immediately. It was a name that could be easily pronounced by a Navajo and even had a Navajo sound to it, but he would have none of it.

When pressed he finally said, "It sounds like a person throwing up!" An alternate name was finally agreed upon, and he lived happily ever after—and "zeke" was incorporated into our family vocabulary as the only word the younger members ever knew for that very unpleasant experience.

Many new names were acquired at a trading post or government institution, and a few were given in an effort to be funny: one young man had a musical sounding name, Ben Jo. Then later two of the *tłʼízí łání* brothers turned up at the Mission as Amos and Andy, the names of two characters in a current radio show favored by a nearby trader.

MODERN NAVAJO NAMES

Many families still retained Navajo surnames but often gave their children first names *bilagáana* style, and a few students had English surnames translated from Navajo. When I attended the Navajo Methodist Mission High School in Farmington, many of my classmates had Anglo or Mexican names: Lee Peterson, Sam Blatchford, Paul Duncan, Eugene Charles, Sam Sandoval, Annie Hartman, Lilly Woody, and Maurice McCabe.

Since Navajos have now scattered so much, I sometimes wonder if there are still Navajos living in Los Angeles, Dallas, or Chicago with family names like Black Goat, Pockets, or Mistaken.

PLACE NAMES

A traditional Navajo would never consider having his name on a landmark to be an honor and would be extremely uneasy about having that name used casually by strangers, so almost no mountain, stream, or other physical landmark carried the name of a Navajo in the 1930s, and few exist even today.

Geographical places were usually descriptive or commemorated some event that had taken place there. Winslow is *béésh sinil,* "iron lying down," meaning the place where the Santa Fe Railway stored its iron rails; Farmington is *tó t'áá,* or "among the waters," as the Animas joins the San Juan there; and Navajos still call Gallup *na'nízhooszhí,* "spanned across," referring to the bridges in that town.

51 | Music at the Mission

Often at night would I hear the haunting sound of a Navajo riding past the Mission in the dark, loudly singing the "Riding Song" in a high, quavering falsetto that ended in a short yelp.

Music at the Mission during the very early years was also a cappella, and the only musical instrument was a small treadle organ. Aunt Clara was the only member of the family who mastered it. She used it regularly in her presentations to visiting Navajos, and it was an important part of her message. They were intrigued by the musical box, referring to it as *béésh hataałii,* the "iron singer."

MOTHER'S MYSTERY PIANO

A momentous musical advance at the Mission occurred in the early 1930s when we acquired an old, ornate upright piano. The legend is this was one of the first pianos made by Story and Clark some time before the turn of the century, and it came to Denver. There it was eventually bought by the family of the government farmer stationed at Teec Nos Pos, named Gresham.

It is still a beautiful old piano, dark red with carved round pillar legs, and my fantasy always was that rolls of bills were hastily stuffed in those pillars by robbers who managed to escape the sheriff but never returned for their loot. Mother would never let me remove the legs and recover that money, and neither will my daughter Mari Jo, who still has it in her home in Corrales. The money may still be there, hidden in that mysterious old piano.

Mother was in charge of the piano, and for nearly a decade it was not only used for evening service every night, it was also the center of our social life. The whole family, sometimes joined by a few young Navajos, gathered in the living room many evenings after supper to sing dozens of old songs, a few such as "Yankee Doodle" dating back to the American Revolution. We had such fun that our songfests sometimes lasted into the wee hours—after 9 o'clock.

Dad played the harmonica and learned to chord a little on the guitar, a popular instrument of the emerging cowboy and western singers. He formed a wire frame to hold the harmonica so he could play both at the same time. Of course this arrangement prevented him from singing, and we needed the fine bass voice he had developed in the men's chorus in Northern Arizona Normal

Clara playing the "iron singer."

School in Flagstaff. Dad also played a small nickel-plated flageolet that sounded something like a penny whistle.

A little M. Hohner harmonica, a Christmas present in the early 1930s, launched my musical career, and after many hours of practice I became moderately proficient in that instrument—the only instrument I ever mastered. I still wonder at the patience of my mother during those trying hours while I was learning to blow the then-popular "Red River Valley." She was probably also disappointed by my failure to apply the piano instructions I received. I continued to play a couple of chords and endlessly picked out tunes by ear. Her patience ended, however, with any indiscriminate banging on her treasured piano by anyone, which she always halted immediately.

DISCS AND NEEDLES

The only other source of music at Immanuel Mission was a portable windup phonograph that someone gave to Aunt Clara, but it later fell into my hands. With it I acquired fewer than a dozen records and Gospel songs, and eventually I added a few others.

The sound was pretty thin and scratchy, but one of the marches of John Philip Sousa, "Stars and Stripes Forever," was my march. As an aspiring world traveler I would have been even more enthralled if I had known Sousa had composed that march while walking the deck on a return voyage from Europe on the SS *Teutonic*—no, not *Titanic*. The constant marches eventually fell into disfavor with the rest of the family, probably because I liked to play them loud and the sound was so poor and scratchy. I eventually discovered that phonograph needles were supposed to be changed often, but I had no source for replacements. I found that cactus needles, which were in abundant supply, produced a soft sound but were even less durable than steel.

I did not have a good voice for *bilagáana* songs and was not encouraged to sing during evening services. However, I could choose my song at Sunday evening's songfest when everyone chose one number, and mine was always "Greenland's Icy Mountains."

This old missionary hymn was written in the glory days of the British Empire by Reginald Heber, as an inspiration for the Church to take up the burden of bringing Christianity to the many lands beyond the ocean, then under British rule. I loved its opening verse:

> From Greenland's icy mountains,
> From India's coral strand,
> Where Afric's sunny fountains
> Roll down their golden sand,
> From many an ancient river,
> From many a palmy plain,
> They call us to deliver
> Their land from error's chain.

"Greenland's Icy Mountains" became popular in the colonial days of England, and Heber's dedication to missions led to his becoming an Anglican bishop to Calcutta, India, where he died at the early age of forty-three.

Undeterred by the tragic history of the composer, my imagination was fired by this hymn, and I called for it every time until Mother became so tired of the piece she refused to play it anymore. I then worked it out, note by note with two fingers, on the piano, but after a time Mother became unreasonable about even that. Thank goodness for my trusty harmonica; I could practice it outdoors.

Yellowhair was also a one-hymn man and always called for the same song, "*nánadzago,*" translated into Navajo by Alice Gorman from the English "When He Cometh." I never learned the English words as we always sang it in Navajo, but I still remember the ending of the chorus: "*bee bi-cha ah daa-tee go / 'a- i laah di 'i-zho'-ni' / bi-ts a'- dini-diin doo.*" I think Yellowhair liked this song because it had a rhythm like a Navajo chant.

Another hymn, "*kéyah diyiinii,*" translated by Allen Neskahi from "There Is a Happy Land" has music identified as "Hindee Air." It is even more of a chant, and it became my hymn of choice when "Greenland's Icy Mountains" was banned.

52 | Romance on the Rez

Here I must first make a disclaimer. At Immanuel Mission we never referred to the Reservation as "the Rez," and I actually never heard that term until after World War II. I might add that neither did we ever refer to Navajos as "Navies," a nickname in common usage then.

Romance played little part in Navajo marriages at that time, and the pairing of two young people usually was a community effort of careful planning by both families. Parents often came to Immanuel Mission to discuss their children, and Aunt Clara was respected as a counselor when she suggested suitable mates for a possible match. Pairings were discussed at length. Most of these sessions resulted in permanent and apparently harmonious marriages.

EARLY ENCOUNTER

A *bilagáana* boy growing up on the Navajo Reservation in the 1930s had very little contact with any other children, let alone girls of his own age, so any affairs of the heart were mostly left to the imagination. My concept of romance was largely founded on my reading, so I had vague ideas of fair young ladies similar to those as described by Sir Walter Scott in *Ivanhoe,* or Longfellow's Minnehaha in his epic *Song of Hiawatha.*

As a preteen, I had little interest in the whole idea of romance, particularly not with the few maidens I encountered only occasionally in the vastness of the Four Corners region of the Reservation. My first involvement in such affairs occurred when Black Goat, the tall, respected head of the family living not far from Immanuel Mission, came down with his five-year-old daughter, a shy, pretty little girl to whom I paid absolutely no attention.

When they first arrived, he presented me with a very nice arrowhead he had picked up along the trail, and I was delighted as I collected bits of pottery, metate stones, and arrow points, and this was a prized addition. Dad and Black Goat then began discussing some business regarding trading meat for a coat, and I sat on a nearby box admiring my new artifact and ignoring everything else. The little girl stood silently watching from behind her father's legs.

Concluding the business session, Black Goat looked at the two children for a moment, then turned to Dad and silently pointed at me and then the girl and brought his two forefingers together, depicting two people going off together into the sunset.

As Navajo marriages were usually arranged by parents, and young people often married in their teens, this was a proper suggestion, but Dad thought it was a little premature. He assumed Black Goat was probably being humorous and suggested perhaps this pairing should be considered a little more. I didn't learn about the exchange until years later, and by then the black-haired young maiden had moved far away into the canyons.

ANNA

Another girl prominent in my early life was Anna, the daughter of Hazel Fairfield, one of the first women who visited Immanuel Mission during its very early days. She and her husband, Walter, had lived with us and helped as interpreters and with many other tasks during those early days.

A bright, personable girl, Anna was a little older than Danny and me and treated us somewhat like younger brothers who needed a lot of instruction, particularly in the Navajo ways of doing things. Danny thought of Anna as his older sister and later wrote of her, "She took me as her own self-appointed charge and took good care of me."

I regarded Anna with somewhat mixed emotions, largely indifferent, but Mother became uneasy and called me aside one morning and queried me about my feelings for the cute little Indian girl. I had no idea what she was talking about until she finally made her point that it would be a long time before I should be interested in the opposite sex. This was probably the first time it had occurred to me that we were all that different.

ELEANOR

My first romantic incident of note occurred when I was seven years old. Roy Foutz, a partner in the Sweetwater Trading Post, was managing the post at that time, and at the end of the school year his family of several young children, including a son called Buddy and his sister about my age, came out to the Reservation for the summer months.

We knew the family, although not as well as the Palmer family, and on occasional visits to Sweetwater I enjoyed playing with them, mostly in front of the store and sometimes running up and down the hill just beyond the water box.

At the end of the summer of 1930, I left Immanuel Mission for a season at the little Red Schoolhouse on the hill just above Grandfather Girdner's ranch on Oak Creek. We set out on the long trip in our little car, along the only practical route at that time: through Shiprock, New Mexico, down Highway 666 to Gallup, and west on Highway 66 to Flagstaff.

About three hours after leaving Immanuel Mission we stopped in Shiprock for our mail. Mother opened the mail as we continued down the road to Gallup, and, to her surprise, found a letter addressed to me. She was more than a little curious, as I never received mail from anyone except my Grandmother Girdner—and she knew we were on the way to see her.

Mother handed the letter to me unopened, but I knew she was curious and I was expected to share the contents with her. It was a charming little letter, neatly printed on ruled paper, from the girl at Sweetwater Trading Post, and she wrote that she would really miss me and hoped I wouldn't forget my girlfriend during my long absence.

Mother asked to see my letter and I innocently turned it over for her inspection. To my chagrin, she was very cool about the whole idea and again made some mention of my immature age of only seven. I knew better than to argue with Mother, and nothing more was ever said.

When I returned to the Reservation the following spring, the trading post at Sweetwater was again operated by Ace Palmer, and I was happy to be reunited with his son Bill. But I never forgot that little girl.

Over a decade later, the Navajo Methodist Mission High School in Farmington produced a tremendous basketball team, though not through my efforts, and we qualified for the 1939 District Tournament, held that year in Kirtland. We were stunned to lose the first game to Fort Wingate, another Navajo school and the eventual winner of the tournament. We went on to win all our other games and finally walked away with the Consolation Trophy. It was much smaller than the one awarded the champion, Fort Wingate, but it did look nice in our brand new but empty trophy case at Mission High.

While at the tournament I spotted my old friend Bill Palmer during one of the games between two other teams, and we retired to a bench in a neutral end zone and were deep in a discussion of the good old days at Sweetwater when a group of cheerleaders walked by.

One gorgeous young woman paused to speak to Bill, and he casually remarked to me, "You remember my cousin Eleanor, don't you?" The girl from Sweetwater Trading Post acknowledged me with a dazzling smile, we exchanged a few pleasantries, and she walked away with her teammates. And my first love vanished into the mists of time.

"TAKE ME BACK TO TULSA, I'M TOO YOUNG TO MARRY"
—Bob Wills and the Texas Playboys, 1941

The last summer we lived at Immanuel Mission I remained at home with Yellowhair on several occasions while the rest of the folks made trips to destinations off the Reservation. One afternoon during these absences a querulous old Navajo woman came by and wanted to make an *'awéé ts'áál,* or cradle board, for an expected grandchild.

Yellowhair was exceptionally gracious and helpful to the old lady, who may have been a clan relative, and he soon found a few small boards, got out a hammer, hand saw, and hand drill, then called for me to operate all these strange tools. In addition to my early adventures in the kitchen, I had also learned a little about carpentry in the shop of the old rock building, from Dad, who was a good carpenter among all his other skills, so I began to measure, saw, and drill. The little old lady closely supervised everything I did but kept up a constant stream of conversation in Navajo during the whole process. With my mind on the project, I only responded briefly.

Yellowhair did his part in keeping up the conversation by expanding on each subject she introduced. Finally she asked me another question, and I absently answered *'aoo',* "yes," and all conversation stopped.

Then Yellowhair asked in the Navajo indirect, diplomatic way, "Are you really married?" That got my attention and lame retraction: "Well, *dooda.*" There was a moment of silence and then the conversation went on, but I paid much closer attention to future questions directed at me.

Soon after the "married" incident, a group of women implored Aunt Clara to take them to Sweetwater. Aunt Clara was very busy at the time but she also needed a few things from the store so, reluctantly, she asked me to make the trip, and I was off with a carload of three ladies.

Jim Palmer was a little surprised to see me and my entourage, but we all completed our transactions with surprising speed and set off for home. One old lady sat up front with me and was very effusive in her comments about my ability to handle a car and then remarked that since I was so mature I must have a wife somewhere. This time I was wise in the questions of Navajo women and carefully evaded committing myself.

53 —Now I Lay Me Down

Just outside the south entrance of the Mission compound there was a hitching rail where visiting Indians tied their horses when they stopped by. Some days only a few visitors would come in, but at other times there would be a dozen ponies hitched to our rail as their riders sat drinking coffee and talking in the large meeting room. Often they would become so engaged in conversation that they would still be talking after sundown, and occasionally several men would decide to remain overnight at the Mission, as most Navajos did not like to ride in the dark.

They would then set up an informal camp just beyond the hitching rail, build a fire, pool what food they had available, and their basic needs were satisfied: a little heat, food, water, and good fellowship. A convenient arroyo just south of the campsite provided the privacy for the only other facilities they might need, and they slept on the ground just as they did at home, watching the stars and telling stories for half the night.

The Mission was prepared for such occasions, and I was in charge of our considerable store of blankets and quilts, which were stored just off the meeting room at the head of the stairs to the attic. So on a cold night I would unlock the door, go up the unlighted stairs to the pile stacked by the "Haskell Trunk," and throw blankets down as each Navajo, in turn, stuck his head in the doorway below and called out the number he wanted.

Blanket issue was a time of joking and kidding around while the guys commented on the sleeping habits of each recipient as I tossed down the requested number of *golchoon,* a word taken from the Spanish word for mattress, *colchón.*

Usually a man would call "*naaki*" for two quilts, but sometimes a Spartan would casually call "*t'áálají*"—"just one"—and his comrades would comment on how macho he was on such a cold night. Three quilts were seldom requested, but one winter night Charlie, now an old man with a sad, careworn face but a sly sense of humor, solemnly called out "*dį́į*"—four! This broke up the entire company and all went laughing out into the dark night. It was Navajo humor, but Charlie did not sleep cold that night.

Airing the blankets at an old-style Navajo camp.

In the morning when the missionaries arose, they would find the Indians had all departed at dawn, leaving only a dead campfire and a great pile of quilts neatly folded and stacked on the outside landing of the main building. One morning I was up before sunrise to go out "hunting" with my rifle. As I slipped past the sleeping Navajos I noticed they were lying in a tight circle, each with a blanket wrapped over his head to protect him from the bad night air and his bare feet pointing toward the smoldering remains of the campfire. This was the Navajo way of sleeping, summer or winter. Day or night, hat and shoes were usually the only clothing a Navajo ever took off.

54 Long Hair vs. Short

Mother was proud of the waist-length hair that she always wore, and for years Dad carefully trimmed it for her every few weeks. One day, as I was watching his technique, Dad started trimming her hair as usual but then suddenly exclaimed, "Oops!" and in one slash of the scissors cut halfway across her hair. Then, before she had time to react, he continued, "Might as well finish the job," and with another great cut Mother had shoulder-length hair.

There was consternation for a few minutes, and then Mother began studying her hair in the mirror and decided she might try short hair for the rest of the summer—and never wore her hair long again.

I learned to cut hair at an early age, by watching Dad, and then started practicing on a very unwilling Danny, but he was always vocal when I tried to force the hand clippers through his hair rapidly without enough clipping action—he complained that I pulled his hair. Neither Danny nor I ever saw the inside of a real barbershop while we lived on the Reservation.

The division between traditional and modern Navajos was evident in the men's hair style. The older Navajos, men and women, wore their hair in the traditional *tsii tł'óół,* a distinct double bundle at the back of the neck that required a lengthy ritual of washing, brushing with a yucca fiber brush, rolling up, and wrapping with a length of white cord. It was a time-consuming process that always required assistance.

Practically all older men wore their hair in this fashion, and these traditionalists were commonly referred to as "long hairs." Many men, however, wanted the convenience of short hair but did not want to undergo criticism for going against tradition. The younger men began to favor a short, military cut, which was difficult to obtain in the camp environment where the only choice was usually between using a knife or a sheep shearing tool, so they would come to the Mission to discuss this serious change in their appearance.

When a young fellow came in for that purpose, he would often sit around for hours visiting with the other Navajos present, patiently waiting for them to leave before casually mentioning he was considering cutting his hair. Aunt Clara would discuss the important decision with him, and point out that it could result in strong

Educated Navajos visiting the Mission.

opposition from his family and traditional older men. However, if he persisted, she would ask for Dad to come and give the young man his first haircut.

Dad was an expert with hand clippers and scissors and was in frequent demand as a barber, especially as his haircuts were free. However, he was not always available, and occasionally a young man would decide he would take a chance with me. Dad was very pleased to be relieved of this chore, and in time I became the barber of choice and developed my own expertise.

I would seat the man on a straight chair and drape a cloth securely around his neck. Then came the moment of truth. He would untie his *tsii tł'óół,* and a great cascade of shiny straight black hair would tumble down to below his shoulders. At this point I often hesitated and stood with scissors poised, hating to cut such beauty.

When we finished, the barbered man would carefully sweep up all the clippings and either burn them in the big stove in the center of the room or take them with him when he left. Ancient fears of witchcraft lingered even in the most progressive young men, and they still were cautious about any hair or nail clippings falling into the wrong hands, where they could be used by a witch to cast a curse.

Yellowhair eventually also learned to cut hair and was quite adept, but the Navajos seemed reluctant to accept his offers and usually asked for Dad or for me. Later we discovered that Yellowhair was charging fifteen cents a head per sitting.

Long and short hairstyles.

Boarding School

Soon after the return from *hwééldi* the education of Navajo children became a prime subject of heated debate that continued for decades. In the original treaty the United States government agreed to provide education to all Navajo children, and a school was started near Fort Wingate as early as 1870. It was the single school established until after the turn of the century when another *ólta' hótsaaigii,* or boarding school, was established in Shiprock to serve the Northern Navajo Agency.

In the early days it was almost impossible to provide a program to take school out to the children on the Reservation. There were no towns or villages. Navajos traditionally lived in scattered camps and moved constantly in search of grazing for their flocks and herds, so there were few Reservation sites where more than a handful of children could attend school without miles of travel every day, walking or riding horses or burros, sometimes in beautiful weather but at other times through snow, mud, thunder and sand storms, flash floods, and frequent subzero temperatures.

The BIA also saw little hope for the Navajos to continue in the old traditional way if their population continued to increase, and they decided that if Navajo children were to have a role in the future they would have to know how things worked in the outside world by learning to speak, read, and write basic English. Children also needed some knowledge of the prevailing culture of the United States, a society that already was an amalgamation of the languages and customs of many other countries.

The alternative to local schools was to gather the children and take them away to boarding schools off the Reservation, where they could be totally immersed in the *bilagáana* way of life. This required a long term of separation from their families, and the children had to learn a completely different social and moral code.

NO, NO, WE WON'T GO!

Most Navajo families did not require much of an excuse to keep the kids home, where there were always chores like herding the family sheep. A traditional Navajo attitude toward an all-white education was recorded in *Boil My Heart for Me* by H. Baxter Liebler, a missionary at Saint Christopher Mission at Bluff, Utah:

> They want us to send our children to school. We need our children to herd sheep, to carry water and firewood. They don't teach anything useful in school. They don't teach how to herd sheep, how to weave, how to track animals. They teach them how to talk American and to read and write.
>
> That is no good. Nobody understands American except only the traders and the teachers. The traders can talk Navajo, so we don't need to learn American to talk with them, and the teachers can get along without. And nobody can read, so what is the use of writing?

THE BYALILLI AFFAIR

One day at a meeting at Immanuel Mission I noticed that one older man in traditional clothing and moccasins, whom they called "Uncle Ed," was walking with a decided limp. I mentioned it to Dad, who told me of an altercation near Teec Nos Pos in the early 1900s, when Superintendent William Shelton was enforcing mandatory school attendance in the Four Corners area, and a local headman called *byalilli* resisted with force.

Captain H. O. Willard was then dispatched from Fort Wingate with two troops of cavalry to quell the unrest. At a hogan just south of the San Juan River, a skirmish resulted in two Navajos being killed and Uncle Ed getting a bullet in his heel.

However, by the time Immanuel Mission was established, BIA elementary and high schools had been built in Shiprock, and many students from the Four Corners area were taken there, while others were sent to Albuquerque and Phoenix. A few were assigned schools far from home: Sherman Institute in Riverside, California; Hampton Institute in Virginia; and Haskell Institute in Lawrence, Kansas.

ROUND-UP DAY

On an appointed day in the fall of each year, some families dutifully brought their reluctant children to Immanuel Mission, a designated stop for the school truck, and we watched as the kids were loaded up and tearfully hauled off to civilization, leaving their known world behind.

CULTURE SHOCK

Upon arriving at the boarding school the frightened little fellows had their hair cut and received a bath, something very strange to them, as bathing was not very frequent in their waterless homeland. Then they were issued *bilagáana* clothing,

Little sheepherder and his favorite goat.

including shoes, and served three regular meals a day for the first time in their young lives.

In *The Scalpel and the Silver Bear,* Dr. Lori Arviso Alvord, the first Navajo woman to become a surgeon, wrote of her own similar experience with culture shock even when she entered college at Dartmouth in 1975: "I thought people talked too much, laughed too loud, asked too many personal questions, and had no respect for privacy. They seemed overly competitive and put a higher value on material wealth than I was used to."

ENGLISH ONLY!

The new schoolchildren missed the hogan, their kinfolk, the sound of sheep and goats milling around, the familiar acrid smoke of wood fires and smell of coffee boiling in the morning, and even the pack of hungry dogs that hung around the camp stealing food, barking, and fighting. But they missed their mother tongue the most.

Many horror stories have been told and much newsprint expended on the brutal treatment of Indian children in BIA boarding schools. Discipline at most boarding schools was strict, almost military. It included uniform dress for boys and girls, short hair, a regular routine of work and study, constant washing for personal cleanliness, and, most despised of all, speaking only English, even in private conversations among themselves.

With all the changes in their familiar life styles it took time for the children to learn the new language and get used to the strange food, and to having always to be on time, a concept almost unknown in Indian society. But the most hated rule, and the one that led to most of the conflict between students and matrons and teachers, was the ban on speaking Navajo, even to each other.

Complete immersion in English was, by far, the most frequent complaint about boarding school by the homesick little children, isolated and completely out of touch with their families, friends, and everything familiar in camp life. The English-only rule was strictly enforced, so the little Navajos would be able to take their place in the prevailing English-speaking society when they finished their education. Few of these children, however, wanted to live in white society, with all its regulations, and only hoped to complete this ordeal and return to traditional camp life at home on the Reservation.

Estimates of the number of Navajos who spoke English on the Reservation at the time were one in ten, and most of these lived near centers of population. Most Navajo families were still nomadic and had no mailing address other than that of the trading post or mission in their general area.

Almost no one in the camps near Immanuel Mission spoke English, so mail had to be translated and then answered for them by the missionaries or a trader. Even this contact by mail was usually impossible, as the family often didn't know what school their children were in, nor did they have any concept of where it might be. There were a few instances of a child actually disappearing for years.

On one occasion we traced a little girl from a local family to Phoenix, only to find she had become seriously ill and died just weeks before. The school hadn't known where, in the vast Navajo Reservation, her family actually lived.

Some Navajo children never adjusted to the strict new society and ran away, particularly if they were "incarcerated" in a school near the Reservation. Usually they were quickly picked up and returned to school, but some remained free for several days, as did three boys from families near Immanuel Mission who escaped to the Carrizo Mountains one winter and wandered about for days, eluding the Navajo police. They were apprehended only after they carelessly burned down a hogan and were tracked down by an infuriated tribesman. Another very young girl ran away from Shiprock School one cold winter's night, never found her way home, and, lost in the freezing wilderness, died alone.

HOMECOMING!

Every spring, word was sent to the traders and missionaries that a truck would be in their area on a certain day to deliver returning students, and at the appointed time Navajos would began arriving early in wagons or on horseback to welcome their children home.

By noon a crowd of eager parents would be gathered in groups in the Mission yard, talking with each other but always keeping an eye on the only road down to the Mission.

A ripple of excitement would run through the waiting group when the truck finally came into sight and slowly made its way down the long road. As it drew near we could see dozens of boys and girls standing in the back, waving and shouting as the truck pulled into the Mission compound. It was hard to recognize the ragged little long-haired kids who had fearfully left last year. Now they were sophisticated gum-chewing young folks with short hair and neat blue school clothing, looking very healthy and well fed.

One year an impatient father intercepted the truck before it got to the Mission, and riding along behind the slow-moving Dodge truck, lifted his little girl onto his horse and started riding away. Just then another child started shouting, and he glanced back to see his own daughter frantically waving from the truck. He had snatched the wrong child! He later learned that she even had a new *bilagáana* name, "Winnie." Needless to say, his friends never let him forget that misadventure.

Resentment of school was not very evident, and nearly all the kids were laughing and talking excitedly in English, and a few were actually boisterous. But as their parents claimed them, they remembered that Navajos felt that showing great emotion was not good form, and one by one, they quietly left for their camps by wagon or on horseback.

End of the day for two young sheepherders at
a camp on a mesa near the Mission.

One boy demonstrated this reserve: coming home after a year at school he arrived at his camp only to find his family all out chasing some scattered sheep. Without a word, he jumped out of the car and joined them in chasing the flock, and when he passed his younger sister he didn't stop his pursuit of an errant goat, only nodded recognition and raced by.

RELIGIOUS INSTRUCTION IN SCHOOLS

During the 1930s the BIA built forty-six new day schools across the Reservation to bring education to the Navajos in every area. Part of the goal was to "Christianize and save them from extinction as a vanishing race" by offering Navajo children religious instruction, both Catholic and Protestant, in both boarding and day schools, on designated days, with parental consent.

By September 1935, a school was under construction west of Immanuel Mission at Rock Point, and before the buildings were completed Aunt Clara had already secured thumbprints from a number of Navajo parents in that area requesting Protestant religious instruction in the new community school.

Dad made the weekly two-hour trip to Rock Point and later wrote: "We at the mission were ready to take action when the schools first opened, and I began teaching released time classes at Rock Point and continued as long as I was on the Reservation." He also commented that teaching in Navajo "tested my Navajo language skill rather severely."

Later, Dad wrote: "The first week of school at Rough Rock I also started a class there, but that was not really practical as it was too far from Immanuel Mission and I agreed to let the Presbyterian missionary at Kayenta, about seventy miles west of Immanuel Mission, take my place after I had made a few trips over there." He couldn't resist pointing out that the missionary at Kayenta taught through an interpreter but that "Clara had spent patient hours teaching us to speak Navajo."

56 Adventures at Round Rock

Dad taught me how to use his prized slide-action .22 rifle, when I was about nine years old, as soon as I demonstrated reasonable competency and a regard for safety in handling the piece. For years I enjoyed getting up at daybreak and, armed with my trusty .22, explored the hills and arroyos around the Mission, ostensibly for game but actually to enjoy the solitary splendor of the early desert morning.

As the price of ammunition, even for .22 shorts, was intimidating for a young boy, I selected my targets with extreme care. I did succeed in destroying a few unfortunate rabbits, and one windy morning I shot a crow carelessly sitting on a fence post a considerable distance away, snatched up my prey, and rushed in to find Dad to take my picture with my trophy.

WALTER SOLMES

In the early 1930s a young man from Chicago and his wife came to the Navajo Reservation to work with the Indians. Walter Solmes was a gun enthusiast and had a beautiful new rifle that he loved dearly, and he and I went "hunting" together several times, but he soon became disgusted with my reluctance to pull the trigger on any living animal I actually got in my sights.

For some months the Solmes stayed at Immanuel Mission, then decided to move on to establish a small outreach station at the Round Rock Trading Post. But after only a few months they decided that Reservation life was not for them and they should leave Round Rock and return to the more civilized streets of the Windy City. They contacted us for help in moving. Dad had a small, home-constructed trailer, so he and I set off on the circuitous route west through Rock Point and then to Round Rock, not far from Immanuel Mission across the canyons but a long journey by road.

It was all new country for me. As we approached Round Rock I was awed by the prominent rock buttes that ringed the place Navajos called *bis dootł'izh,* "blue clay." I saw that the only building at Round Rock was a small rock trading post building with a windmill and a water tank, but the place was well known for an incident that had taken place there over forty years earlier.

SMELLY GOAT

David L. Shipley, who was known as *tl'ízí niłchxon,* or "smelly goat," to the Navajos, was the unpopular government agent at the time. He decided to round up the quota of thirty-four children for this area who should be attending the boarding school at Fort Defiance, but he was frustrated by a stubborn resistance from the Navajos around Round Rock, led by a local headman, *łii łizhin,* meaning "Black Horse."

In October of 1892 Shipley sent orders to this group of recalcitrant parents to come to a meeting at the trading post on a certain day with the children who were to be picked up. He arrived in Round Rock on the appointed day with a posse of Navajo police and Chee Dodge and Frank Walker as interpreters, and they found a crowd of some fifty Navajos had gathered to meet them.

The Navajos at first seemed to be friendly, and soon they were engaged in a game of cards, playing for cartridges, and won most of the ammunition of the policemen.

The next day, a meeting started quietly, but the Navajos soon learned that Smelly Goat would not be deterred from taking their children away and became angry and threw Shipley down and beat him, breaking his nose, then dragged him to a point on the bank of the arroyo behind the trading post where some of the enraged Navajos started shouting that they should push Smelly Goat off the cliff and be done with him!

After a furious shouting match, cooler heads prevailed, and several Navajos and the posse pulled Shipley back into the safety of the trading post, and the door was barricaded. Although they were inside, they had only two rifles and two pistols and about fifty rounds of ammunition, while the angry crowd outside had more ammunition, as well as the rifles they had stashed nearby the day before.

After another day of siege and fruitless negotiation, one of the Navajo policemen managed to escape that night and rode back to headquarters. Soon a Lieutenant Brown arrived at Round Rock with a detachment of ten armed soldiers, and after more discussion everything quieted down, and the posse left—without the children. And early the next year Shipley resigned as agent and left the Navajo Reservation forever.

TARGET ON THE TANK

We stayed at Round Rock overnight packing up Walter Solmes's household goods. Early next morning we were loading boxes and discarding many other items on a dump out behind the trading post when we noticed that on one trip back from the dump, Walter stopped just inside the fence by a large water tank the trader had built to supply the post with running water, an unheard-of luxury on the Reservation. He reached up to put a small pickle bottle on the tank.

Solmes then walked back, picked up his beloved rifle and handed it to me, saying, "Take a shot at that jar and if you miss, let your Dad try, then I'll knock it off." I was torn between accepting the challenge and the fear of shooting a hole through the water tank, but tentatively raised the rifle, took careful aim, and shot just the top off the bottle. But it remained on the tank and I passed the rifle to Dad.

Dad was pretty handy with a gun and couldn't resist the challenge either, and his shot shattered the jar, leaving just the bottom, a thin line of glass, lying on the tank. Without a word he handed the rifle back to Solmes.

Walter took his gun, looked at the sliver of glass remaining on the tank, then turned, pointed his piece in the opposite direction, and casually remarked, "Let's see if I can hit that rock way out there by those bushes."

FIRE IN THE HOLE

We returned to the task of moving, and I was putting a box of dishes and cooking utensils in the trailer when I noticed smoke coming up through a box of clothing and shouted, "Something's burning!"

Walter rushed out of the house and started throwing things about. Finally pulling out one smoldering glove, he searched a little more and found a fruit jar that had focused a beam of early morning light on a bag of clothes and started them smoldering.

After putting out the fire, we completed emptying the little apartment, covered the entire load with a canvas, tied it down, and with our loaded trailer and our artillery, left the trader, his trading post, and his water tank...intact.

57 | Trips to *Tóta'*

SHOPPING WITH YELLOWHAIR

As Yellowhair almost never ventured off the Reservation, it was a special occasion one day when Mother couldn't join us on the trip to *tóta'* (Farmington) and Yellowhair decided to go to town with Dad and me.

I was about eight at the time, and Mother entrusted me with her grocery list as I had often helped her in this most important activity of our trips. We usually only shopped about once a month, so the list was formidable, and Yellowhair thought he should accompany us and help me. Dad stopped at the *ch'iyáán ndahaniihi* (grocery store) to let Yellowhair and me off to do the grocery shopping, and he went on to the garage and other important stops that had to be made while we were in the big city.

This was before the day of the supermarket and comparison shopping by just walking through the aisles and selecting whatever caught the eye. At that time there was much less selection, and shopping was done by standing at a counter and ordering from a list as the grocer and his assistant gathered the requested items and placed them on the counter. Items from the high top shelf were retrieved with a pair of long-handled tongs, and bulk items were taken from bins and barrels out on the floor.

This procedure was not too different from that at the trading post, except that here the transactions were conducted in English, and I made only one payment after I had completed the selections. A limited selection was available, and as I was familiar with Mother's preferences, all proceeded smoothly for a time, and the groceries quickly piled up on the counter.

Then Yellowhair decided I wasn't taking enough time to really consider what I was ordering and started discussing in Navajo the merits of the items we were buying. He knew that Mother wouldn't drink Arbuckle's coffee, but he thought perhaps the coffee of the man in the yellow gown might be better than the coffee with the picture of the empty cup on the label.

Also, as he knew almost nothing about vegetables other than he didn't care much for any of them, he often suggested alternates, and I had to explain to him why Mother wanted what I was ordering. These discussions soon became frequent and lengthy, and I was glad when we finally finished the list and Dad came by to pick us up for the long trip home.

On the next trip to Farmington Mother resumed her duties as official purchasing agent for the Mission, and when she entered the store the owner immediately questioned her about the previous shopping event. "Was everything O.K. with what your boy and the old Navajo bought last month?"

Mother replied that everything was fine, and asked if there had been a problem. "No," the grocer explained. "Except that the old man seemed to question just about everything the boy selected, and sometimes there was a lot of conversation—of course it was all in Navajo and I had no idea what they were talking about, but I think the kid speaks Navajo as well as the old man."

A SHOCKING EXPERIENCE

On another occasion Mother, Danny, and I were staying with the Neff family on a trip to Farmington. When I went back into our room one afternoon I found Danny sitting on the floor by an overturned chair with a slightly dazed look on his face. After he recovered from his shock he explained the overhead light did not respond to the switch so he had climbed up on a chair and unscrewed the bulb. Dust had accumulated in the socket but he couldn't reach it—so he had stuck in his tongue to lick it out.

Actually, it wasn't too different from Benjamin Franklin's great discovery, but Danny didn't get as good press as Ben did. To the contrary, Mother became very upset when she learned of this episode.

NAVAJO METHODIST MISSION

By the early 1930s we had established a close association with the people at the Navajo Methodist Mission, a boarding school for Navajo children, and the superintendent, C. C. Brooks, was a personal friend of Grandfather Holcomb. When we were in Farmington we often stayed as guests at the Navajo Mission and sometimes took our meals in the school dining room. I had never seen such a mass of well-scrubbed Navajo youngsters and, like them when they first arrived, was bewildered at the noise and confusion of such a large group eating together.

58 Education On and Off the Reservation

BOOKS, BOOKS, BOOKS

I do not know when I learned to read. But Mother must have started me at a very early age, and things just progressed, and soon I was reading everything I could lay my hands on, even the fine print on bean cans. Mother tried to limit my book time by imposing a quota of fifty pages a day on my reading but soon decided it was better to let me set my own pace.

An enlightening event for me took place on a visit to the Methodist Mission when I was perhaps six years old. We were being shown around the school when our guide opened the library door to the most wondrous sight I had ever seen in my life! Shelves and shelves of books from floor to ceiling completely around the room with even some tables stacked with books, books, and books! I stood astounded that so many books could be found in one place.

The librarian must have been impressed by my reaction and told me to select a box of books of my choice to take home with me. This was better than Christmas and came more often! For the next five or six years, my trips to Farmington almost always included a stop at the Navajo Methodist Mission to return a box of books and choose another boxful.

When I didn't make the trip to Farmington myself, the librarian would often pick out a selection she thought I would like and send them out with anyone who came to Farmington from Immanuel Mission. Those surprise boxes of books would always be a mystery to me. "What great books would be waiting for me this time?" I wondered. I was happy, however, to receive anything in print.

Mother was a little more selective and looked over every shipment with a critical eye. She didn't want me reading unsuitable material. I only remember one volume she wouldn't let me read, however, the original version of the *Wizard of Oz*. She probably didn't want me to become interested in wizards—too much like witchcraft.

Needless to say, this was one of the first books I read when I finally had unsupervised access to a library. But I was a little disappointed to find just a story with nothing very wicked, other than the witch.

GRANDFATHER'S LIBRARY

H. A. Holcomb spent most of his later days in his study, a snug little room with its own wood stove, desk, and bookcases holding his wonderful collection of fascinating leather-bound books. By then his time was mostly spent reading and carrying on an extensive correspondence with people in the United States and foreign missions.

I think this dedication to books and learning, as well as the strange exotic postage stamps he gave me for my growing collection, helped create my lifelong interest in faraway places.

Once or twice when Grandfather was away, I slipped into this cozy den and carefully took down and examined the many volumes with interest. Nearly all were theological works, which included various editions of the Bible. One leather-bound book particularly confounded me and I struggled with the text for some time until Mother finally informed me it was a Greek edition of the Bible.

I examined every other book at the Mission but remember very few titles, with the exception of one huge biography of Hudson Taylor, an early missionary to China. I was curious and started to read, but after wading through a dozen chapters before reaching the account of the birth of his father I decided that book was too long for me.

COMPTON'S ENCYCLOPEDIA

Over the years, Mother continued to work on our education and taught us many subjects informally at home. For source material she and Dad purchased the full set of the 1923 edition of *Compton's Encyclopedia,* and this became the most important factor in my entire early education.

I was fascinated with the articles and spent so much time reading that this was when Mother set a quota of only fifty pages a day. But I eventually succeeded in getting this extended, and over the years worked my way through the entire twelve volumes from Achaean to Zymology. To this day I have an amazing fund of archaic facts stored away, useful only in playing Trivial Pursuit (now an archaic game itself).

FICTION

Mother had a taste for fiction, and I tried reading some of her books, such as *Ramona* by Helen Hunt Jackson, but I remember finishing only one, *Lorna Doone,* a tale of the Dartmouth moors that fascinated me, though it was every bit as dark and gloomy as the actual moors we visited in England many years later.

Soon after Dan was born the folks bought me the first of the Thornton Burgess series of animal stories, and I eagerly read that little book and looked forward for the next volume to appear, sometimes on my birthday, sometimes as a Christmas present, and sometimes just a surprise present from my parents. I followed the antics of Jimmy Skunk, Paddy the Beaver, Jerry Muskrat, and Old Mister Buzzard, and they became household names as I studied the Harrison Cady illustrations of all the little creatures that ran through the pages.

Sometimes it was only with some difficulty that I could visualize the environment of green grass, trees, and abundant water in which these little fellows frolicked, but over the years my Burgess books became a respectable collection, and the last time I saw them they were a worn set of old books in my grandson Aaron's bookcase—quaint stories and characters of a time long gone by.

As I acquired more and more books, the tall apple-box bookcase in our room became filled with, in addition to the Burgess books, my own eclectic collection including *Robin Hood, Christopher Columbus,* and *The Pathfinder,* and to this day I have always had crowded bookshelves.

The book quest became a habit I have never been able to break, and fifty years later, during a three-day Girl Scout meeting in Milwaukee, while my wife, Marjorie, was busy attending official meetings I was rummaging all day through musty old bookshops. One day I returned to our hotel room with seventeen tomes and Marjorie started referring to me as a "bookoholic." By this time, however, I had limited my expenditures mostly to material relating to the Navajo Indians and have now built a respectable library of over 1,000 books on that subject alone.

SEARCH FOR A FORMAL EDUCATION

In the early 1930s, Dad wrote that the problem of school for the children was "heavy upon us." The new day school at Rock Point was for Indian children only, and the established BIA boarding school fifty rough miles away in Shiprock did not accept white children either. The public school in Shiprock at that time was a one-room, one-teacher institution with perhaps two dozen students in all eight grades, and the closest school in Arizona was over 200 miles away.

Over the next few years my parents tried everything possible to provide an education for their kids, but nothing was really successful, and Mother and Dad knew that sooner or later they would have to take their family somewhere nearer schools.

My education had started, however, while we were still living at the new rock house and I heard the words "East side, west side, all around the town" sung on the radio and asked Mother what it meant. She identified it as "Sidewalks of New York," the campaign song for Al Smith, and of course I asked, "What's a campaign?"

My always thorough mother started with the story of the Teapot Dome oil scandal, continued through the unexpected death of President Harding, and went on to vice president Calvin Coolidge's becoming president. She explained that when Coolidge's term was almost over he declared, "I do not choose to run," and the race for president was now between Herbert Hoover and the Democrat,

Al Smith. After this preamble she led me into the kitchen and diagrammed on the blackboard there the entire election process from primaries to the final vote by the Electoral College. Strangely enough, I was fascinated by the process and have followed, but not always participated in, politics ever since.

VOLUNTEER TEACHER

Our first "full-time teacher" was a very serious middle-aged lady originally from Scotland, who wrote and asked if we could help her become a missionary to the Indians. She had neither missionary experience nor any knowledge of Navajos, but she was determined that she was called to serve the Indians.

The folks saw this as a way to start educating their boys, and, after more earnest discussion and prayer, accepted her offer. So she came out to Immanuel Mission to teach kindergarten and first grade, and a rudimentary study space was set up in the new rock house. Our formal education began on the kitchen table.

It was a severe cultural shock for a middle-aged Scottish lady when she realized she was in the howling wilderness and responsible for two small boys who had no idea what was happening. Unfortunately, she spoke no Navajo, and English with such a Scottish burr that the little fellows just gazed at her when she gave instructions. They were polite and disciplined but had no idea of how to behave in a classroom.

On the first day of school we were sitting quietly at the kitchen table with our work before us when Mother came into the room. Immediately Danny and I started showing her what we were doing, but our teacher sternly interrupted and told us to pay strict attention to our lessons only. A few minutes later a Navajo wagon drove into the compound, and when we heard strange voices and the jingling harness just outside, we both jumped up excitely and ran to the window to see who was coming. Our teacher was scandalized and marched us back to our seats with a lecture on proper behavior in school.

We sat subdued but still not understanding the concept of classroom behavior nor the language she was speaking. After a few days the dear lady decided she had completed her missionary career and departed the Navajo Reservation for parts unknown.

MIDDLE VERDE SCHOOL

Education of the children continued to be a problem for my parents for the entire time we remained on the Reservation. Now, realizing that Danny was too young for school and that I needed to learn to live in the company of my peers, the folks decided I would have to go down to Oak Creek for school, and we made the long trip to the Girdner ranch in Yavapai County for Christmas.

A few days after New Year's, Aunt Eva and Mother took me along on a post-Christmas shopping trip to Cottonwood and visited a number of shops. But

I only remember one item, a magazine cover picture of old Father Time, with his long beard and carrying his sickle, leaving the world and meeting naked Baby New Year coming in to replace him.

Aunt Eva, who had followed Dad to what is now Northern Arizona University in Flagstaff, had become the first Girdner to graduate from college, and her first job was as an elementary teacher at the Indian Agency of the Apache–Yavapai tribe in Middle Verde. Mother and Dad decided I should stay and start at a regular school with her. So, when they took Danny and returned to the Reservation after the holidays, I remained behind and went to Middle Verde with Aunt Eva.

She boarded with Indian Agency Superintendent Frey and his family and was now sharing her room with the frightened little boy from the Navajo Reservation. We had a single room with a double bed, and Aunt Eva explained the house rules. "See that blanket down the middle of the bed? That is your side and this is my side and if you ever cross over that line you will regret it, mister!" I never crossed over that line.

Every weekend we drove back to Oak Creek in Aunt Eva's new green Essex coupe, a mark of success for a young woman just out of Northern Arizona Normal School. The distance to the ranch was about fifteen miles, but the primitive road made this weekend trip a major excursion. Now people commute farther every day and drive home for lunch.

The first grade was a study in black and blond. Most of the students were Apache Indian youngsters with jet-black hair, but a few were tow-headed kids from the families of local farmers and miners with names like Kovacevich and Killebrew, recently arrived from Austria, Serbia, Croatia, and other Balkan states, and I became the only redhead. Aunt Eva was responsible for turning this motley crew into semi-educated Americans.

A LITTLE TALK WITH THE WIND

It was an interesting term, and I learned many things in my new environment, including a number of colorful words and expressions that I had never heard at home. One windy evening after school, I went out to the swing yard behind the superintendent's house, climbed up on the crossbar at the top, and began practicing all the new words I had learned from the older boys.

When it came time for supper that windy evening, I was nowhere to be found, and Aunt Eva went looking for her missing nephew. She finally located me, and ever after loved telling how she found her shy little lost nephew, perched on the very top of a swing set and shouting the worst words she had ever heard out into the windstorm.

I had my first encounters with accidents involving children at Middle Verde School. First, my friend Harold, the superintendent's son, fell and broke his arm as he worked the rings in the schoolyard, and I stood by and watched as he was rushed to the hospital. Then came my first experience with violent death. A little Apache girl in first grade with me lived very near the school, and one evening she was kicked in the head by a horse. Her father rushed her to the Agency, but she died very soon after, and in a few days our entire school attended the tiny little girl's funeral.

At the end of the term Aunt Eva drove Grandfather Girdner and me back to Immanuel Mission. This surprised my folks, as it was one of the first times Grandfather had left his ranch on Oak Creek since his arrival in Arizona in 1907, over twenty years earlier. My first year at school had introduced me to the great world out beyond the Reservation, but I was delighted to be back home in familiar Navajo country. We had a wonderful week in Aunt Eva's little green car, exploring some remote parts of the Reservation I had never seen before, including the Four Corners, way out on a desolate, windblown plain near Teec Nos Pos, but only a little over thirty miles from Immanuel Mission.

Dad recorded the occasion by taking a picture of Aunt Eva, in full Navajo dress, sitting in four states at once atop the little stone marker.

BEULAH NEFF

Later that year, my parents hired a teenage girl, Beulah Neff, to continue our education, and she came to Immanuel Mission in the summer after she graduated from Farmington High School. In September, Mother and I drove into town and picked her up. This was unusual because Mother almost never drove. She didn't trust either the car or the Reservation roads, and her fears were confirmed that night on our return from *tóta'.*

All went well for most of the trip home, and we were only eleven miles from the Mission when the Model A Ford stopped dead in its tracks and stubbornly resisted all efforts to start again. Mother knew it would be futile for her to look under the hood to find the problem, let alone fix it in the dark, so she and Beulah stood in the bright moonlight and held a hushed discussion about what to do. Finally they decided to go for it: walk the eleven remaining miles home.

Stumbling along with them, my overactive imagination began taking over until I began to see all kinds of snakes and frogs and evil spirits in the shadows of the bushes along our way. I had almost worked myself into a panic when I saw a snake in the sandy track and cried out in alarm.

Mother, who had just about come to the end of her patience, told me to quiet down. Beulah, however, stepped over and fearlessly seized the snake by the tail and held it up in the moonlight: "Look, sport, it's just an old stick!" She had my complete confidence from that moment on, and we trudged down the road to reach the Mission just before daybreak. Dad immediately set out for the car on foot, located the problem, repaired it, and had the car back home before noon.

Beulah, still a high-spirited teenager herself, got along wonderfully well with Danny and me in the classroom, and the sessions passed quickly. She really enjoyed riding, and many afternoons she and I galloped the surrounding hills and mesas on the two Mission horses, and I would point out familiar rock formations and plants, giving the Navajo name for each.

Beulah was interested in learning Navajo, and I was all too happy to teach my teacher the names of these items. Occasionally I would ask her to repeat the words because she had a little difficulty in pronouncing some of them, and in time I grew slightly cocky about my ability to speak Navajo and was constantly asking her the name of some plant or animal. However, I was soon to learn humility. One day I was singing the hymn "*kéyah diyiinii*" and stopped suddenly to remark, "Bet you don't know what that was!" I was astounded when she replied, " 'Happy Land,' you dummy—the tune is the same as in English."

I realized then that she was still the teacher and I was only the student.

Just out of high school, Beulah dressed differently than the girls and ladies on the Reservation, and her attire was no doubt a subject of many conversations. One young man, attending services one night at the Mission, grew curious about just what she was wearing under that short dress, if anything, as she sat across the room from him with carelessly crossed legs.

He was leaning intently forward when Grandfather Holcomb suddenly thought of something left unattended in the other room, jumped from his chair, and started across the room. The young man ducked, sprang up from his seat, and was seriously considering running as Grandpa rushed right by him and out of the room.

I was innocently unaware of what was happening, but Mother had been watching, and to my amazement, she laughingly recounted the whole episode the next noon at dinner.

After Beulah returned home, we occasionally stayed overnight at the Neff home in Farmington. I liked Beulah's mother, who was great with kids and always had a plate of cookies or other goodies on hand. The Neff house was just down the hill from Farmington High School, and late one night her younger brother suddenly burst into the living room practically drenched in sweat.

Mother was startled and exclaimed, "What happened to you?" He laughed and said, "I just finished the basketball game and came home to shower." This gave me pause as I hadn't thought of basketball as that violent a game.

Beulah's father, however, was a gruff old man. He had retired from farming a place somewhere up on the La Plata River, and I don't think he ever adjusted to life in town. One evening he was reading his newspaper while I was in the room quietly reading a book. Suddenly he snapped his paper and exploded. One word: "Damn!" He was not looking at me, so I decided he had taken issue with his news, not me, but I was always exceedingly wary around him thereafter.

One memorable afternoon Mother and Mrs. Neff were busy, so Beulah and a teenaged friend volunteered to entertain me. We were walking around Farmington as they showed me the sights of the "big city," when Beulah spotted the marquee on the theater, and exclaimed "*Grand Hotel* is showing!" And the next thing I knew I was sitting in a theater.

The movie starred people whom they seemed to recognize but I had never heard of: John and Lionel Barrymore, Greta Garbo, and Joan Crawford. I was a little bewildered but learning quickly. As the Hayes Office censored all movies at that time, there was no profanity or nudity, and when a couple was on a bed they always had to have one foot on the floor. However, in spite of the censor, this movie had a little harmless smoking, prostitution, gambling, drinking, robbery, and murder.

Mother actually didn't say much when I reported my great experience, even though movies were strictly off-limits and at the Mission the glorification of a dissolute life style was not only sinful but also considered to have a bad influence on young people.

Dad, though, once admitted that he had been to a movie while stationed at Camp Pike. He and some army buddies were strolling through Little Rock when they spotted a picture of the sheriff of Yavapai County on a movie poster, and they bought tickets for a "short visit back home." Nevertheless, he was careful to add that "movies weren't really a good idea for me."

That was the last time I saw Beulah. Just a few months later I was stunned to hear Beulah had suddenly died while on vacation in Colorado, and I had to adjust to the loss of someone very close to me.

THE LONG ROAD TO OAK CREEK

In 1933 I returned to Oak Creek for the second semester of third grade, and we started for the ranch by way of Highway 666, still an unpaved road that passed through Gallup. Coal mining was the most important activity at that time, with miles of tunnels underground and some seventy coal-train carloads leaving Gallup daily.

These large coal mines were manned by miners from around the world, so there were few, if any, other places in our whole country where so many strange languages were spoken. Starting with English and Navajo, they also conversed in Cornish, Croatian, Dutch, Danish, Belgian, Bulgarian, French, Greek, German, Hungarian, Norwegian, Polish, Russian, Romanian, Spanish, Serbian, Swedish, Swiss Italian, Japanese, and even some Hopi and Zuni, all working together in the coal mines of that area on the edge of the Navajo Reservation. Arguments among miners at that time must have been fascinating.

Continuing unrest among the miners, and finally a strike in 1933 at Gamerco, caused Governor Arthur Seligman to declare martial law. He sent the New Mexico National Guard to restore order, and they were camped just north of Gallup.

As we approached the town that day, we saw trucks, tents, and a lot of uniformed men walking around, and then we came to a barricade across the road manned by several soldiers. Dad stopped the car, and our excitement rose as an armed soldier stepped up to the car and began questioning Dad through the open window. A harmless family with young children, we were waved on, but Dad couldn't resist a few comments about his military experience, so they had a short discussion before we moved through the barricade.

As we drove on down the highway toward Flagstaff, I eagerly asked if that was a real soldier. Dad replied, "He sure was," but he and Mother laughed at my next innocent query: "Did you know him?"

NEW OAK CREEK CANYON ROAD

Late that afternoon we were leaving Flagstaff when Dad decided that rather than take the old Schnebly Hill route he would try the "new road" down Oak Creek Canyon. All went well until we started down from the rim and discovered that the single track was barely passable. I don't think we got over about ten miles an hour with frequent stops as Dad negotiated our way around piles of road equipment and materials, mud, and big rocks.

About halfway down the canyon we encountered a huge pile of boulders in the track, and we had to wait while Dad had a long discussion with a lone guard with a lantern. I was sitting in the back seat just behind the driver and opened my window. It was pitch dark outside, and all I could see was the bobbing up and down of the lantern just ahead, and all I could hear was a faint rustling sound of water, drifting up from Oak Creek somewhere in the unseen depths of the black chasm below.

With the help of the man with the lantern, Dad successfully inched the car around a small landslide on a single track with nothing between us and the abyss, and we were on our way again.

About midnight we struggled wearily up to the big gate at Shady Vale Ranch. Just as the headlights swung off the lane we saw something on the ground just inside the gate—Grandfather Girdner, in a big cold-weather sheepskin coat and bundled up in a blanket, waiting for his eldest son and his family to come home. He jumped up, pushed open the big iron gate of the ranch, and greeted us with a cheery shout, "Merry Christmas!"

CHRISTMAS AT OAK CREEK

At the Mission our big celebration was always on Christmas Eve, but this year it was celebrated early on Christmas morning. Excited family filled the old ranch house, talking, catching up on family news, reciting experiences, singing, eating, playing games, and checking those loads of mysterious packages piled on separate chairs under the big decorated tree.

Finally we were allowed to gather by the tree and open those mysterious packages and boxes on our chairs, with everyone excitedly displaying and shouting with delight about each present.

Most of the people at this gathering were relatives that I really didn't recognize, and many others were complete strangers, including Vendla Sides, who was to be my new third-grade teacher at the Red Schoolhouse, and Grandmother's younger brother, Don Lockhart, and his family, Dust Bowl refugees who had just arrived from Kansas and had leased the small ranch just across Oak Creek. That was the same ranch where Mother had lived with Grandmother Holcomb and Uncle Lee Holcomb years earlier.

To my dismay someone mentioned that Aunt Sue Lockhart taught piano back in Kansas, and Mother saw the golden opportunity for a musical education for her son. Before the folks returned to Immanuel Mission, arrangements had been made for weekly piano lessons at their ranch on the other side of Oak Creek.

Every Saturday morning thereafter I faithfully crossed the creek and sat at the piano trying to decipher the music Aunt Sue set before me, and every weekday after school I stopped at a little stone chapel that Grandmother had persuaded her sons to build at the foot of the hill, and I practiced my lessons over and over again on the old piano standing in the corner of the one room of that frigid place.

Eventually Mother realized I had absolutely no musical talent whatever and abandoned hope for any musical career for me. At the end of the school year, when she came to take me back to the Reservation, she brought Aunt Sue a nice Navajo blanket as thanks for her efforts with a reluctant little boy, and also a beautiful saddle blanket for me—in spite of my lack of accomplishment.

That blanket stayed with me during all my life of wandering about the globe and remains today as one of the very oldest treasurers from my days on the Navajo Reservation.

RED SCHOOLHOUSE

After Christmas, Mother and Dad returned to Immanuel Mission with Danny, and I remained at the ranch with Grandmother Girdner, to attend the Red Schoolhouse on the hill behind the Girdner ranch. I usually walked, but when it snowed my uncle Dale, who was also living at the ranch, would sometimes take me up by horseback—giving me no little prestige with my fellow students.

I was in the third grade in room one, which served grades one through four. The other room was for grades five through eight, and all students were some shade of white, except one little Apache boy who soon became my special friend.

KENNON LOCKHART

Another gain from these many treks across Oak Creek was that I got to know the only Lockhart son, Kennon, a tall, slim fellow four years my senior and a serious radio fanatic. One Saturday after I had completed my weekly piano lesson he took me up to his room in the attic of the old ranch house to see his workshop: a large cardboard box half full of assorted wireless equipment, and another box turned upside down for a workbench, where he spent hours putting together all kinds of experimental radios.

One crisp December morning, when I arrived for my lesson, I found everyone crowded in the living room listening to a shortwave broadcast from one of Kennon's amateur radios: King George V's Christmas message to his subjects of the British Empire coming in loud and clear from London.

Kennon Lockhart and I had a number of adventures together: He taught me how to swim in Oak Creek, hiked with me up the steep Sheep Head hill behind the Lockhart ranch, and was even part of a "talented" group of students from our school who went to Jerome and presented a very amateur program of songs and recitations for radio station KIUP.

Kennon was also part of Uncle Dale's expedition to explore the red rock country near what is now Sedona, climbing the hills with Grandmother, Aunt Eva, and me. That adventure almost resulted in disaster when Grandmother started sliding off one of the high cliffs and was rescued only by Uncle Dale's competent work with a lariat.

INEZ LOCKHART

In the spring of 1934, Inez Lockhart, who was a cousin of Kennon's, came to help further the education of the missionary kids on the Navajo Reservation. A girl just out of Clarkdale High School, Inez arrived just in time to drive Dad, Mother, and me to Gallup to catch the train for our big trip to the Midwest. Then she returned to Immanuel Mission to start a life among the Indians as a lone white girl with only the company of Aunt Clara, Yellowhair, Danny, and Helen, who was still just a baby.

Inez also proved to be an excellent teacher. She lived with the Girdner family of five and Yellowhair in the big adobe house. Aunt Clara had moved into the smaller rock house, where Helen's former little nursery room was converted into a tiny, narrow classroom with a work table and three chairs. There Inez organized a busy program, dividing the day into regular periods for each subject.

She ran a tight ship with firm discipline, but related well with us and kept her two students busy and interested. She would start Danny looking at a book, coloring a picture, or working on a construction project, then turn to me for a lesson in arithmetic, which I hated and never mastered, or English, geography and history, all of which I loved, especially history. We had one history book

I especially appreciated, the *Van Dyke History of the World,* which traced the story of man from the days of prehistory to the present. Of course there wasn't as much history then as there is now.

Inez also attempted to teach me the rudiments of Spanish, but I became a little uneasy when she started explaining that in Spanish the sex of a subject was indicated by the use of *el* and *la,* and she soon decided I wasn't ready yet for another language. Inez had a good grasp of Spanish, but she had difficulty with Navajo words and sometimes had problems when she was alone at the Mission with Yellowhair, as at first he wouldn't respond to her English.

Then one morning she was sharing our big kitchen range with a young Navajo woman who was cooking a pot of cornmeal for her family camped just outside. Suddenly the woman became distressed and turned to Inez, waving her right hand in circles and exclaiming *"béésh 'adee', béésh 'adee'."* Inez had no idea what *"béésh 'adee'"* meant and was beginning to panic when Yellowhair, who had been washing dishes and ignoring the conversation behind him, turned and handed Inez the utensil he was washing, said "spoon," and turned back to his chores without another word.

From then on, Inez always spoke to Yellowhair in English, and he seemed to understand what she wanted, responding to any request she made of him with *"ah biite"* which was how "all right" sounded to him.

On another cold day, Inez was alone in the kitchen when our old friend Brown Hat came in. He had mellowed over the years and now had no problem, just wanted to buy a loaf of bread. Inez got a loaf out of the bin and asked him for the customary dime, and the old man grunted and, to her consternation, slowly started unbuttoning his pants.

To her great relief there was another pair of pants under the first, but he began unbuttoning the second pair while Inez stood holding the loaf of bread, possibly with a fleeting thought that it should be a baseball bat. The old fellow continued fumbling in the pocket of the third pair of pants until he finally found a dime. Brown Hat always dressed for the season.

At the end of the school year Inez returned to Oak Creek, and Dad remarked that she had done a splendid job as a volunteer: "We felt she should be earning something, and again our home schooling plan came to an end."

Seventy years later I visited Inez at the Arizona Pioneers' Home in Prescott, Arizona, and as we were reminiscing about that summer I asked how she got along with Aunt Clara during our absence at the Chicago World's Fair. Without hesitation she replied, "Clara Holcomb was a wonderful woman, but she didn't encourage a difference of opinion."

59   A Century of Progress

The greatest field trip of my life came in the summer of 1934 after I returned to Immanuel Mission from Oak Creek. Dad and Mother were planning a trip to visit a number of Plymouth Brethren assemblies in the Midwest that were supporting Immanuel Mission, and I was determined to go with them.

Mother did not feel right about spending Mission money for a ten-year-old child's pleasure trip until I mentioned the funds I had accumulated from money I had been given over the years. Then we found that the $40 I had saved in a Farmington bank was just enough to cover my train ticket. I paid my own way and was off with my folks for the mysterious "Back East." Billed as a "visiting Indian missionary," Dad spoke at many evening services at assemblies in St. Louis, Kansas City, Minneapolis, Detroit, and many smaller towns in the Midwest as we worked our way east.

UP FRONT IN ST. LOUIS

In St. Louis we stayed with two maiden sisters who were teachers and loved to travel, and I was fascinated by the stories of their adventures in faraway places on their summer vacations. They traveled extensively in Europe and were just returned from Paris, where they had spent days in the museums, including adventures in the Louvre.

The year before they had cruised the Caribbean on the S.S. *Morro Castle* and were highly agitated when the news broke that it had burned at sea with a loss of 135 passengers and crew, then finally run aground on the beach at Asbury Park, New Jersey.

This was a weird story of a luxury cruise ship that ran a weekly "Whoopee Cruise" during the last days of Prohibition, from New York City to Havana for only $75, including two nights in Cuba. But on this excursion the captain suddenly died during a gale-force wind on the last night of the cruise. Then at 3 a.m. flames engulfed the *Morro Castle,* and the chief engineer commandeered a lifeboat and, with part of the crew, escaped, ignoring the floundering passengers, many of whom had jumped overboard into the icy Atlantic.

FIRST TIME UP FRONT

One of the ladies we were visiting in St. Louis took me to her classroom one afternoon and introduced me as a visitor from New Mexico, then invited me to join the activities in an art class. I got my first, and only, lesson in watercolor, in which I attempted to portray a scene of *diné tah*.

At the end of the lesson she held up my Navajo painting for the class to admire and then asked me to come up and talk to them about my life with the Indians. I hadn't expected to do this but walked forward and stood alone in front of a sea of white faces and improvised my first lecture. To my surprise, it was enthusiastically received by my captive audience, and the questions that followed ran into overtime after the closing bell.

CHICAGO, CHICAGO, THAT WONDERFUL TOWN

The highlight of our 1934 trip was a week in Chicago as guests of Mother's old friend, Dr. H. A. Ironside, where we had a room high up in the Plaza Park Hotel on Lincoln Park. He and his wife had left Oakland in 1929 and moved to Chicago as the new head pastor of Moody Memorial Church. He had been awarded an honorary doctorate degree by Wheaton College in 1930.

We arrived in Chicago on a Sunday evening, dropped our things at the Plaza Hotel, and, still dressed in our traveling clothes, were rushed to the evening services already in progress at Moody Memorial Church.

We entered a 4,000-seat auditorium, the largest I had ever seen, which was filled with well-dressed people, and we were crowded embarrassingly into a center pew right down in front. We were barely seated when Dr. Ironside stopped his sermon in full flight and introduced his "dear missionary friends from the Navajo Reservation in New Mexico," and then, to my further consternation, he asked us to stand and to be welcomed by thunderous applause, the first in my young life.

I was further awed the next night when we were invited to join Dr. Ironside and his wife, Helen, for supper in their apartment at the top of the Plaza Hotel. I stood amazed at their big window, looking down on Lincoln Park below us with the dark mass of Lake Michigan to the left and the lights of the city of Chicago spread for miles around us. Immanuel Mission and Sweetwater Trading Post, with all the country between them, would fill only a tiny portion of what was down there.

We remained at the Plaza Hotel for nearly a week and, looking back on that experience, I am somewhat amazed that Mother let me go down alone to explore that part of Clark Street and even cross the street to visit Lincoln Memorial Museum, on the edge of the park. Fortunately I didn't get lost and always found my way back to the Plaza.

One evening we were dinner guests in the home of a doctor and his wife, a registered nurse, both employed at a large Chicago hospital. The other guest was her brother, also a surgeon, and the conversation soon turned to "shop talk" that was quite graphic but intensely interesting to a boy from the outback. I tried to join the discourse by excitedly telling of hearing a fire alarm the night before in the street below the Plaza, only to be dismissively informed that such things happened all the time in the big city.

Several times we walked together along the shore of Lake Michigan, which to me looked as blue and huge as the Pacific. Although Mother told me it was one of the Great Lakes, I was not fully convinced it was not a part of an ocean, but I didn't have the opportunity to check to see if it was really salty.

LUNCH AT MARSHALL FIELD'S

One day we visited Marshall Field's, where our department store tour cumulated in lunch at my first cafeteria, located at the top of the towering building. Mother, with her San Francisco experience, led the way to show her bemused husband and young son how it was done. She briskly picked up a plate and started with a selection of salad and then pointed to several other dishes, indicating Dad should select one, thinking they would share when they got to their table.

Dad didn't get the drill quite right and took both. Then he passed the word on to me that Mother recommended both. I dutifully took his advice, and seeing an array of other tempting items, helped myself to a few of them also.

When we checked out, Mother had a tray of her favorites, Dad had all those and a few selections that appealed to him, and I had everything recommended by them and my own selections of several other items I had never seen before, such as watermelon cut in balls. My tray was so loaded I could hardly move without dropping the whole thing, so a helpful waitress carried it for me, laughing and shaking her head and saying I couldn't eat that much food in a week.

Everyone else at the table also thought it was funny and made remarks about my eyes being bigger than my stomach. That challenge struck a stubborn streak in me, and after everyone finished they had to sit and watch me until I finally downed the last bite and left an empty tray.

My career almost came to a sudden end as we departed that great department store. Surfeited with my enormous lunch, I carelessly stepped off the curb on State Street immediately in front of a large black automobile turning the corner. Dad snatched me back, and we were amazed that the black uniformed chauffer had jammed on his brakes and waited without changing his bored expression— more high adventure for a ten-year-old boy from the Navajo Reservation.

I realize now that herding a bewildered kid through the bustling maze of a large city must have been trying experience for his two weary, but very patient, parents and am truly thankful for all their patience.

THE CHICAGO WORLD'S FAIR

The nation's premier show of the years 1933–1934 was the "Century of Progress" Exposition, and the Girdner family spent several days discovering all the wonders of science and technology, including a demonstration of brand-new television. I was fascinated by all the wondrous sights, but most particularly by the exhibits of many nations: France, England, Palestine, and my favorite, the "Black Forest Village."

This German exhibit featured a wonderful skating performance that astounded a boy from the desert who had never even seen ice skating before— one man actually skated on stilts and showed us how get up from a sitting position on the ice. Little did we know that within less than a decade we would be locked in a deadly World War with these charming people.

Early one morning, after about a week in Chicago, a lady from an Assembly arrived at our hotel to drive us around Lake Michigan to our next destination: Holland, Michigan. She pulled up in her car during early morning rush hour in Chicago, and we had just started out of town when Dad remarked that all the traffic was coming towards us, and she suddenly realized she was driving on the wrong side of Michigan Boulevard.

She finally found the correct lane, and we continued on our way out of the city and along the edge of Lake Michigan, through many towns and open areas of fertile farmland, all so different from anything on the Arizona desert—including billboards, flowers, and even blackberries growing in thickets along the road.

EGG SANDWICH

We stopped for gasoline at a surprisingly rural little crossroads, and Dad and I went into the station with our driver, where I was surprised to see a lunch counter and suddenly became very hungry. Dad said we couldn't stop and eat, but he would buy me a sandwich, and the attendant brusquely asked, "What kind ya want?"

I was at a loss for words but finally stammered "egg," thinking of egg salad sandwiches like we had at home. He turned, cracked an egg, threw it on the grill for about a minute, slapped it between two slices of bread, and handed it over, muttering, "Egg sanwich." I had been taught to eat anything I was given, so, regardless of how it looked, just shut my eyes and ate.

We stayed a few days in Holland, where Dad worked with the local Assembly, and we also had occasion to visit some of the local attractions and learned a great deal about Dutch life and customs before moving on to Ypsilanti, Michigan.

CAMPBELL COUSINS AGAIN

Mother's older sister, Aunt Ruth Campbell, and her family, whom we had not seen for five or six years, lived in Ypsilanti, Michigan, just outside of Detroit, where Uncle Dick worked for Ford at Rouge River.

My cousin David was now sixteen and had just learned to drive, and Bob, a little younger, rode a bicycle. I could do neither, and Ruth, who was my age, immediately took it in hand to teach her cousin to ride a bike like every other American boy. She ran alongside the wavering bicycle, insisting I get back on every time I crashed.

The two families had a great time together, driving around to see Detroit and other places all around wonderful, green Michigan. We even attended a Webster family reunion on a grassy hillside in the country where I met dozens of tall, red-haired Websters, although I had no idea how they were related to me.

THE DETROIT TIGERS

After about a week with the Campbell family, Mother and Dad left for scheduled meetings in Detroit, and I remained with my cousins, who immediately introduced me to the all-American game of baseball.

That year, 1934, was a glorious one for the Detroit Tigers. They had won the American League pennant and were headed for the World Series when I arrived on the scene and soon joined my cousins as a loyal fan of the team, particularly my favorite player, catcher Mickey Corcoran, but I never could understand the fervor that made them stop one afternoon in Detroit to buy a paper for the scores, when there was a perfectly good paper waiting for them at home with the same scores.

Subsequently the "gas house gang" beat the Tigers in the World Series, and history was to repeat itself seventy-two years later when the Tigers again played the Cardinals in another World Series—with the same result.

After leaving the Campbells we spent a few days in Detroit with a cousin of Mother's who owned an ice and coal business. I understood coal; we had occasionally used it at the Mission. Ice, however, was something we only saw outside in the winter at home (until we eventually got our Electrolux refrigerator, that is), but here in Michigan the system seemed reversed, and ice appeared at houses in the summertime.

I was particularly fascinated with the little cards people put in their windows in different positions so the delivery men down in the street would know how much of a block of ice they wanted lugged up to their apartment that day.

FIRST TRIP ABROAD

For me, the best part of our Detroit stay was the afternoon Dad took me to Canada, the first trip abroad for either of us! We took a streetcar (another first) and rode through miles of dreary suburbs to downtown Detroit, where we boarded a bus that took us down under the water and through a glistening new tunnel dedicated just three years before by President Hoover. And suddenly we were in a foreign city!

At first, Windsor, Canada, didn't look much different to me than Detroit, USA, and everyone seemed to speak pretty good English, but when a big Scot came striding down the street in full kit, jacket, tartan kilt, and swinging sporran, I realized I was really out of the United States, and my horizons suddenly expanded. Forget Africa; I would see all the countries out there in this great, wide world!

On the train home after our great adventures Back East and "abroad" in Canada, I became concerned about how we would ever get back to our Reservation home when we finally arrived in Gallup. Even with Mother's confident prediction, "Somebody will be there to meet us," I was uneasy, but sure enough, Inez Lockhart and our battered little green car were waiting at the station when we got off the train.

I have often wondered since how a teenage girl could have negotiated 150 miles over the primitive dirt roads of the 1930s Navajo Reservation alone in an old Model A Ford.

MISSION MUSEUM

Even before our trip to the Century of Progress, I had started a museum to display important artifacts that we had collected around Immanuel Mission, and I put them in the basement next to my room.

Almost all our storage at Immanuel Mission at that time was up in the attic with Mr. Haskell's trunk, but a very few large items had ended up in the basement. One of these was the big shipping crate that came with the piano from the Grisham home at Teec Nos Pas, and after the piano was uncrated the sturdy box stood in the corner for several months.

Before our great expedition through the civilized part of the United States I had come up with a splendid use for that old crate and asked Mother if I could have it. With a rather bemused expression, she consented, and I went to work on a rather ambitious project for a preteen youngster.

First, I managed to turn the big crate around to face a corner of the wall so that it made a very small room, 6 x 8 feet. Then I nailed in shelves and laid out my extensive collection of potsherds, arrowheads, the head of a stone ax, pieces of petrified wood, colored rocks, a metate, several grinding stones, and an old Navajo bow, for exhibit in our own private "Mission Museum."

After the great expedition to the Chicago World's Fair in 1934, the museum was expanded to include a rare (at least in Arizona) Osage orange from a tree in a Kansas hedge, several Canadian coins, and a small can printed "Century of Progress" that I had actually "manufactured" myself simply by pressing a button and watching it roll down an incline at the Continental Can display at the World's Fair.

Later I covered the enclosed space with a barn door, and the resulting four-foot space between the door and the overhead became a deck that was accessed by rope ladder and became the nautical extension of the museum. Dad soon lost interest in coming up to visit the deck, and Mother didn't want Danny climbing up my makeshift swinging ladder, so I happily spent many a private hour imagining a cruise on the deck of my own ship, the S.S. *Immanuel Mission*. Of course, anything pertaining to ships was entirely imaginary, as the nearest body of salt water was the Pacific Ocean at San Francisco—discounting, of course, the Great Salt Lake.

60 ┤Navajos vs. *Waashindoon*

Since the Ulysses S. Grant administration, the goal of the Bureau of Indian Affairs had been the eventual assimilation of all Indians into mainstream America. To accomplish this, the federal government first turned to Protestant missionaries and asked them to assume the task of Christianizing and assimilating the Indians, by educating the children in the strange new ways of the white man.

All future generations would then be equipped to take their place in mainstream American life. This was a more reasonable goal than that of a number of individuals, particularly Westerners, who subscribed to the position that "the only good Indian was a dead Indian" and advocated that all "redskins" be exterminated and the land made available to white people who knew how to put it to good use.

The actual administration of Indian affairs under a succession of appointed commissioners produced a turbulent history over the years, but at the time of the founding of Immanuel Mission the general policy of assimilation was still being pursued, with indifferent success.

Albert Bacon Fall was a colorful individual and longtime resident of New Mexico who had been involved in feuds, gunfights, lawsuits, and political maneuvering since 1883. With the assistance of a number of political cronies, such as Elfego Baca, he managed to be one of the two first New Mexico senators elected in 1912. Thomas B. Catron, the other senator and a large landowner in southern New Mexico, had a similar reputation, described by a contemporary newspaper editor who had never heard of political correctness as "a record that would stink a Ute right out of his tent."

Fall served two terms in the U.S. Senate and was then appointed secretary of the interior by President Warren G. Harding in 1921. This meant Fall took over direct control of the Bureau of Indian Affairs and soon was micromanaging its activities to the advantage of oil interests.

Oil had been discovered in the Four Corners area in the early 1920s, and the Standard Oil Company wanted to lease Navajo lands and start operations in the area. However, the BIA could not lease lands without consent from the tribe, and at that time there was no tribal entity of Navajos that could give consent.

Secretary Fall, champion of oil companies, called a meeting of headmen in the spring of 1922, but the Navajo leaders didn't play the game and rejected all leasing proposals.

NAVAJO TRIBAL COUNCIL

The existing six Navajo agencies were then consolidated into a Tribal Council made up of representatives from the chapters, or local divisions, so Navajos from all over the Reservation could make decisions for the tribe. Nevertheless, any meeting of the council could only be convened by a representative of the Secretary of the Interior, who also had to be present at any meeting of the council before any real action could be taken. *Waashindoon* also held the power to make appointments for the tribe as necessary.

The council was to meet annually for a two-day session, but had very little power for Navajo self-government, other than allowing them to approve recommended actions. Herbert J. Hagerman, a former territorial governor of New Mexico, was appointed as a special commissioner to the Navajos, with power to approve leases on behalf of the people, and power of attorney was retained by the federal government. Next the Navajo Tribal Council was reorganized in 1923, and Hagerman negotiated 4,800 acres of Reservation land for Continental Oil leases. Drilling started at the Rattlesnake Dome pool, some eight miles west of Shiprock.

Albert Fall's activities culminated in the "Teapot Dome" scandal of the 1920s, in which he was the principal figure. His downfall came when his leasing of oil reserves to private oil companies made the national headlines, and in 1929 he entered history as the first United States Cabinet member to serve time in federal prison. Kathleen P. Chamberlain recounts many of these events in *Under Sacred Ground*.

Ja'kali and the Indian New Deal

TRANSITION PERIOD

Franklin D. Roosevelt swept into power in 1933, at the depth of the Depression, and appointed political liberal Harold L. Ickes as secretary of the interior. Ickes had previously headed the Indian Defense Association, a group dedicated to the preservation of Native American culture, and he originally wanted to be appointed Commissioner of Indian Affairs.

John Collier was chosen by Ickes to be Commissioner of Indian Affairs. The new Senate majority leader favored his own brother-in-law (a longtime employee of the BIA) for the position, but both Ickes and Collier had favorable connections with the new president, and Collier, an outspoken antagonist and severe critic of the Republican-controlled Bureau of Indian Affairs policy, was now in control of the programs he had long denounced.

The fifty-year-old Collier had worked for years as a social worker, adult educator, and lobbyist for the American Indian Defense Association. He had long opposed the policy of assimilation, comparing it to the treatment given newcomers to this country, and claiming that "immigrants in rapid, planned Americanization become disorganized."

To stop this destruction of cultures, Collier had arranged parades and other protests to save the culture and customs of the new, defenseless people arriving in the United States from foreign countries. As editor of the reform journal *American Indian Life,* Collier not only saw the treatment of the Indians as an extension of this policy, but he was convinced the Indian way was better, asserting in the journal that "only Indians had the 'fundamental secret of human life.' "

He was confident, however, that intense social engineering would stop this pernicious policy of assimilation and foster an Indian society in which the old ways, customs, and traditional religion could be restored and practiced in a protected atmosphere unaffected by the dominant white American culture.

Collier immediately launched a program to protect and preserve and develop the "arts, crafts, skills, and traditions." He hoped to revive the old Navajo ceremonies and religious rites. Yet his vision of a great religious revival of traditional ceremonies brought him into direct conflict with the Christian missionaries, as well as with the Indian Rights Association position that the

Flock of sheep rounded up in a brush corral for the night.

Navajo religion was primitive and pagan, and promoting it would only isolate the Navajo as a tiny minority, unable to function as part of modern life. The tribe, they argued, would therefore always remain permanent wards of the government.

WHERE DID ALL THE PASTURES GO?

The major problem facing the Navajos at that time, in addition to the 1934 drought, was erosion all over the Reservation. A nomad lifestyle of grazing sheep, goats, and horses, coupled with a tremendous increase in population to over 50,000 members, had resulted in a severe soil-conservation problem.

When Immanuel Mission was established in 1922, a small wash nearby drained runoff water from the mesa when it rained. Although rain was infrequent in that sandy country, cloudbursts did sometimes dump great amounts of water in a few minutes, and then the little wash would become a raging torrent. Within a few days the wash would be completely dry and dusty again.

Over time we noticed the channel growing deeper through erosion, and by the late 1940s, when I revisited Immanuel Mission, I was astounded that the small arroyo had become a canyon, over ten feet deep and enlarging with every rainstorm. Topsoil was going down to Walker Creek, on to the San Juan, then down the Colorado, eventually to become a part of the silt accumulating behind the new Hoover Dam.

INDIAN NEW DEAL

A bill introduced by Senator Burton Wheeler of Montana and Edgar Howard of Nebraska resulted in an Indian New Deal. Called the Indian Reorganization Act of 1934, it changed the direction of federal policy toward all the Indian tribes.

Collier had a simple solution to the erosion problem on the Navajo Reservation: "Livestock was killing grass? Kill the goats, sheep, and horses that were eating the grass." Collier proceeded with a mandatory stock reduction program, not only calling for the elimination of thousands of sheep and horses and all goats, but also requiring the Navajos to pay the bill, either in labor or in cash.

This program immediately ran into huge resistance and was furiously denounced in gatherings at hogans, trading posts, and missions, and it brought on a storm of unrest with the new governmental interference with the Navajo way of life. If someone just mentioned *ja'kali* (John Collier) and the proposed new regulations, immediately heated discussions and comments would follow, which often led to quite colorful speculation as to what he wanted to do to the People.

Some districts along the southern edge of the far-flung Navajo Reservation favored the plan, but to Collier's dismay, Jake Morgan, our old friend during the building days of Immanuel Mission, who would later become the fifth tribal chairman, from 1938 to 1942, arose as the most aggressive voice in the debate over assimilation. Some referred to him as the "Apostle of Assimilation."

Morgan was overwhelmingly supported in the Shiprock area by those Navajos who opposed the proposed stock reduction plan, which they saw as destroying their traditional way of life. Jake Morgan and Robert Martin were quoted as warning the Navajos that if they voted for the act, "their reservation would be allotted, their sheep and goats taken away from them, and their property, both tribal and individual, made subject to taxation."

The Navajos remained divided on the entire program, with some favoring it and others opposed. Morgan continued to bitterly denounce the whole effort and referred to it as the "Back to the Blanket" movement that would make the Navajos a "monkey show for tourists." The traders on the Reservation also opposed the reduction of the Navajo herds, as it threatened their livelihood as well as the Navajo ability to barter. Other educated Navajos took the more moderate position that the Navajo culture was no different than various other cultures that made up the American system, and acculturation of the Navajo people in the United States was inevitable.

Dad, as an enumerator of the 1934 U.S. census that was under way at this time, often heard a fearful rumor: "*Ja'kali* counted the sheep and goats and began killing them off. Now he is counting Navajos...?"

RESERVATION POLITICS

Navajos were citizens of the United States, and some had even served in the armed forces, but none of those living on the Reservation had a vote in state elections, on the grounds that they were wards of the federal government and did not pay state taxes.

To bring self-determination to the Indians, the government set a federal referendum to accept or reject the new program, but before a vote could take place it was necessary to designate dozens of local polling places. Mostly trading posts were selected on the Navajo Reservation, but some schools and missions were also designated as places to vote, and one polling place was scheduled at Immanuel Mission.

During the days leading up to the voting, lively debates continued with all Navajos visiting the Mission, since every Navajo who came by wanted to discuss the latest machinations of the infamous *ja'kali* and to express concern about the proposed stock reduction. In our area most, when queried on their position, would just grin and hold up a thumb and forefinger to form a circle: "Against."

VOTING DAY AT IMMANUEL MISSION

On voting day in June of 1935, a number of government representatives arrived and set up tables in our kitchen. A stream of people poured in all day long, and we were kept busy serving coffee and trying to maintain some sort of order. Navajos had congregated by the dozens, lining up to vote. Few could read or write, and the simple instructions to vote by marking an X for "yes" or drawing a circle for "no" on the ballot led to some highly imaginative results.

Many Navajos wore as ornaments their little round metal census tags that were assigned in 1925, to indicate they were enrolled in the tribe.

Now many put their census tags on the ballot and traced a circle. Some ballots had neither a circle nor an X but were decorated with a drawing of a horse or other animal. A few were marked with both an X and a circle, and a few others showed an X with a circle around it.

As the official position of Immanuel Mission was to be neutral in this election, we took care to remain apart from all voting. But I just happened to be standing nearby when the box was opened, poured out onto the kitchen table, and sorted into three piles of ballots—"For," "Against," and "Both." There was considerable discussion about ballots in the "Both" category, but it was finally agreed that they would not be counted. Only the votes with a single circle or X were counted. The measure was overwhelmingly defeated by the Navajos.

STOCK REDUCTION

Early on, the new Collier Administration had put a team of young experts on the Reservation to study the problem, and soon they fenced off a number of

Navajo men rounding up sheep for a sheep dip.

small areas near the Mission to study the effect of limiting grazing. But the Navajos soon discovered that the grass was indeed greener on the other side and started lifting their smaller sheep over the fence to browse on the lush, protected patches before the experts were able to complete their studies.

The inevitable recommendation was to stop all overgrazing on the Reservation as soon as possible, and a drastic stock reduction program was developed. It called for immediate reduction of Navajo horses and sheep, and a quota system was devised to reduce all flocks by a set percentage. Late in 1934 this program to reduce flocks, particularly goats, led to the slaughter of a large number of animals on the Reservation. Another proposal, the eradication of prairie dogs as a grass-conservation measure, was apparently defeated when Navajo elders made the plea that "without these little brothers there would be no one to cry for rain."

The Navajo people had rejected stock reduction, but Commissioner Collier proceeded to "rehabilitate the Indian economic life and develop the initiative destroyed by a century of oppression and paternalism," and he initiated a program to reduce the number of sheep and horses that overgrazed the Reservation. Kenneth R. Philp describes Collier's long career in *John Collier's Crusade for Indian Reform, 1920–1954.*

Morgan continued to fight Collier's policies. In 1937 he led a delegation from the tribe who appeared before the Senate Indian Affairs Committee to request the removal of Collier and a return to the authority of the old tribal council to deal with Navajo affairs. Yet although Morgan bitterly opposed the stock reduction, later on after becoming chairman of the Navajo Tribal Council in 1938, he was more cooperative with other government programs.

Superintendent Albert H. Kneale, who by that time had moved on to the Pima Reservation in central Arizona, wrote later: "I would not question the honesty or sincerity of this administration. But honesty and sincerity in combination with crass egotism, with ignorance of the matters to be administrated, with intolerance, with bigotry, with prejudice, with obstinacy, are without virtue." He went on:

> With all the emphasis of which I am capable I state that the health and happiness, well being and properties of dependent peoples should never be subject to the whims of an individual whom chance has elevated to the position of Commissioner of Indian Affairs, nor should these things be permitted to become the toy of theorists nor the tool of politicians.

It was best for the missionaries to remain silent, if not neutral, during these exchanges, always keeping in mind the importance of the separation of church and state, but this became almost impossible when Collier expedited his policy of returning to the traditional life by encouraging and subsidizing the practice of the old native religion.

The federal government's policy of promoting separate but equal religious practices was questioned, but subsidization of religion on the Navajo Reservation continued. Almost fifty years later on Oct. 31, 1978, the *Wall Street Journal* reported:

> Medicine men may lose their federal subsidies. Health, Education and Welfare shelled out $585,790 over six years to a Round Rock, Arizona, program to give 28 medicine men 10 years of training—some medicine but mostly ceremonies and taboos. HEW may not be able to fund an $81,000 one-year renewal.

The comprehensive Collier program to reduce stock and protect Navajo rangeland from overgrazing was well intended, and many improvements were brought to the old Navajo way of life, particularly programs in education, hospital and medical service, and erosion control. But the drastic killing of stock did tremendous damage to the traditional Navajo way of life and demoralized the Navajos. The controversy continued over the years, with many vocal expressions of views. Uncompromising positions were taken by the opposing sides, and the question of assimilation has continued, and to this day the Navajo Nation still has its old-way "Traditionalists" and the more progressive "Moderns."

John Collier was to serve as Commissioner of Indian Affairs for twelve years and did not resign until 1945.

62   Oak Creek Redux

n 1936, the year I entered seventh grade, the folks decided that Danny and I should go back to Oak Creek for school and took us to the ranch to stay with our Girdner grandparents. For a time all went fine, and Danny and I enjoyed living together in the old shack outside, just behind the kitchen. It was private and had D.C. electric lights, but it had no heating, so the place became quite brisk as winter came on.

Danny worked with Grandpa doing farm chores, feeding chickens and pigs, helping with the milking and other chores, and he enjoyed being outside and around livestock.

My tasks were inside. I kept the woodbox filled, washed dishes, and helped Grandmother with the cooking. I liked baking, which was my hobby at the Mission, and often prepared my specialty—cookies. I was not as pleased, however, with preparing some of the other dishes, particularly chicken. This started with dispatching the bird with the same ax I used to chop wood—and that was only the beginning of a long, messy procedure.

Grandmother was quite happy to have her number-one grandchild with them, and we got along famously and had great conversations. Grandmother told many a story of her own early days in the frontier in Dumpling Valley of east Tennessee, where she was a fourth-generation member of the Scotch Lockhart family in America. I learned Lockhart history back to a crusade in the early 1300s, when Sir Symon of the Lee accompanied Robert Bruce, and when Bruce was killed, his heart was brought back in a locked box. Sir Symon carried the key to the locked box, hence the name Lockhart.

TENT THOMAS FAMILY

One family had lived on Oak Creek for years, occupying temporary shelters that earned them the name "Tent Thomases." The boys were good ranch hands but found higher education a little difficult, and they often spent several years in the same grade. I knew two of the boys in school, but seventeen-year-old Lester got kicked out for refusing to stand when we sang patriotic songs early in the term, and only his younger brother, Jesse, and his sister remained in school.

Jesse was in the fifth grade, a big fellow, always aggressive and sometimes hostile. Every time I looked back at his desk during class he would be just sitting there, his pale blue eyes staring at me with absolutely no expression on his blank face. I stayed strictly out of his way, and for several months I tried to avoid him, as Grandmother Girdner was a dedicated peace activist, and every morning she would hand me my lunch with the stern admonition, "Now Alwin, don't fight." Besides, Jesse was considerably larger than me.

Soon, however, I moved up to live with Uncle Stanley, whereupon I decided not to turn the other cheek anymore, and the next time Jesse made a routine rude suggestion to me I replied in kind, prepared to take the issue to the mat. To my surprise Jesse just looked at me for a moment, then turned and walked away.

After a few anxious days Jesse again approached me at recess one morning, drew me aside, and whispered a proposition in my ear. "You and me is the biggest guys here. Let's stick together and we can run this school!"

YAVAPAI COUNTY JAIL

While we lived there at the ranch, Grandfather Girdner was called for jury duty and went off to Prescott, the Yavapai County seat, for a couple of weeks. When he came home the first weekend Grandmother decided to go back to Prescott with him for the second week, leaving Danny and me to "batch" at the ranch. Then Uncle Stanley had occasion to go to the county seat himself and took his two nephews over for the day.

Grandfather gave us a tour of his courtroom and then walked us through the jail, with the sheriff as our escort. As we walked down a long stark row of cells, a Navajo stuck his hands out between the bars, calling "agháhwiizídí, agháhwiizídí." When I stopped to talk with him, the sheriff turned to see what the talk was all about, exclaiming, "Well, he's been asking for something for a couple of days but we can't figure out what he wants." I relayed the Navajo's message: "He's asking for castor oil." And the mystery was solved; all it took was an interpreter.

When our parents came down to Oak Creek for Thanksgiving, they decided changes should be made. Danny would return with them to the Reservation, while I would move up to stay with Uncle Stanley at his house across from the little rock church, on the other side of the ranch and a little closer to the Red Schoolhouse up on the hill.

Uncle Stanley and Aunt Leona and their two preschool children, Nina and Leon, just about filled his small house, so he set me up in a heavy waterproof tent in his front yard and put in a steel army cot with a tiny battery-operated light overhead. I also had a small box that served as a clothes cabinet and held a few books below and my clock on top. An early snow furnished welcome insulation to the tent, and with four heavy wool blankets I survived the winter very well. I spent many a chilly night reading by my bright little light.

One book the folks gave me for Christmas was *Oliver Twist,* that dreary story of the misadventures and endless misery of a poor boy in London, which even today reminds me of those cold nights in a tent. I never did like Charles Dickens anyway.

SHEEPHERDER OFF HIS RESERVATION

A few days before school was out, our neighbor on the Cox Ranch, just east of Shady Vale, decided to run some sheep on his field and imported a small flock to the fenced pasture just below Uncle Stanley's house. Although the field was tightly fenced, he hired a herder to tend his sheep. We watched the proceedings with great interest, and before long I realized the herder was a young Navajo.

As soon as Uncle Stanley learned this, he suggested I go down and talk with the Indian, but I deferred this. It wasn't Navajo custom just to walk up to a stranger and strike up a conversation, and I wanted to give the question a little time. Uncle Stanley was curious, however, to know if he really was a Navajo and kept insisting that I go down and find out.

Finally, on a Saturday morning when there was no school, I climbed down the steep hill and casually walked along our side of the fenced high ditch that separated the two ranches, usually known as a barrow ditch. But the youngsters called it the "burro ditch" because it carried water on its back.

Of course the herder saw me as soon as I started down the hill, and he sat down, leaning his back against a post of the Cox fence so we wouldn't have to actually meet. Much to the disgust of the family that had gathered at the edge of the hill to watch me, I just ignored him, passed behind him, and followed the ditch on down to Oak Creek. I walked around in the creek bottom for a while, then started back toward the hill, where the herder still sat gazing into the distance.

As I came up behind him again, I paused and casually asked, "*díkwíi dibé?*" He didn't look around but indifferently replied, "*neeznádiin.*" So he had 100 sheep. I remained standing, looking at his flock. Then I put one foot through the lower strand of fence and a hand on the fence post.

Another pause, and I asked, "*háadisha?*" and he mentioned his home, a place south of Immanuel Mission but unfamiliar to me, so I just gave a small grunt.

Our desultory conversation continued for some time as I talked to his back while he sat on the other side of the fence gazing at the hill, giving short answers to my inquiries. Finally, his curiosity got the better of him, and he slowly stood and casually turned to see if this was really the white kid talking—then reached through the wire *'anit'i'* for a very limp Navajo handshake.

He then became quite voluble and began telling me stories of his amazing adventures herding for the *bilagáana* on other ranges. Suddenly it was noon, and we were still talking when Leon came down to tell me dinner was ready, so I went back up the hill and answered a barrage of questions.

Monday it was back to the Red Schoolhouse as usual. A few mornings later the sheep were gone. Our neighbor had decided he was not a sheep man, and I never saw my Navajo friend again.

MY SOFTBALL CAREER

That year I was in the "Big Room" of the two rooms of the Oak Creek Red Schoolhouse, and we had a very unusual teacher, a man with the German name of Osterfoss. Just out of Northern Arizona University, he had an enthusiastic love for sports, but our little school had no equipment for sports except a couple of old bats and a softball. However, he energetically set to work with his inexperienced boys and girls, and in short order actually developed a respectable team in which I guarded third base.

That spring, in our last game of the season, we played Bridgeport, a school from over on the Verde River, a team that featured one big fellow with a moustache. He drove a smoking ball directly into my hands, we won the game, and I received a round of surprised applause from the few parents gathered 'round to see the big game of the year. Mr. Osterfoss remarked that it was a case of "catch it or go through you," but it proved to be the greatest moment of my entire life in sports.

MYSTERIES OF THE CRYSTAL SET

During that winter Uncle Stanley got me interested in crystal set radio, and he and I put together a rudimentary pin and crystal arrangement, but I was very disappointed to receive only a few murmurs from space.

Then one afternoon after school, Kennon Lockhart stopped by to look over my little rig after he got off the yellow bus from Clarkdale High. He put on the headphones, and, after just a little positioning of the pin on the crystal, handed them back to me, and to my astonishment the signal came in clear, all the way from Jerome, over fifteen miles away!

In December of 1936, I was over at Kennon's house when he tuned in to the broadcast when Edward VII gave up the throne of England to marry the woman he loved, the twice-divorced Wallis Simpson. Unfortunately we missed the prime minister's reaction when he commented: "He was Admiral of the Fleet but he's now the third mate of an American tramp."

RCA VICTOR

Eighteen years later I entered a management-training position at RCA Victor in New Jersey, and, before leaving, dropped by Prescott to visit Grandfather Girdner at the Arizona Pioneers' Home.

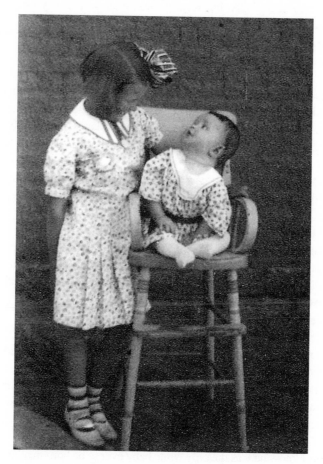

Ronnie and big sister Helen.

Grandfather casually mentioned that Kennon was also at RCA, but I thought he must be mistaken. After all, Grandpa was over ninety years old and might be a little confused, but soon after I reported at Camden, Kennon called my department to welcome me to New Jersey and invited me to dinner at his home.

I was a trainee at RCA, but Kennon was well on his way up the ladder to a key position. He was playing an active part in the development of color TV, as a member of the early team that went up to New York to run test broadcast patterns, sent from there to Camden, New Jersey, at night after regular programs went off the air.

These sessions were critical, as RCA was in competition with CBS to be the first to develop a standard system, and David Sarnoff often attended these experiments. The test crew was made understandably nervous by Sarnoff's presence and was very formal in approaching him, all except for Kennon. He received several warnings from the concerned project chief about showing proper respect for "the General," who was the founder of NBC and head of RCA, but Kennon's treating him as a member of the crew was well received by Sarnoff.

RONALD GLEN GIRDNER

When I returned to Immanuel Mission from Oak Creek I found another brother had joined the family, Ronald Glen. He was supposed to have been born in the hospital in Farmington, but that plan didn't eventuate. Dad succinctly noted: "I delivered my third son, no doctor, misestimated."

Later he elaborated:

We went to Farmington and Marie was admitted to the hospital at the expected time but after vain efforts to induce labor we returned to the Mission to wait another week. On September 16, 1937, Ronald came. Marie was a licensed midwife and had coached me enough so that I delivered the baby with no mishaps.

As far as I know he was the only white baby ever to be born in all that area.

MAMIE PARKER

With the money saved by avoiding hospital bills, my parents paid Mamie Parker, a recently divorced woman with a small baby, to come out to Immanuel Mission. For a short time she helped Mother in the multiple duties of running the household and taking care of the three younger children of the growing Girdner family. When it came time for Mamie to return to her father's home in Aztec, Dad and I drove her and her baby back to New Mexico on what proved to be a very eventful trip.

We stopped for lunch in Farmington, parked the car, and started walking down the street to my favorite, Mandarin Café. Dad was carrying the baby, Mamie was walking beside him, and I was trailing along beside them, when we crossed a side street and saw an old Navajo standing in a doorway about halfway down.

We didn't really know him but had seen him around Sweetwater several times, and as we walked on down the street Dad looked back and ruefully remarked, "I'm going to have a hard time explaining my being in Farmington with a young woman and a baby when old *hastiin* gets back to the Reservation."

Aztec is on the Animas River, fourteen miles above Farmington, and Mamie's father, Sherman S. Howe, had a farm near Aztec Ruins National Monument. He appeared to be a thin old farmer in work clothes but warmly welcomed us and asked us in for a drink of water. As we sat visiting, Mr. Howe casually asked if we would like see a few Anasazi things he had picked up around his farm. We certainly did! So he led the way out to his chicken house, shooed off a couple of hens, and opened a large bin half full of feed.

Propping up the lid with a board, he began rummaging around in the bran and uncovered a splendid Mesa Verde–style pottery bowl, put it gently on a shelf, and continued digging around until he had uncovered over a dozen unbroken bowls, pots, and mugs, and lined them up for our amazed inspection. He then explained that they were just a few of hundreds he had found over the years as he worked his farm. Many had been unearthed as he ploughed and others as he dug ditches and irrigated his fields and orchard.

What we were holding in our hands that day in a chicken coop was a tiny portion of Sherman Howe's personal collection, which later became part of the displays now at Aztec Ruins National Monument and other museums throughout the Southwest.

We learned later that Sherman S. Howe came from a very early pioneer family in the Aztec area and was one of seven or eight schoolboys who in 1882, with their teacher, found a way down into the archaeological site that later became known as West Ruin. As he wrote in *My Story of the Aztec Ruins*, they were the first to crawl into its dark, dusty rooms. In the 1920s Sherman Howe was part of the American Museum of Natural History crew that restored the Great Kiva of the Aztec Ruins National Monument, under the direction of Earl Morris, and he remained active at Aztec Ruins National Monument well into his eighties.

63   Eveready Batteries

In the summer following my return to Immanuel Mission after my freshman year at Navajo Methodist Mission High School in Farmington, Yellowhair was invited to a wedding in a camp somewhere in the *tsegi* canyons south of Immanuel Mission.

I do not know exactly why he was asked, as we did not know the family well, but he was probably a clan relative of the bride. As our parents were already in Oak Creek, Yellowhair asked Aunt Clara for permission for Danny and me to accompany him. With some reluctance Aunt Clara said we could go, and just before sunset on the appointed day the three of us set off on the trail to the canyon.

It was nearly dark when we caught, on the cool evening air, the pungent smell of cedar smoke, then almost at once we heard dogs up on the rim above us. Suddenly the animals were swarming all around us, snarling and barking furiously as we walked the final short distance to a blazing campfire surrounded by the figures of a group of men, standing around talking quietly. Just beyond were a couple of large hogans.

We joined the men without a word of greeting. Soon Yellowhair fell into conversation with several in the group while Danny and I stood silently by, uneasily eying the pack of hungry dogs that had followed us up the hill and were now suspiciously sniffing around the two strange *bilagáana* boys.

After a time another man emerged from the nearby hogan, greeted Yellowhair, and acknowledged the two white boys, then showed us into the hogan, where we were pleased to be given a place on the south side with the men. For an interminable time we sat cross-legged on the floor as the Navajo conversation flowed around us and the bride and groom, who were seated at the west side of the hogan.

Finally, when the hogan was filled to overflowing, all fell silent, and the medicine man started the ceremony. I was familiar now with the wedding basket of corn mush and the ritual of dipping one's fingers in for a portion as it was passed to us, but I was unprepared for the feast of frybread and mutton stew that followed.

Danny was too shy to take anything. However, I recognized the *náneeskaadí* and took a piece. I also recognized the mutton stew, but didn't take any and quietly passed it on to Yellowhair on my right. The Navajo men immediately noticed this and made several comments about the refined eating habits of white boys, followed by a lot of laughter.

I wisely didn't reply, but Yellowhair was discomfited by all the jesting and made his own speech. I did not fully comprehend what he said but it was in defense of the *bilagáana yázhí,* and soon the small talk died down and the wedding advice began. The elders talked in turn, each explaining, in endless detail, what was expected of the new wife, the duties of the husband, and the harmony that should prevail every day in their future life together.

The hours dragged by. First Danny and then Yellowhair fell asleep, as the men talked on and on and the happy couple sat as if in a trance, although the new husband occasionally nodded his head to acknowledge some sage advice. Finally, all fell silent, the fire died down, and we sat on in the dark. My legs were numb from being folded under me for hours on my sheepskin, and I began thinking of the precipitous trail across the canyon and the long walk back to the Mission.

As midnight approached, I became increasingly restless and finally nudged Yellowhair awake. "*Shináái,* perhaps we should go home?" He said nothing, but after a time arose and, without a word to anyone, started picking his way out of the hogan, closely followed by a semi-comatose Danny and then by me.

There was a sharp chill in the air when we lifted the blanket and stepped outside. The conversation of the men had died to a murmur, and many had stretched out on the ground wrapped in their blankets and were already sleeping under the bright, cold stars, their feet to the smoldering fire. We spoke to no one but silently started down into the dark canyon with Yellowhair leading the way, occasionally flashing his flashlight down the trail as we slowly negotiated our way and eventually reached the bottom.

We crossed the sandy streambed, climbed up the north side of the canyon, and started the long trudge home. Yellowhair strode alone at a brisk pace, flashlight in hand. To conserve his batteries he would walk for a minute in the dark and then shoot a quick beam of light to see a few steps ahead, turn it off, and walk for a few more seconds before sending another flash up the trail ahead.

As the night progressed the moon came up and cast enough light over the desert for us to see ahead, but as our eyes adjusted to the dim trail Yellowhair continued shooting bursts of light ahead. When the flash blinked off, we were temporarily blind, and I grew irritated, wishing he would just walk on without the flashlight as it was possible to follow the trail in general by moonlight, but I think he was afraid of stepping on a rattlesnake lying in the warm sand of a trail when the air turned chilly.

We arrived home just before dawn and, for perhaps the first time in my life, I slept until noon.

Decades later, I was living in Dallas when Eveready ran a series of ads, each featuring a "True Adventure" in which their product served to avert some life-threatening disaster, and it occurred to me that there might be a story in our canyon adventure of thirty years before. I also remembered the black cat logo on the batteries we used, so I wrote a short account of our "adventure" and submitted it to the Eveready Company.

Much to my surprise, Eveready accepted my effort, and their artist prepared a strip, with the first panel showing us with an ancient Indian going down a steep canyon trail. The second panel showed one of us had fallen off the cliff and hung clinging to a small tree while a prowling mountain lion watched from a dark thicket above.

Apparently I had climbed down to help because the final panel showed the old Indian, with an inappropriate Hopi haircut, shining a great beam of light from his trusty flashlight with Eveready batteries, and rescuing us both!

Eveready sent copies of the proof to me, to Dan in Nebraska, and to Yellowhair, still at Immanuel Mission, each with a check for $50 and a release form. Yellowhair and I both signed the release and cashed our checks, and Yellowhair had a petty cash fund for the rest of his life that he always referred to as "Alwee's money," but Dan found the story too fantastic for his approval and wouldn't sign the release, so the strip never ran.

64 Officer of the Day

After my return from Canada and the big cities Back East in 1934, I considered myself an experienced man of the world. Even my parents seemed to accept the fact I was old enough to take on some responsibility, and over the years there were several occasions when Mother, Dad, and Aunt Clara left on short trips away from Immanuel Mission and left me in charge, with Yellowhair and sometimes Danny.

I was not expected to conduct any religious services but did carry on all other Mission activities, feeding the livestock, milking, and cooking the meals as well as dealing with Navajos that came by.

This gave me an opportunity to try the exotic recipes I found in Mother's big cookbook, and my audience of two received all the benefits of my efforts—sometimes saved by the return of the cavalry before I prepared dinner.

Baking powder biscuits were usually a favorite of the family, so one night when I was in charge I decided to experiment with an outdoor recipe from my Boy Scout Handbook that called for little more than flour, baking powder, and water. The results were not as good as I had expected and Danny refused to eat his serving; however, Yellowhair was supportive of the would-be chef and diplomatically asked for another serving of *tsé łigai*—white rocks.

On another day, when Dan and I were alone with Yellowhair, I expected the family to come home in time for dinner that night and prepared a sumptuous meal, topped off with a special dessert—ice cream. Preparing the ice, which was gathered from the outdoors after a freeze, and cranking the ice-cream freezer were Yellowhair's specialties, so I left the hard work to him and put together the ingredients for the treat.

When it came time for the flavoring I decided on a surprise. Tonight we would have peppermint! There was a bottle of the strong liquid in the medicine chest, used for treating head colds and toothache, so I opened it, then hesitated: "How much?" I had no idea, but two tablespoons sounded about right, so in it went. It was St. Patrick's Day and Helen's birthday so, as a final touch, I added a generous amount of green cake coloring.

Yellowhair then took over and worked on the back porch grinding away at the freezer to the rhythm of a Navajo chant. After nearly an hour he called me to check the mix—it didn't seem to be freezing. On unpacking and opening the can I discovered we had failed to put in the dasher, so we just had a can of bright green, cold milk. Yellowhair didn't find the situation as funny as Danny and I did, but when we had added the necessary part, faithfully went back to chanting and grinding his freezer.

The folks arrived late with a guest, and I was gratified by how well my dinner was received. Our guest, a government man, was exceptionally complimentary in his comments, and everyone was impressed until I proudly served my surprise dessert! The shock of the garish green color was the first surprise—but that was not all.

Somewhere in the lengthy process of preparation something had gone seriously wrong, as the ice cream was also very, very strong. After the first bite, everyone rejected their servings of green ice cream and refused to eat any more, all but the government man and faithful Yellowhair, who asked for seconds.

Maybe he just felt he had too much invested to let our joint effort go to waste.

65 Farmington 1937

At the beginning of my eighth-grade school year, Mother and Dad knew it was time to make a decision on their children's education, and Dad wrote:

> By that time we knew that there was only one way to have the children in school: Leave the Mission and find work somewhere near school, yet we tried to compromise and work out another try. We rented a small house in Farmington and Marie enrolled three children in school and then I went back to the mission and Yellowhair and I lived in the adobe house and Clara lived in the rock house.

The Farmington house was owned by a Mr. Newton, an older man with deep Southern roots and accent. This was my first exposure to regional dialect, and I was intrigued by his comments and words he used. One day soon after moving in, Mother mentioned something that needed to be repaired, and he replied, "Ah was jus' fixing to do that!"

Mother and I, with the three younger children, soon established a daily routine. She stayed home with Ronnie, Danny and Helen entered elementary school in Farmington, and I registered for the eighth grade at the Navajo Methodist School, about two miles west of our house. It was the only mission school for American Indians supported by the Methodist Episcopal Church and maintained by the Home Missionary Society.

Every weekday, rain, shine, or snow, I made the round trip hike from our rented house on the edge of Farmington, across two fields, over a little stream then called the Glade, and out along the highway to the Navajo Mission School. This proved to be physically beneficial for me and, combined with a dogged determination to play basketball in competition with healthy young Navajos, kept me in excellent physical condition that winter.

We were also almost without transportation. We did not have a car in town and there was no local public transportation, so our shopping was restricted to only what Mother and I could carry home in paper bags, until the occasional weekend when Dad brought the car in from Immanuel Mission to be with us.

Alwin and Howard Montgomery a few days before Alwin left the Mission in 1938.

Those weekends were always festive occasions. We did all our shopping, drove to church on Sunday, and sometimes took sightseeing trips around Farmington. One momentous afternoon we crossed the San Juan River and drove along the south side for several miles, just to be back on the Navajo Reservation for a short time.

Sometimes Dad would surprise us and buy a small treat on our Sunday afternoon tours. I was especially pleased the one special time he bought *two* "Three Musketeer" bars, cut them in half, and there were six pieces, one for each of us.

The Episcopal Hospital for Navajos was on the southern bluff above the San Juan, and Yellowhair was once brought there for treatment. He thoroughly enjoyed his stay, as he had never in his life had such comfort and attention. Danny and I made one long hike across the river to visit him before he returned to Immanuel Mission.

Our family joined the Federated Church of Farmington, composed of members of several Protestant churches that had no congregation of their own, and I became active with a youth group for the first time. This was my first social contact with teenage white boys and girls. The boys of the church also had a group, with the somewhat pretentious title Ancient Order of Shepherds, which church elders called "the sheepherders," and I was invited to take part in their meetings and to become a regular member.

BSA

I was also interested in the local Farmington Boy Scout troop, as I had long read *Boy's Life* magazine and was very familiar with its founder, Dan Beard, and the principles and activities of that organization. Mr. Jackson, a member of our congregation, was scoutmaster of the troop. But our family didn't have funds for more than the essentials of food and housing, and it seemed unlikely that I would join either the Shepherds or the Boy Scouts of America (BSA).

A men's group at the Federated Church took an interest in the new missionary kid, however, and contributed funds for me to join both groups. The Shepherds cost fifteen cents a month, and that, plus a year's dues in the scouts, were paid in advance. I had enough money remaining to buy an official khaki BSA shirt and blue and yellow kerchief, and the mother of a neighbor boy found his old scout hat for me, so I became a regular member of the Farmington troop of the Boy Scouts of America, wearing most of the official uniform—except the trousers and shoes.

Both organizations gave me further opportunity to mix with fellows of my own age, and I appreciated the opportunity to learn *bilagáana* ways, but at the same time I had a deep feeling of resentment for being an object of charity and determined never again to fail to pay my own way.

ROCKY MOUNTAIN CLIPPER

One day the barnstorming *Rocky Mountain Clipper* came to Farmington, and on Saturday morning, while baking my favorite "double deck" cookies, I heard an announcement on the radio that tickets for a flight over Farmington were available, "today only."

Tickets came at an enormous price, but I had an accumulation of change saved for a special event and immediately decided this was that special event! I turned the task of finishing my cookies over to an aunt who was visiting us and set off for the airport, located on the hill just above Navajo Methodist Mission.

As I was climbing the hill a car pulled up beside me, and the driver asked me the way to the airport. It was a hot day and I gladly told him to just go on up the hill, and then innocently remarked that I was also headed for the airport.

"Good for you," replied the driver and gunned the car up the hill, leaving me in a hot swirl of dust. I eventually made it up to the airport and was relieved to see I was on time and people were still buying tickets. I purchased one, and, with mounting anticipation, climbed up a ladder and boarded the airplane.

It looked like a decrepit old school bus, big but not anywhere near as big as the new Pan American Clippers just starting the commercial overseas flights that ended the practice of cruising the world on ocean liners. I was one of the last to board and found a seat just behind the big man standing at the controls. He needed a shave and didn't look a bit like Lindbergh, but he closed the door, and with a tremendous roar we charged down the short runway to the edge of the hill and were suddenly airborne.

At first I was conscious only of noise and of a feeling of lifting until we cleared the hill, but when we leveled off and started a big circle I suddenly saw the little town of Farmington spread below us along a small brown stream of muddy water—the San Juan winding down the valley.

Then just ahead I spotted a blue monolith thrusting up on the barren plain—Shiprock! And just beyond the blue mass of Carrizo Mountains on the horizon was *dine' bikeyah* (Diné Land), and Immanuel Mission, and the canyons of *tsegi hoch cho* that were still home for me!

66 Navajo Methodist Mission High School

y the time I had completed the eighth grade I was well adjusted to my Navajo fellow students at Navajo Mission High School. We had many things in common, I spoke their language with a near perfect accent but only a limited vocabulary, and I was familiar with Navajo customs and their way of thinking. I even had a limited knowledge of their tradition: the myths, witchcraft, taboos, and curses that still deeply troubled traditional camp Navajos.

GIRDNER THE GARDENER

The next year Dad was offered the position of dairyman and gardener at the 832-acre campus of the Navajo Methodist Mission High School. He took charge of the considerable farm operation of barns, fields, and orchards and was assigned a crew of older Navajo boys to work afternoons at various work projects, tending orchards, planting fields, and doing chores in the barns with the cows, hogs, and other livestock.

The Girdner family moved to a nice house on the south edge of the campus in the fall of 1938, and I entered the high school as a freshman. Classes were held in the new main high school building that included classrooms, a few teachers' residence quarters, and an excellent gymnasium, all completed just the year before, during my eighth-grade year at the school.

Dad was also responsible for heating the buildings and dormitories of the school, and during the winter months he hauled coal in the big red mission truck from a small mine some miles west of Farmington. A Navajo student and I occasionally made the coal trip with Dad as "helpers." On one occasion we were invited to go with the mine crew down into the tunnels to see how coal was mined. This proved to be an extremely interesting event for me but also motivated me to get an education and qualify for any career other than digging in a dark tunnel underground.

After spending almost my entire life in the interior of the Navajo Reservation, living in Farmington just off the far corner of the Reservation still seemed like exile to me, as it did to the entire Navajo student body. In addition to this, I was also a minority within a minority and, with the family of the school Superintendent C. C. Brooks, one of only three palefaces in the entire high school. Marie Brooks was a senior, and sophomore Bob Brooks was a year ahead of me.

I had one advantage over Bob, however. I understood enough of what was being said about us by our teammates when they spoke sarcastically to each other in Navajo, usually comments about our abilities in the gym.

BASKETBALL, BASKETBALL, BASKETBALL

Navajo boys were excellent in various sports, but I soon learned their three favorite sports were basketball, basketball, and basketball. Track was new that year at Mission High and almost as important to the fellows as basketball, but not one of the top three.

I had some knowledge of the game, but my basketball practice at the hoop on the side of the windmill at Immanuel Mission had not really prepared me for the aggressive physical contact that organized basketball required, so I found this game sometimes less than a pleasant experience. I gave it my best shot, but very seldom changed anything on the scoreboard.

Although I was not a good player I usually traveled with the Navajo Mission team on the excursions to play other high schools in New Mexico and southern Colorado, and one cold, disastrous afternoon in Durango, Colorado, I was assigned to guard a certain Durango player. Coach Willard Bass had trained me to watch the eyes to determine what my opponent's next move would be—however, this fellow turned out to be cross-eyed and faked me out every time.

If my performance on the floor never excited the crowd, I always got attention as the only redhead on the team. I spent most of my time warming the bench—sometimes with Maurice McCabe, who was a much better basketball player than I ever was. We became good friends and always found the opportunity to congratulate each other on an occasional good move on the floor.

One dark, snowy night we were on the way home in our bus from a basketball game at Fort Lewis. We took a shortcut home, and at a canyon crossing we were stopped by the guard, a bundled-up old man with a flashlight, who told us the bridge was unsafe. Then after flashing his light around the students in the bus, he remarked, "Just a bunch of kids? Go ahead." Everyone on the bus took this as hilarious and kept shouting out: "Bunch of kids. Go ahead!"

Later that night we stopped for dinner in Durango, Colorado, trooped off the bus into a small café, filled all the available tables, and began a loud conversation. Speaking Navajo was usually discouraged in our classrooms, but on this special evening, with everyone excited, it became the language of choice.

Several old cowboys sitting at the bar turned and watched us laughing and shouting about the great game—which seems to indicate we won—then turned back to the bar and engaged in a long, intense discussion. Finally, one old fellow turned and leaned over and asked me, confidentially, "We know

Alwin's visit to Mesa Verde as a freshman at Mission High
in his brand-new Boy Scout uniform.

these kids are all Indians but—what are you?" Surprised, I replied, "Oh, I'm a half-breed."

Politically incorrect—but the cowboys asked no more questions, and the Navajos, who were following the exchange, roared with delight. I was lucky this didn't result in a new nickname, but I remained forever "*n'alwol*" to my teammates in some obscure reference to my running ability, or maybe the lack of it.

I continued my scouting experience while living at Navajo Methodist High School, walking to town every Wednesday night to scout meetings and taking part in various scouting activities. We marched in the Farmington Armistice Day Parade; worked traffic control at the community Easter sunrise service—held, of all places, in the underground Big Kiva at Aztec Ruins National Monument; and made weekend camping excursions to Durango, Colorado, in a big open truck.

I soon achieved the advanced rank of Second Class Scout and also earned my first merit badge—in bookbinding! The only time I missed taking part in scout activities was when our troop marched in a parade for the dedication of the new bridge across the San Juan at Shiprock. I didn't have a complete official uniform, but I don't know if I was more disappointed by not marching or by missing a return to the Navajo Reservation, even if only for one day.

My regular scout troop days were over when we moved to Arizona in the fall of 1939; however, I became a "Lone Scout" while living on the ranch on Oak Creek and finally achieved my "Eagle" award in my junior year at Clarkdale High School, when it was presented one memorable night in 1941, by Eugene C. Pulliam, publisher of the *Arizona Republic,* who came up from Phoenix to the Verde Valley with several scouting officials for the ceremony.

67 Adiós, Siempre Adiós

t the end of the school year in 1939, I went back to stay with Aunt Clara and Yellowhair for my last summer at Immanuel Mission. The rest of the family stayed in Farmington until August, then came out to the Mission for a few weeks before moving permanently to the Girdner ranch on Oak Creek, where I would complete my high school years attending Clarkdale High School. Aunt Clara followed them to Oak Creek in her car to help in the big move and, expecting to be gone for three or four days, gave us her expected return date and left, leaving Yellowhair and me to run the Mission.

As a number of Navajos dropped by over the next few days, we were kept busy with many tasks, and I lost track of time until one evening Yellowhair asked, "*ha'át'iish nat'aa?*" Then I realized Aunt Clara was already a day late in returning, but only answered his question about when she was returning by suggesting that perhaps she had a lot of things to do.

Two more days went by, and every night Yellowhair asked again, "When is she coming back?" as if I had some special means of communicating with the absent one. Finally, a few nights later, quite late in the week, we saw the lights of a vehicle bobbing down our road and my wayfaring Aunt Clara arrived with a tale of much tribulation.

She had started home as planned, but a serious problem developed with the car, and it was necessary for her to take it to a garage for major repairs before she could continue. Rudy Zweifel, the district range rider based at Teec Nos Pos, found her stranded in Shiprock and made a special trip to Immanuel Mission to deliver her safely home.

Not long afterward, a group of Navajos, angered by the stock reduction program, kidnapped Rudy Zweifel and his wife and kept them several days before releasing them, scared but safe.

LITTLE LOST BABY

A few days after Aunt Clara's return from Oak Creek, a young Navajo couple with a tiny baby set up a temporary camp at the foot of the mesa about a mile north of Immanuel Mission. We knew the baby was very ill, and Aunt Clara had sent medicine, warm wrappings, and fresh milk up to the camp every evening.

Black Boy, Alwin's favorite pet during his time
on the Reservation.

The morning before I left Immanuel Mission for the final time, the young man suddenly appeared at the Mission very early and stood silently just inside the kitchen door. Aunt Clara acknowledged him, didn't say anything but just stood, with all color gone from her face, looking at him. After a long minute of silence there was a terse three-word conversation: The Navajo exclaimed *"ha'átish?"* ("What?") She asked, *" 'awée'?"* ("Baby?") and he answered, *"ádin"* ("Gone").

There were only three of us at the Mission: Aunt Clara, Yellowhair, and me. Yellowhair was not about to become involved and immediately left the room. Aunt Clara just looked at me, and I went to the old rock building, picked up a shovel, and followed the young man out the gate and up the hill without a word.

We arrived at the camp where the young mother, barely a girl herself, was sitting under the shade with the tiny wrapped bundle on the sand beside her. All their meager belongings were stacked neatly not far away.

Digging was easy in the sandy soil, and it took just a few minutes. We placed the baby in the little excavation, packing the sand down firmly, then went a few yards away and gathered some large rocks to cover the grave, leaving the girl sitting in the shelter, quietly crying. When we had finished our work, the young man motioned for me to follow, and we started running down the hill in a zigzag course through the rabbit brush and salt bushes, brushing our legs against the undergrowth to confuse and lose any evil spirits following us.

We returned to the camp and found the girl had heated a pot of water, and we used an empty baking powder can to pour the hot water over each other's hands, vigorously washing them and our faces. Still without speaking, we shook hands; I shouldered my shovel and walked back down the hill to Immanuel Mission, alone.

LAST DAY AT IMMANUEL MISSION

The next day Aunt Clara and I started for Shiprock, where I was to catch the "stage," an old bus from Cortez, Colorado, that made regular runs to Gallup. Our plans were good but, as Aunt Clara would say, "Man proposes, God disposes," and we did not allow time for a flat tire at Red Wash, and when we finally got to Shiprock we had missed the stage.

Aunt Clara, always a resourceful woman, spotted a truck bearing a Colorado license, which was being refueled at the trading post, and she walked over and started negotiating with the driver. A minute later she hurried back to our car, where I stood watching, and went directly to the point as usual: "Get your suitcase. These fellows are going to Gallup and have agreed to take you for a dollar. I have already paid them."

After a hasty goodbye, I climbed into the cab of the truck, already occupied by two fellows, and as we pulled away, I looked back and saw Aunt Clara standing by the road waving her handkerchief. I waved back, we went down the hill, and I could no longer see her. I had started on the journey that was to take me away from the Navajo Reservation, forever.

THE ROAD TO GALLUP

The truckers seemed pleased to have a paying passenger; however, they carefully warned me that if we were stopped I was just a friend riding with them down to Gallup. As I sat there between the driver and his young partner, they began inquiring about my background, and when I said I had lived with the Indians most of my life, the younger man immediately began asking questions about life on the Reservation.

I was hesitant to discuss my personal affairs, and when he asked what I did every day, I tried to put him off with general answers, but then he persisted with a specific question, "So, what did you do yesterday?" I gave him a short, truthful answer: "Well, yesterday I buried a baby." They looked at each other and we rode on to Gallup in silence.

Late that night I arrived in Flagstaff by train, and as I started walking back east on Highway 66, it started to rain. I plodded on toward my destination, the summer camp at the Southwest Bible Conference grounds, not knowing whether to curse my luck or pray for a ride, and finally settled on the latter.

A minute later, one of the speeding cars splashing by screeched to a stop, the red tail light winking in the dark, and as I ran up to it, a young man leaned out and curtly asked where I was going, then motioned for me to get in. We drove on for several miles, with the only sound the swish of windshield wipers, and then arrived at the conference grounds driveway. He let me out without a word, and I thanked him and ran up the short road to the conference buildings as he made a screeching U turn and roared back toward Flagstaff in the rain.

I located the summer cabin of a family we knew, worked the window open and crawled through to find a bed with the mattress rolled up for the winter. I hung my wet clothes up to dry and curled up in the mattress for the rest of the night. The next morning I sealed up the cabin, walked up to the groundskeeper's house, and picked up the bicycle my folks had left for me when they moved to Oak Creek. It was still raining as I cycled through Flagstaff and out to the rim of Oak Creek Canyon. My goal was to finish a 50-mile bike ride to qualify for a merit badge required to attain the rank of Eagle Scout. Water began dripping down my face as I pedaled my way through the forest along the new road out to the rim and then down the treacherous hairpin turns of the canyon that took me to Sedona.

It had stopped raining by the time I turned off the highway, and my bike suddenly dropped into a rut in the dirt road and stopped, but I continued over the handlebars and found myself rolling in the dust. Bruised and bloodied, I was determined to finish my trek and cycled on. I was approaching Page Springs when I spotted the school bus being parked by my Uncle Stanley Girdner. I had completed my 50 miles so I ended my cycling adventure with a free ride home to the Girdner ranch in his car.

68   Graduation and Beyond

The nine seniors of the Class of 1939, three years ahead of me, were the first class to graduate from Mission High School. The executive secretary of the sponsoring Home Mission Council of the Women's Home Missionary Society delivered the school's first commencement address in English, assisted by our old friend of Immanuel Mission days, Jake Morgan.

World War II, however, scattered my classmates to the far corners of the earth, and I was only to see one ever again. In early 1943, when I was a freshman at the University of Arizona during the early days of the war, the Navy had established a training school there in the desert to train men to go to sea, and for a time regular students and future sailors shared the same facilities.

Many Navajos joined the armed forces during World War II, and I understand that at least three of my classmates from Navajo Mission High served with the acclaimed "Code Talkers" of the U.S. Marine Corps in the Pacific theatre, an activity that was kept highly secret until a few years ago, but which has since been the subject of many books and even movies.

When I enrolled in the University of Arizona in the fall of 1942, I also enrolled in the ROTC cavalry unit. Wearing the khaki uniform, cap, and boots for drill, I was hurrying back to Cochise Hall one noon to change to my more comfortable civilian attire before afternoon classes, when someone on a passing truck of sailors yelled *"nsinilwod!"* Although I couldn't identify the particular sailor, I knew he had to be from Mission High School. No one else ever called me *nsinilwod* ("runs back and forth" in reference to playing basketball in high school).

That afternoon the mysterious sailor turned up at my room in Cochise Hall. He was John Benally, a Navajo from Toadlena who had entered the Methodist Navajo Mission in 1929 as a primary student and stayed the course to become a member of that first high school graduating class of Mission in 1939, a year after I had left New Mexico for Arizona.

John and I had a great session of catching up, and a few days later went to a movie together in downtown Tucson and made plans to get together again, but he was suddenly shipped out. I never saw him or any of my other Mission classmates again, although James Nahkai and Sam Sandoval later gained recognition as members of the Navajo Code Talkers.

MAURICE MCCABE

My fellow bench-sitter and good friend, Maurice McCabe, played a key role in the formation and early days of the Navajo Nation, twenty years after our days at the Navajo Methodist Mission.

Maurice was named Executive Secretary when the Navajo Tribal Council created that position. Since he coordinated the administration and departments of the tribe and was responsible for the budget, he has been called the "architect" of modern Navajo government. In their time Maurice McCabe and President Paul Jones were considered the two most powerful figures in the Tribal Council and played an active role in the 1958 negotiations with the oil companies over treaty rights and drilling arrangements on the Navajo Reservation.

Maurice contributed in other ways as well. Harry Goulding, a longtime trader in the Monument Valley area from as early as 1925, was involved in the establishment of the first Navajo Tribal Park at Monument Valley. In Samuel Moon's biography of Goulding, *Tall Sheep,* Goulding gives Maurice McCabe the credit for selling the idea to tribal members and describes the scene:

> He would lean his elbow comfortably on the piano, and make about a thirty-minute talk, sometimes more than that, as to what the Navajos were thinking about and what they were going to have to do. He never wrote anything, there was nothing [written] down. It just flowed out of him like water coming out of a spring, and beautifully so! You could have heard a pin drop in there...he went over and put it up to the tribal council. It was the first Navajo Tribal Park.

Maurice died unexpectedly in 1974.

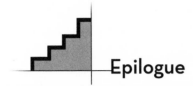

Epilogue

A fter the Girdner family moved to Oak Creek in 1939, Aunt Clara and Yellowhair remained at Immanuel Mission, where they were joined by a young man, Howard Montgomery, who worked there for several years before meeting and marrying one of the teachers at the Navajo Methodist Mission. His wife, Helen, remained at Immanuel Mission for years after Howard died, occupying our old room next to Yellowhair's den. I think she enjoyed Yellowhair's nightly Navajo chanting, and she was with him when the old man died.

HAZEL FAIRFIELD
Over thirty years after leaving the Navajo Reservation, my work with the New Mexico Credit Union League took me back to the Navajo country for meetings, first in Farmington and then in Gallup, and I took the opportunity to detour by way of Immanuel Mission, this time over splendid paved highways, except for the last few miles of the original unpaved road.

Helen Montgomery was still there, and it was wonderful catching up with people and happenings after three decades, especially about Yellowhair, who had died only a short time before. Hazel Fairfield was the only Navajo I saw who remembered me, and she hugged me and burst into tears in a much more emotional meeting than any we could have had in those days long past. We talked at length about the times we had together. She also told me about her only daughter, Anna (Blackwater), who was to remain near Immanuel Mission to the end of the century.

AUNT CLARA
Aunt Clara completed her lifelong work with the Navajo Indians when she moved to Oak Creek to be with the family in the winter of 1944. She was there when I arrived home from Pearl Harbor, and we had a few days to visit before I had to return to Tucson for summer session at the University of Arizona.

Superintendent Albert H. Kneale, who of course played a key role in obtaining Navajo approval for the original petition and establishing the Immanuel Mission, wrote a poignant tribute to her in his autobiography, *Indian Agent:*

A Sunday walk at the Mission.

The Navajo Reservation knows Miss Clara Holcomb no more. No longer, does she ride the lonesome and interminable miles of sheep trails seeking her beloved Navajos. The lowly hogan is no longer her habitation.

The end came July 9, 1945.

My Reservation days are brightly colored in my memory, and all the time that followed as I learned to live in the *bilagáana* world now seems much dimmer. Again and again as I look back across it all, I remember moments in middle life when I was finishing a painting, and my wife used to say, "It's done. Don't hesitate. Sign it and hang it on the wall!" and so, after all these years, I will.

Acknowledgments

Many thanks to my entire family for their support, encouragement, and occasional prodding to finish this account. A heartfelt thank you to my children: Allen Girdner for his diligence in promoting my book, Sharon Magee for her consistent motivation, Kennan Girdner for his continued interest in my writing progress, and Mari Jo Girdner Vigil, who has served countless hours as my literary agent extraordinaire.

Thank you so much to my grandsons Matthew Girdner for creating the maps depicting the Reservation landmarks of my childhood and Glen Magee who was instrumental in setting up my manuscript on the computer to facilitate my writing. My grandson Julian Addison Honeycutt gets a special recognition for a summer of processing dozens of old negatives to produce fine prints from my original file of ancient Reservation negatives.

Thanks to the people of the Cline Library at Northern Arizona University, Barbara Valvo and Peter Runge, who have also been most helpful, as has Bunnie Foster at Avant Ministries, who provided the copies of the Holcomb's 1894–1915 reports to the Gospel Missionary Union. Winona Wallace of the Museum Department of the City of Ketchikan, Alaska; Bruce Dinges, Editor of the *Journal of Arizona History*; Nancy Jones, Archivist with Menaul Historical Library; Greg Staley at Immanuel Mission; Dr. Russell Ewing of the Historical Department of the University of Arizona; and many thanks to my Publisher, Editor and the staff of Rio Nuevo Publishers, particularly Susan Lowell Humphreys for her countless hours fine tuning my manuscript.

Resources and Suggested Reading

Alvord, Lori and Elizabeth Cohen Van Pelt. *The Scalpel and the Silver Bear*. New York: Bantam Books, 2000.

Barker, Florence A. *Journals ca. 1922–1938*. Northern Arizona University, Barker, Florence collection.

Bernheimer, Charles L. *Rainbow Bridge: Circling Navajo Mountain and Explorations of the Bad Lands of Southern Utah and Northern Arizona*. Danbury, CT: Warren Press, 2007.

Blue, Martha. *Indian Trader: The Life and Times of J. L. Hubbell*. Walnut, CA: Kiva Publishing, 2000.

Brown, Kenneth A. *Four Corners: History, Land, and People of the Desert Southwest*. New York: Harper Perennial, 1996.

Chamberlain, Kathleen P. *Under Sacred Ground: A History of Navajo Oil, 1922–1982*. Albuquerque: University of New Mexico Press, 2008.

Conrad, Howard L. *Uncle Dick Wootton*. Des Moines, IA: Time-Life Books, 1980.

Cummings, Byron. *Indians I Have Known*. Arizona Silhouettes, 1952.

Dolfin, John. *Bringing the Gospel in Hogan & Pueblo*. Charleston, SC: BiblioBazaar, 2009.

Dyk, Walter. *Son of Old Man Hat: A Navaho Autobiography*. Lincoln: University of Nebraska Press, 1967.

Evans, Will. *Along Navajo Trails: Recollections of a Trader 1898–1948*. Logan: Utah State University Press, 2005.

Faunce, Hilda. *Desert Wife*. Lincoln: University of Nebraska Press, 1981.

Forrest, Earle R. *With a Camera in Old Navaholand*. Norman: University of Oklahoma Press, 1970.

Gillmor, Frances and Wetherill, Louisa Wade. *Traders to the Navajos: The Story of the Wetherills of Kayenta*. Albuquerque: University of New Mexico Press, 1979.

Girdner, Alwin J. "Navaho–United States Relations." Tucson: University of Arizona Department of History, 1950.

Goossen, Irvy. *Getting Acquainted with the Navajo Field*. Flagstaff, AZ: Southwestern School of Missions, n.d.

Hannett, A. T. *Sagebrush Lawyer*. New York: Pageant Press, 1964.

Haile, Father Berard. *Navajo Windway and Chiricahua Windway*. St. Michaels, AZ: St. Michaels Press, n.d.

Hegemann, Elizabeth Compton. *Navaho Trading Days*. Albuquerque: University of New Mexico Press, 2004.

Heyman, Jr., Max L. *Prudent Soldier: A Biography of Major General E. R. S. Canby 1817–1873.* Cleveland: Arthur H. Clark Co., 1959.

Howe, Sherman S. *My Story of the Aztec Ruins.* The Basin Spokesman, 1955.

Kane, Wanden M. *What Am I Doing Here?* Palmer Lake, CO: The Filter Press, 1979.

Kluckhohn, Clyde M. *To the Foot of the Rainbow: A Tale of Twenty-five Hundred Miles of Wandering on Horseback through the Southwest's Enchanted Land.* Glorieta, NM: The Rio Grande Press, 1992.

———— and Leighton, Dorothea. *The Navaho: Revised Edition.* Cambridge: Harvard University Press, 1992.

Kneale, Albert H. *Indian Agent.* Caldwell, ID: Caxton Printers, 1950.

Liebler, H. Baxter. *Boil My Heart for Me.* Salt Lake City: University of Utah Press, 1994.

Lister, Florence and Robert Lister. *Earl Morris and Southwestern Archaeology.* Tucson: University of Arizona Press, 1968.

Marriot, Alice. *The Ten Grandmothers.* Norman: University of Oklahoma Press, 1983.

Matthews, Washington. *Navajo Legends.* Salt Lake City: University of Utah Press, 2002.

McNeley, James Kale. *Holy Wind in Navajo Philosophy.* Tucson: University of Arizona Press, 1981.

McNitt, Frank. *Richard Wetherill–Anasazi: Pioneer Explorer of Southwestern Ruins.* Albuquerque: University of New Mexico Press, 1974.

Moon, Samuel. *Tall Sheep: Harry Goulding, Monument Valley Trader.* Norman: University of Oklahoma Press, 1992.

Morris, Ann Axtell. *Digging in the Southwest.* Santa Barbara, CA: P. Smith, 1978.

Nusbaum, Deric. *Deric in Mesa Verde.* New York: G. P. Putnam's Sons, 1926.

————. *Deric with the Indians.* New York: G. P. Putnam's Sons, 1927.

Philp, Kenneth R. *John Collier's Crusade for Indian Reform, 1920–1954.* Tucson: University of Arizona Press, 1977.

Peters, De Witt C. *The Life and Adventures of Kit Carson, the Nestor of the Rocky Mountains, from Facts Narrated by Himself.* General Books, 2010.

Richardson, Gladwell. *Navajo Trader.* Tucson: University of Arizona Press, 1991.

Saner, Reg. *Reaching Keet Seel: Ruin's Echo and the Anasazi.* Salt Lake City: University of Utah Press, 1998.

Staley, Jeffrey L. *Reading with a Passion: Rhetoric, Autobiography, and the American West in the Gospel of John.* New York: Continuum Publishing, 2002.

Thybony, Scott. *Burntwater.* Tucson: University of Arizona Press, 1997.

Wagner, Sallie. *Wide Ruins: Memories from a Navajo Trading Post.* Albuquerque: University of New Mexico Press, 1997.

Wetherill, Louise Wade and Harvey Leake. *Wolfkiller: Wisdom from a Nineteenth-Century Navajo Shepherd.* Layton, UT: Gibbs Smith, 2007.

Wuest, John B., O.F.M. "Letter about Navajo Ministry." *Provincial Chronicle* v. 20, 1948.

Young, Robert and William Morgan. *The Navajo Language: A Grammar and Colloquial Dictionary.* Albuquerque: University of New Mexico Press, revised edition 1987.

About the Author

Alwin J. Girdner had two nicknames when he was growing up in Diné Tah (the Navajo Reservation). In English the redheaded boy was called "Rusty," and in Navajo he was *chee yazzie,* or "Little Red." After leaving Diné Tah in 1939, he traveled in 114 countries before returning to New Mexico, where he now lives in Albuquerque. Girdner holds degrees in business and Southwestern and Latin American history from the University of Arizona. He is a native speaker of Navajo and through the years he has studied and maintained lifelong ties to Diné (Navajo) culture.